AF552829

MORAL VALUES OF INTERMEDIATE STUDENTS

MORAL VALUES OF INTERMEDIATE STUDENTS

By

Dr. N. Amareswaran

Deptt. of Education
Sri Venkateswara University
Tirupati (Andhra Pradesh)
(India)

DISCOVERY PUBLISHING HOUSE PVT. LTD.
NEW DELHI-110 002

First Published-2010

ISBN 978-81-8356-587-5

Published by:

DISCOVERY PUBLISHING HOUSE PVT. LTD.
4831/24, Ansari Road, Prahlad Street
Darya Ganj, New Delhi-110002 (India)
Phone: 23279245, 43764432 • Fax: 91-11-23253475
E-mail: parul.wasan@gmail.com
info@discoverypublishinggroup.com
Website: www.discoverypublishinggroup.com

Printed at:
Ārora Offset Press, Delhi – 92

DEDICATED TO

My Beloved Parents

N. HAMSA

and

N. MUNIRATHNAM REDDY

Foreword

At present the nations across the globe are finding it difficult to solve the problem of mismatch between the Moral Values of their populace and positive human capital development. Due to the surge of print and electronic media sensationalizing the infraction of Moral Values making mountain out of anthill, industrialization, globalization, the Moral Values in every society are taking a nosedive. This trend is spreading like a virulent virus across mankind and national governments. It is also learnt that some national governments are sponsoring terrorism resulting in loss of innocent lives. To obviate all these ills in the society the government is promoting national integration through songs, dances, dramas, youth festivals etc. Even some of the school children are kept in schools of other states for considerable period of schooling to integrate their cultures and augment national integration.

This study assumes transcending importance since it has embarked on the attitude of intermediate students on Moral Values, who are at the transitional stage of concretizing their Moral Values which act becomes the bedrock of societal building. The objectives of the study are apt and non-pedestrian. The antecedent variables such as socio-demographic, psychological, self-concepts and study habits are well conceived which have a bearing on Moral Values. The subjects (intermediate students) included for probing come from variegated backgrounds (rural and urban) and colleges manned by government, aided and private managements thus nullifying danger of getting one-sided responses due to mono-cultural situations.

The findings of the study and suggestions given to inculcate Moral Values in students of different educational institutions would provide food for thought for the policy makers and administrators if they heed and put them into practice. As the plant creeper behaves on how to occupy the gradient of a mesh or ladder provided by the gardner, the children can be moulded on values, as they are tender enough to internalize them. As the adage-charity begins at Home, imbibing Moral Values should start at home, schools and colleges concomitantly.

Finally, this book is of immense value to teachers and educational administrators who can take a cue out of it to imbibe Moral Values in student fraternity who eventually occupy the positions in legislatures, judiciary and executive echelons of governance.

Dr. (Mrs). S. RATHNA KUMARI
M.A., Ph.D.
Professor, Dept. of Economics
S.V.University
Tirupati-517502
Andhra Pradesh
India

Preface

Modern mass society presents a sharp contrast, as the young grow up. They are faced with confusions, delays and discontinuities. Adolescents in particular are uncertain about themselves. Some are in conflict with themselves, bewildered an insecure.

Values are usually influenced by the changing philosophical ideologies, cultural and religious perspectives, social, political and geographical conditions. In modern emerging society, there has been a revolutionary change in the field of values due to many factors in addition to the influence of modern culture, industrialization, modernization, urbanization, globalization and multinationals.

Values are the guiding principles, decisive in day to day behaviors as also- is critical life situations. Values are a set bring of principles or standards of behavior. Values are regarded desirable, important and held in high esteem by a particular society in which a person lives.

Today there is lot of degradation of values in every walk of human life. Individuals are crazy for material wealth. Money making is the main motive of the initial stages of the child. Schools and Colleges are institutions which can shoulder the responsibility of including Moral Values among the people and students. Though there are considerable numbers of studies on Moral Values in relation with certain psycho-sociological variables at school and college level. The present study is concentrated on Intermediate Students. Intermediate Students are adolescents and they are the citizens of future generation. It is necessary to know what is right and wrong; which is good and bad; which is good way and bad way and how to behave with others especially with elders. Hence there is a need to take research activities in the area of Moral Values.

There are so many factors influencing Moral Values, i.e. Study Habits, Self-concepts, Personality Factors and Socio-Demographic Factors/Variables. In this study different types of statistical techniques were used - critical ratio, one-way anova, multiple regression and factorial analysis. The main aim of the study was to predict the multiple effects of the independent factors on attitude of Intermediate Students towards Moral Values.

The present book is aimed to identify the influence of certain psycho-sociological factors on attitude of Moral Values of Intermediate Students. Data was collected from 1200 Senior Intermediate Students from 16 Junior Colleges.

Subject-matter of the book has been divided into six chapters. In the first chapter brief introduction of the topic is given. Chapter II deals with a brief review of related literature. Chapter III deals with the present study, chapter IV gives an account of methods employed in the investigator. Chapter V consists of analysis of the data, results and discussions. Chapter VI gives the summary, major findings, conclusions, educational implifications, recommendations and suggestions for further research.

This book is prepared to know the attitude of Intermediate Students towards Moral Values. This book is more useful not only for teachers but also parents. The present government is planning to introduce Philosophy/Psychology at intermediate level to develop Moral Values in the students. I do not know to what extent I have succeeded in my attempt, but I feel this book is more useful for all.

Any suggestions and criticisms will be gratefully welcomed and acknowledged.

Dr. N. Amareswaran

ACKNOWLEDGEMENTS

Now I am very happy to express my distinct pleasure to my beloved Parents, Teachers and Friends. First of all I am thankful to our Honourable and Dynamic Professor B. Ramachandra Reddy Garu, M.A., M.Sc., M.Ed., M.Phil., Ph.D., B.L., Dip. In A.Ed. & Dip. In Stats., Vice-Principal of S.V.U. College of Education and Extension Studies, Head of the Department of Education and former Principal of I.A.S.C., and former Dean of Education Sri Venkateswara University, Tirupati for his planning, best suggestions, advise and benevolent guidance, unending constant encouragement and exuberant style of inspiration in the prosecution of this work *Moral Values of Intermediate Students*. Diction is not enough to express my profound sense of gratitude and I wish to place on record my sincere and heart full regards to him. I am grateful to him for his keen and personal interest, constructive criticism and able guidance. My sincere thanks are due to him for having provided necessary facilities in connection with the investigation.

I am very much thankful to Prof. D. Usha Rani, Principal, S.V.U. College of Education & Extension Studies, Tirupati for her constant encouragement for the completion of this work.

I am thankful to Prof. Y. Venkatarami Reddy, Registrar, S.V.University, Tirupati and Prof. V. Narayana Reddy, Registrar, Simhapuri University, Nellore for their encouragement in this work.

I wish and take this opportunity to express my deep sense of gratitude to respected Dr. D. Ramakrishnaiah, M.A., M.Sc., M.Ed., M.Phil., Ph.D., former professor and Head, Dept. of Education, Sri Venkateswara University, Tirupati; Dr. V. Dayakara Reddy, M.A. (Soc.), M.A.(Eco.), M.Ed., Ph.D., Professor, Principal I.A.S.E., Chairman BOS in Education and former Head of the Department of Education, Sri Venkateswara University, Tirupati; and Dr. M. SYAMALA, M.A. (Edu.), M.A.(Soc.), M.Phil., Ph.D., Associate Professor, Dept. of Education, S.V. University, Tirupati; for the encouragement and suggestions and guidance they have given me now and then in completing this book.

I feel it is a golden opportunity to say thanks to my beloved family members, my mother Mrs. N. Hamsa Garu, my father Mr. N. Munirathnam Reddy Garu, Sisters Miss. N. Koteeswari, M.A. (Eco.), Mrs. N. Vanaja and Mrs. N. Jamuna; brothers Mr. N. Udayasankar and Mr. N. Amarnadh, uncles Mr. M. Munikanna Reddya, M. Ranganadha Reddy and M. Ramachandra Reddy; aunties M. Dhanamma, M. Padma and M. Govindamma and other relatives.

I express my deep sense of gratitude to my well wishers Dr. C. Manchala, School Assistant, Z.P. High School, M.R. Palli, Tirupati, Dr. E. Prabhakar Reddy, Academic Consultant, DDE, S.V.University, Dr. C. Sheela Reddy, Assistant Professor, Dept. of Political Science and Public Administration, Dr. S. Rathna Kumari, Professor, Dept. of Economics, Dr. D. Jamuna, Professor, Dr. S. Viswanath Reddy, Assist. Professor, Dept. of Psychology, Dr. P. Bhaskar Reddy, Dr. D. Kiran Kanth Choudary, Principal, College of International Studies, Dr. B.C. Obul Reddy, Associate Professor, Dept. of Philosophy, Dr. N. Savithramma, Head, Dr. T. Vijaya, Associate Professor, Dept. of Botany, Dr. K. Manjula, Dr. K.V. Sucharitha, Assist. Professors, Dept. of Home Science, Dr. T. Bharathi, Dr. D. Aruna Jyothi, Assist. Professor, IASE, Dr. K. Sudha Rani, Associate Professor, Dept. of Adult Educatin, Dr. T. Kumaraswamy, Head, Dept. of Adult Education, Dr. P. Adhinarayana Reddy, Dr. M.C. Reddeppa

Reddy, Professors, Dept. of Adult Education, Dr. V. Kodandarami Reddy, Professor, Dept. of Econometrics, Dr. K. Viswanatha Reddy, Professor, Dept. of Anthropology, Sri K.M. Bhanu, Assistant Professor, Dept. of Mathamatics, Dr. K. Raja Reddy, Dr. Y. Yagama Reddy, Dr. G. Jayachandra Reddy, Director, Cente for Southeast Asian and Pacific Studies and Dr. C. Venkat Reddy, former Principal, S.K. University, Anantapur.

I wish to express my deep sense of appreciation and gratitude to Mr. P. K. Subramanyam, Mr. M. Munaswami Pillai, Mr. & Mrs. M. Ramesh Babu, Mrs. A. Leelavathi, Mrs. A. Bhavana, Mrs. Ramesh Naidu, Mrs. Padma, Mr. Penchalaiah, Mr. K. Munaswami, Mr. Venkata Krishnaiah, Mr. Kumar, Mrs. Ankamma, Mrs. Gayatri, Mrs. N. Padma Kumari, Mr. Vivekananda, Mr. Vasu, Mr. Pancharatnam Mr. Umamaheswar, Mr. Vijaya Bhaskar, Mr. Praveen, Mr. Gagadeesh and all non-teaching faculties of all departments in Sri Venkateswara University, Tirupathi.

I like to express my profound sense of gratitude and thanks to my friends and scholars Dr. Madhu, Dr. Anil Kumar Reddy, Dr. Pulla Reddy, Dr. Sankar Reddy, Mr. M. Mohan Reddy, Mr. Papaiah, Mr. Pranil Kumar, Mr. Bhaskar Reddy, Dr. K. Sudhakar, Dr. Anil Kumar, Dr. Bhuvaneswara Chowdary, Mr. E. Mahadeva Reddy, Mr. Hari Babu, Mr. Subbarama Krishnaiah, Mr. Elmalai, Mr. Hussain Reddy, Mr. Hari, Mr. E. Anjineyulu, Mr. Morarji, Mr. Lakshmipati, Mr. Raveendra and Mr. Ravi, Mr. P. Dhanumjaya, Mr. S. Purushotham, Mr. N. Hemadri, Mr. P. Udaysankar and Mr. N. Kesavulu, for their better co-operation and encouragement at all times.

I am thankful to all the Mess and Hostel staff for their comfortable accommodation and food.

My fore most thanks to all the Intermediate Students of selected colleges in Chittoor District. My special and heart full thanks to their keen interest in answering all the given questionnaires.

I am thankful to all Teaching and Non-Teaching staff of selected Junior Colleges in Chittoor District those who helped me in all the ways.

My special thanks to my former teachers Mr. Rajgopal Reddy, Mr. Subramanyam Reddy, Mrs. Jnanamba, Mr. Changama Naidu, Mr. Koteeswara Rao, Mrs. Syamala, Mr.Raju, Mr. Sampurna Chandra, Dr. Dayanada Reddy, Dr. Bhanumathi, Dr. Subramanyam Reddy, Dr. Chandrasekara Rao, Mr. Muralikrishna, Mrs. Meri and others; my old friends Mr. Ajay, Mr. Kumar, Mr. Devendra, Mr. Janardhan, Mr. Hari, Mr. Ashok, Mr. Ashok Babu, Miss. Latha, Mrs. Kavitha Raj, Mrs. Dhanalakshmi, Mrs. Manjula, Mrs. Jyothi, Miss. Sasikala, Mrs. Kamesh, Mr. Suresh, Mr. Vijay, Mr. Ashok (CTR), Mrs. Thimma Reddy, Mrs. Amaranadh, Mrs. Mamatha, Mrs. Sathyavathi, and all my neighbours, those who helped me in the direct or indirect ways.

Last but not least, I am thankful to all other personalities who have helped me directly and indirectly in completing my research work successfully.

God is truth and Truth is God. I am thankful to Lord Rama, Goddess Seetha, Lord Venkateswara, Lord Siva, Lord Hanumana, and Lord Kanipaka Varasiddi Vinayaka for their blessings in all the times.

Once again I thankful to all my beloved Parents, Teachers, Friends, Scholars, Teaching staff, Non-teaching staff, Relatives, Well wishers and God.

N. AMARESWARAN

CONTENTS

Acknowledgements vii

Abbreviations xiii

1. Introduction 1

2. Review of Related Literature 34

3. The Present Study 107

4. Methods of Investigation 127

5. Analysis and Interpretation of Data 170

6. Summary, Findings, Conclusions, Recommendations and Suggestions 237

Bibliography 264

Index 283

ABBREVIAITIONS

ANOVA : Analysis of Variance

BC : Backward Caste

Cf : Cumulative Frequency

Cpf : Cumulative Percentage Frequency

CV : Coefficient of Variation

df : Degrees of Freedom

et.al. : All other Authors

f : Frequency

FIG : Figure

HSPQ : High School Students Personality Questionnaire

K_U : Kurtosis

M : Mean

Md : Median

Mo : Mode

MS : Mean Sum of Squares

N : Number of Sample Subjects or Number of Observations

NCERT : National council of Educational Research and Training

NPE : National Policy of Education

OC : Open Category

Q_1 : First Quartile

Q_3 : Third Quartile

QD : Quartile Deviation

R : Range

SC : Schedule Caste

SD : Standard Deviation

SE_M : Standard Error of Mean

SES : Socio Economy Status

SHI : Study Habits Inventory

Sk : Skew ness

SS : Sum of Squares

ST : Schedule Tribe

TLM : Teaching Learning Material

VN : Variable Number

1

INTRODUCTION

- ❖ Be good, see good and do good. That is the way to God.
- ❖ Money comes and goes; but morality comes and grows!
- ❖ Good and bad, peace and agony, pain and pleasure, all these originate within man and not outside him.
- ❖ The past is beyond recovery. We are not sure of the future. The given moment is the right time. Do not delay; do right action.

—Sri Sathya Sai Baba

Moral values are things held to be right or wrong or desirable or undesirable. While morality is sometimes described as 'innate' in humans, the scientific view is that a capacity for morality is genetically determined in us, but the set of Moral Values is acquired, through example, teaching, and imprinting from parents and society. Different cultures have very different moral value systems. Moral Values, along with traditions, laws, behaviour patterns, and beliefs, are the defining features of a culture.

In Evolutionary psychology, Moral Values are seen as part of cultural evolution. Nationalists believe that a society needs one set of values to hold it together, and that 'multi-culturalism' is not desirable as it tends to lead to conflict. People enforce Moral Values by parenting, peer guidance, conscience, disapproval, shunning, and only in some instances by law. They were effective in small communities before laws were formalised. They can also be sustained by the concept of 'status', a concept which has many different meanings in different societies. There is today significant disagreement over what role status plays in contemporary society and of what it actually consists.

The development of any nation depends mainly on the standards of its educational institutions. Education is the most powerful and effective instrument for inducing radical changes in the behaviour of students. Education is the process through which an individual is developed into individuality and a person into a personality. Education should be individualized and personalized to the utmost and should constitute preparation for self-learning.

Education, according to Indian tradition, is not merely a means to earn a living, nor is it only a nursery of thought or a school for citizenship. It is an initiation into the life of spirit, a training of human soul in pursuit of truth and the practice of virtue. Aristotle, however, held that education exists exclusively to develop man's intellect in a world of reality, which men can know and understand.

DEFINITION OF EDUCATION

"I think an education is not only important, it is the most important thing you can do with your life."

—Dean Kamen

"The roots of education are bitter, but the fruit is sweet."

—Aristotle

"Education is the most powerful weapon which you can use to change the world."

—Nelson Mandela

"Education is not a problem. Education is an opportunity."

—Lyndon B. Johnson

Definition of Education

- ❖ The act or process of educating or being educated.
- ❖ The knowledge or skill obtained or developed by a learning process.
- ❖ A programme of instruction of a specified kind or level.
- ❖ The field of study that is concerned with the pedagogy of teaching and learning.
- ❖ An instructive or enlightening experience.
- ❖ The process of acquiring knowledge and understanding.
- ❖ Knowledge and understanding acquired through study and training.
- ❖ The process of teaching, especially at a school, college, or university.
- ❖ The theory of teaching and learning.

Education encompasses both the teaching and learning of knowledge, proper conduct, and technical competency. It thus focuses on the cultivation of skills, trades or professions, as well as mental, moral and aesthetic development.

MAN AND EDUCATIION

Man has created education, yet it has become indispensable in his life; for man seeks education for betterment of his life, both inward and outward, and even for survival. It is no wonder, therefore that the U.N.O., in its Universal Declaration of Human Rights, proclaims: "Everyone has the right to education" (Article 26). Not only is this, 'educability' now considered as one of the capacities which distinguish man from other species. Man is educable, whereas other animals and birds etc., are not, although some of them can be trained to do certain things. Hirst and Peters rightly state:

> "We distinguish now between 'training' and 'education', whereas previously people did not. We would not now naturally speak of educating animals and we would never speak in this way of plants. But we do speak of training animals and of training roses and other sort of plants."

Man cannot only create objects, machines, institutions and ideas, but also can envision a life which he can be or become if he wills. To elaborate a little more—man imagines the concept of a chair or a machine with some particular form, qualities or functions and builds it with a degree of perfection, approaching that of the concept, depending on his ability. Similarly man can envision a life with certain qualities: truthfulness, love, tolerance, peace etc., and can become the being he envisions. To explain in the words of Maslow, "being" is "that which the person is" and "becoming", "that which the person could be", Gordon W. Allport can be aptly quoted in this connection. He writes:

> "If the prejudiced style of life can be learned and certainly it is not innate-then surely the tentative style or in Gandhi's term, 'equi-minded outlook' can also be acquired."

Thus man can envision lives with different styles, virtues, states etc., and can become like those. Creativity of this kind, envisioning a life and devising ways for becoming the envisioned personality can very well be termed as "creativity in the field of being and becoming".

In ancient India, the highest conception of education was: *Sâ Vidyâ Yâ Vimuktaye* (Learning or education is that which liberates or makes one liberated). Although other aims were there, certainly there had been a stress on 'to-be'—to be a liberated person (*jivanmukta*) and to be completely free in ultimate sense. In modern age, quite for a long time education has been conceived as that which helps to achieve-mostly outward things. But it seems, there is a revival of the interest in a kind of education that helps 'to be'—kind of person. The emphasis on 'to be'—to be a 'lifelong learner' and to be a 'complete man' by the International Commission on the Development of Education, and naming of their report as 'Learning to Be', symoblises such an interest.

IMPORTANCE OF EDUCATION

"The central task of education is to implant a will and facility for learning; it should produce not learned but learning people. The truly human society is a learning society, where grandparents, parents, and children are students together."

—Eric Hoffer

"No one has yet realized the wealth of sympathy, the kindness and generosity hidden in the soul of a child. The effort of every true education should be to unlock that treasure."

—Emma Goldman

"The only purpose of education is to teach a student how to live his life-by developing his mind and equipping him to deal with reality. The training he needs is theoretical, i.e., conceptual. He has to be taught to think, to understand, to integrate, to prove. He has to be taught the essentials of the knowledge discovered in the past-and he has to be equipped to acquire further knowledge by his own effort."

—Ayn Rand

"The aim of education should be to teach us rather how to think, than what to think rather to improve our minds, so as to enable us to think for ourselves, than to load the memory with the thoughts of other men."

—Bill Beattie

Education is the process of instruction aimed at the all round development of boys and girls. Education dispels ignorance. It is the only wealth that cannot be robbed. Learning includes the Moral Values and the improvement of character and the methods to increase the strength of mind.

Education plays an important role in the progress of an individual's mind and country. Ignorance and poverty are major speed-breakers in the developing country and can be overcome easily through education.

Generally, at the start of a very young age, children learn to develop and use their mental, moral and physical powers, which they acquire through various types of education. Education is commonly referred to as the process of learning and obtaining knowledge at school, in a form of formal education. However, the process of education does not only start when a child first attends school. Education begins at home. One does not only acquire knowledge from a teacher; one can learn and receive knowledge from a parent, family member and even an acquaintance. In almost all societies, attending school and receiving an education is extremely vital and necessary if one wants to achieve success.

However, unfortunately we have places in the world, where not everyone has an opportunity to receive this formal type of education. The opportunities that are offered are greatly limited. Sometimes there are not enough resources to provide schooling. Furthermore, because parents need their children to help them work in factories, have odd jobs, or just do farm work.

Since it is not traditional, in some places, to receive a formal education, the one who receives an education is usually envied, praised and even admired by members of the community. Children sometimes look at other children with awe. Just the same way as one child might envy another because he got a new pair of sneakers, and wishes he could have too. There is a sense of admiration but at the same time there is a sense of jealousy as well. Seeing your peer does better than yourself causes some tension and jealousy because of the scarce opportunities available. As a child, it's hard to understand why there is a difference.

Learning subjects in school is not enough. One can learn History, Mathematics, Science in school, and be "book-smart". In addition, one can learn how to live life by knowing what to say when, acting a certain way in certain situations and be "street-smart". These two types of knowledge are extremely essential to be successful in life. For example, you can have all the "book" knowledge in the world about a certain profession, but if you don't know how to behave with your co-workers and or your superiors, having "booked" knowledge won't get you too far.

But no matter what, education is the key that allows people to move up in the world, seek better jobs, and ultimately succeed fully in life. Education is very important, and no one should be deprived of it.

THE TEACHER

Each person can trace contribution of some teacher who helped that person to transform into a good human being with a more positive self-image, more self-confidence, more commitment and motivation to pursue excellence. This role of a teacher is universally acknowledged. In education, a teacher is one who helps students or pupils, often in a school, as well as in a family, religious or community setting. A teacher is an acknowledged guide or helper in processes of learning. A teacher's role may vary between cultures. Academic subjects are emphasized in many societies, but a teacher's duties may include instruction in craftsmanship or vocational training, spirituality, civics, community roles, or life skills. In modern schools and most contemporary occidental societies, where scientific pedagogy is practiced, the teacher is defined as a specialized profession on the same level as many other professions.

In the 13th chapter of the "*Bhagavadgita*" the characteristics of a real teacher are laid down as follows: absence of pride, free from hypocrisy, non-violence, forgiving nature, straight forwardness, service of the preceptor, purity of mind and body, steadfastness and self-control.

In line with this, centuries ago in this land of Vedas the teacher devoted all his time for the upliftment of his pupils in all directions - knowledge, morals, values etc. He was called the '*Guru* or *Acharya*'.

Guru Brahma Guru Vishnu Guru Devo Maheshwaraha

Guru Saakshat Para Brahma Tasmai Sree Gurave Namaha

Guru is verily the representative of Brahma (Creator), Vishnu (Preserver) and Shiva (Transformer). He creates, sustains knowledge and destroys the weeds of ignorance. Every person can salute such a Guru.

DEFINITION OF VALUE

According to *Cambridge Dictionary of Philosophy*, the value is the worth of something that philosophers discerned these main forms of intrinsic, instrumental, inherent and contributory value.

Values are described as the socially defined desires and goals that are internalized through the process of condition, learning and socialization.

Values are goals set for achievement and they motivate, define and colour all our activities cognitive, affective and conative. When education builds up true values in the life of our student, it has equipped the ship of students with RADAR and compass to sail clear on the stormy sea of life.

Values reflect different philosophical positions. The concepts of values are closely associated with the concept of man.

According to Jules Henry in "Culture against Man" (1963), values are something that we consider good such as love, kindness, quietness, contentment, fun, honesty, decency, relaxation and simplicity.

According to Carl Rogers in *Freedom to Learn* (1969), valuing is the tendency of a person to show preference.

According to Louis Raths, Merril and Harmin and Sidney B. Simon (1966) in *Values and Teaching*, values are due to the out of experiences may come certain and guides to behaviour. These tend to give direction to life.

According to Shepard B. Clough (1960) in *Basic Values of Western Civilization*, in a summary states that values have been variously viewed as preferences, criteria, objects and possessions, personality and status characteristics and states of mind that are absolutes, inherent in objects present in man and stages of mind and identical with his behaiour.

According to John Dewey "the value means primarily to prize, to esteem, to appraise, to estimate; it means the act of cherishing something, holding it dear and also the act of passing judgment upon the nature and amounts of values as compared with something else".

According to Parker, "values belong wholly to the inner world of mind. The satisfaction of desire is the real value; the thing that serves is only an instrument. A value is always an experience never a thing or an object".

According to Mukerjee "values are socially approved drives and goals that are internalized through the process of conditioning, learning or socialization and that becomes subjective preferences, standards and aspirations".

According to Alloport's "the term value means the relative prominence of the subject's interest or the dominant interest in personality".

According to Derek Rowntree's (1960), "Dictionary of Education" that the moral and aesthetics, principles, believes and standards that give coherence and direction to a persons decisions and actions. Where such values are held by or are imposed upon the majority of people in a society they may be known as social values.

In statistics, the different quantitative and qualitative in which an entity can be with respect to some variable that is different categories and measurement.

Values simply stated, are the determiners in the man that influence his choices in life and that decide his behaviour.

Values as indicated are inherent, in individual man but they are additionally inherent although perhaps less definably so, in collective man in a given culture that is or in a combination of cultures. Whatever the exact nature of human society, values exist in some form. In a primitive society, they reside in developed society they reside in written documents as well as in the intangible of social mores and expectances.

IMPORTANCE OF VALUE EDUCATION

Seven sins

Wealth without work,
Pleasure without conscience,
Knowledge without character,
Commerce without morality,
Science without humanity,
Worship without sacrifice,
Politics without principle.

—**Mahatma Gandhi**

Education in general and value education in particular occupies a prestigious place in the modern context of the contemporary society.

The problem of value education of the young has assumed increasing prominence in educational discussions during recent times. Parents, teachers and society at large are concerned about values and value education of children.

The world-wide resurgence of interest in value education has been explained as the natural response of the modern industrialized societies to the fast erosion of Moral Values in all aspects of life and the crisis of values experienced in modern times. It is common place to say that sweeping political, economic and social changes have overtaken human civilization during the past few centuries and these have been largely responsible for the predicament of the modern man. In the case of India, however, the picture appears to be slightly different. While there is no doubt that technological development, however little it might be, compared to the western societies, and is one factor that has contributed to the value crisis that the Indian society is facing today. There are also other factors like personal greed, meanness, selfishness, indifference to others' interests and laziness that have brought about large scale corruption in almost all spheres of life-personal and public, economic and political, moral and religious. One can even say that our fall in moral standards is not so much due to industrialization as to the lack of it. Perhaps, we can achieve better moral standards in our democratic way of national life if we become more industrialized and thus overcome mass poverty and the general feeling of insecurity which gives rise to greed.

The Education Commission (1964-66) says that:

> "a serious defect in the school curriculum is the absence of provision for education in social, moral and spiritual values. In the life of the majority of Indians, religion is a great motivating force and is intimately bound up with the formation of character and the inculcation of ethical values. A national system of education that is related to life needs and aspirations of the people cannot afford to ignore this purposeful fore."

The great defiance in the education in this millennium is, without doubt, to give special emphasis in man's, dignity and values, with a special vision that conceives him as creator who doesn't limit only to watch the established order, by the contrary, he dynamically participates in the changes that benefits the human race.

In the years of history, man's dignity has occupied a preponderant place, but actually we observe a deplorable decadency and crisis in the fundamental values, so we have to recover the course of our own humanity existence before that is forgotten in history route.

Today we have a society that the only practices are profits, earns, commerce and the great shares in which man is only and object, not a subject, so disposable as the same products that we make for only one use. For this reason, is that education development must essentiality contributes to the knowledge and significance of man as a person, and by no way allowed its mutilation, or worst, its own reduction as a thing of learning.

The values present a true perspective of the development of any society or nation. They tell us to what extent a society or nation has developed itself. Values are virtues, ideals and qualities on which actions and beliefs are based. Values are guiding principles that shape our world outlook, attitudes and conduct. Values however are either innate or acquired. Innate values are our inborn divine virtues such as love, peace, happiness, mercy and compassion as well as the positive moral qualities such as respect, humility, tolerance, responsibility, cooperation, honesty and simplicity.

DEFINITION OF MORAL VALUES

Moral values are evaluations of actions generally believed by the members of a given society to be either right or wrong.

Moral values refer to those values which are related to an individual's character and personality conforming to what is right and virtuous. They reveal a person's self-control. Examples: honesty, integrity, sense of responsibility, compassion etc. the realm of Moral Values is rather a debatable one. For example: according to sage Yagnavalkya, as a moral value '*dharma*' signifies the cultivation of the virtues of non-injury, sincerity, honesty, cleanliness, control of the sense, charity, self-restraint, love and forbearance. It may be observed that this list includes both social values (values that refer to the good of others) and individual values (values that serve to develop one's own character and will).

IMPORTANCE OF MORAL VALUES FOR THE PRESENT GENERATION STUDENTS

We know today's children are tomorrow's citizens. It is necessary to take care about present generation students. If we inculcate moral values in the students, the future generation will live happily. So it is necessary to give more importance for moral education.

Moral education involves social education but extends beyond it insofar as it covers the way the individual deals with his own powers and potentialities as well as how he behaves in his relationships with other people and the community at large. It is as much concerned with striving for personal wholeness as with generating a responsible attitude towards others and an understanding of right and wrong behaviour.

The most constructive factor in moral education is a happy, purposeful, stimulating home life which encourages the child to explore his powers while offering living guidance and setting appropriate limits to behaviour.

Indian culture is rooted deeply in her spiritual values and unless these values find their way into the life of students, education will lose its significance and will not fulfill its function of endowing the students with a vision to live by and with ideals to work for. Therefore, in deference to the cherished goals of democracy, socialism, humanism and secularism, it is very essential that our education system should evolve a new positive morality which could effectively be built into the school curriculum.

According to Peters J.

"The growth of morality and value is complex psycho-social phenomenon."

Morality is not something to be taken lightly. It is a form of thought and action, parallel to other forms, such as science, history and the study of literature. One should understand that science alone cannot promote a country's progress and prosperity. Equal importance should be given to character formation education also. There is no anti-thesis between religion and science. This has been clearly defended in the statement of Einstein that

"Science without religion is lame and religion without science is blind."

Hence, moral education deserves the status of a school subject in the curriculum. But, unfortunately the present system of education has not taken proper cognizance of this vital aspect of personality.

Modern mass society presents a sharp contrast, as the young grow up. They are faced with confusions, delays and discontinuities. Adolescents in particular are uncertain about themselves. Some are in conflict with themselves, bewildered an insecure.

Values are usually influenced by the changing philosophical ideologies, cultural and religious perspectives, social, political and geographical conditions. In modern emerging society, there has been a revolutionary change in the field of values due to many factors in addition to the influence of modern culture, industrialization, modernization, urbanization, globalization and multinationals.

Values are the guiding principles, decisive in day to day behaviors as also is critical life situations. Values are a set of principles or standards of behaviour. Values are regarded desirable, important and held in high esteem by a particular society in which a person lives.

Value education means inculcating in the children a sense of humanism, a deep concern for the well being of others and the nation. This can be accomplished only when we instill in the children a deep feeling of commitment to values that would build this country and bring back to the people pride in work that brings order, security and assured progress.

Value education refers to a programme of planned educational action aimed at the development of value and character. Every action and thought of ours leaves an impression in our mind. These impressions determine in our behaviour at a given moment and our responses to a given situation. The sum total of all our impressions is what determines our character. The past has determined the present and even so our present thoughts and actions will shape our future. This is a key principle governing personality development. The human values are resolved having lasting impact necessary for bringing about change in thought and conduct, in the 21st century.

If there is righteousness in the heart there will be beauty in character. If there is beauty in character there will be harmony in the home. When there is harmony in the home there will be order in the nation. When there is order in the nation there will be peace in the world.

At the boyhood state, individual physical development is concerned, during manhood and old age intellectual and spiritual values start dominating the corporal values. Therefore while imparting moral education, educators must keep in minds that the young must be educated.

Prizes may be given to the deserving persons for showing honesty, bravery, truth etc. The award should be given during school gathering. Contests may be organized on values of life.

According to Father of Indian Nation Gandhi

"If wealth is lost nothing is lost

If health is lost something is lost

If character is lost everything is lost"

So, best of all things is character.

LIST OF VALUES

(a) List of 'A-Z' Values collected by the investigator is given below:

1. Abundance
2. Acceptance
3. Accessibility
4. Accomplishment
5. Accuracy
6. Achievement
7. Acknowledgement
8. Activeness
9. Adaptability
10. Adoration
11. Adroitness
12. Adventure
13. Affection
14. Affluence
15. Aggressiveness
16. Agility
17. Alertness
18. Altruism
19. Ambition
20. Amusement
21. Anticipation
22. Appreciation
23. Approachability
24. Articulacy
25. Assertiveness
26. Assurance
27. Attentiveness
28. Attractiveness
29. Audacity
30. Availability
31. Awareness
32. Awe
33. Balance
34. Beauty
35. Being the best
36. Belonging
37. Benevolence
38. Bliss
39. Boldness
40. Bravery

41. Brilliance
42. Buoyancy
43. Calmness
44. Camaraderie
45. Candor
46. Capability
47. Care
48. Carefulness
49. Celebrity
50. Certainty
51. Challenge
52. Charity
53. Charm
54. Chastity
55. Cheerfulness
56. Clarity
57. Cleanliness
58. Clear-mindedness
59. Cleverness
60. Closeness
61. Comfort
62. Commitment
63. Compassion
64. Completion
65. Composure
66. Concentration
67. Confidence
68. Conformity
69. Congruency
70. Connection
71. Consciousness
72. Consistency
73. Contentment
74. Continuity
75. Contribution
76. Control
77. Conviction
78. Conviviality
79. Coolness
80. Cooperation
81. Cordiality
82. Correctness
83. Courage
84. Courtesy
85. Craftiness
86. Creativity
87. Credibility
88. Cunning
89. Curiosity
90. Daring
91. Decisiveness
92. Decorum
93. Deference
94. Delight
95. Dependability
96. Depth
97. Desire
98. Determination
99. Devotion
100. Devoutness

101. Dexterity
102. Dignity
103. Diligence
104. Direction
105. Directness
106. Discipline
107. Discovery
108. Discretion
109. Diversity
110. Dominance
111. Dreaming
112. Drive
113. Duty
114. Dynamism
115. Eagerness
116. Economy
117. Ecstasy
118. Education
119. Effectiveness
120. Efficiency
121. Elation
122. Elegance
123. Empathy
124. Encouragement
125. Endurance
126. Energy
127. Enjoyment
128. Entertainment
129. Enthusiasm
130. Excellence
131. Excitement
132. Exhilaration
133. Expectancy
134. Expediency
135. Experience
136. Expertise
137. Exploration
138. Expressiveness
139. Extravagance
140. Extroversion
141. Exuberance
142. Fairness
143. Faith
144. Fame
145. Family
146. Fascination
147. Fashion
148. Fearlessness
149. Ferocity
150. Fidelity
151. Fierceness
152. Financial independence
153. Firmness
154. Fitness
155. Flexibility
156. Flow
157. Fluency
158. Focus
159. Fortitude
160. Frankness

161. Freedom
162. Friendliness
163. Frugality
164. Fun
165. Gallantry
166. Generosity
167. Gentility
168. Giving
169. Grace
170. Gratitude
171. Gregariousness
172. Growth
173. Guidance
174. Happiness
175. Harmony
176. Health
177. Heart
178. Helpfulness
179. Heroism
180. Holiness
181. Honesty
182. Honor
183. Hopefulness
184. Hospitality
185. Humility
186. Humor
187. Hygiene
188. Imagination
189. Impact
190. Impartiality
191. Independence
192. Industry
193. Ingenuity
194. Inquisitiveness
195. Insightfulness
196. Inspiration
197. Integrity
198. Intelligence
199. Intensity
200. Intimacy
201. Intrepidness
202. Introversion
203. Intuition
204. Intuitiveness
205. Inventiveness
206. Investing
207. Joy
208. Judiciousness
209. Justice
210. Keenness
211. Kindness
212. Knowledge
213. Leadership
214. Learning
215. Liberation
216. Liberty
217. Liveliness
218. Logic
219. Longevity
220. Love

221. Loyalty
222. Majesty
223. Making a difference
224. Mastery
225. Maturity
226. Meekness
227. Mellowness
228. Meticulousness
229. Mindfulness
230. Modesty
231. Motivation
232. Mysteriousness
233. Neatness
234. Nerve
235. Obedience
236. Open-mindedness
237. Openness
238. Optimism
239. Order
240. Organization
241. Originality
242. Outlandishness
243. Outrageousness
244. Passion
245. Peace
246. Perceptiveness
247. Perfection
248. Perkiness
249. Perseverance
250. Persistence
251. Persuasiveness
252. Philanthropy
253. Piety
254. Playfulness
255. Pleasantness
256. Pleasure
257. Poise
258. Polish
259. Popularity
260. Potency
261. Power
262. Practicality
263. Pragmatism
264. Precision
265. Preparedness
266. Presence
267. Privacy
268. Proactivity
269. Professionalism
270. Prosperity
271. Prudence
272. Punctuality
273. Purity
274. Quality
275. Quiet
276. Realism
277. Reason
278. Reasonableness
279. Recognition
280. Recreation

281. Refinement
282. Reflection
283. Relaxation
284. Reliability
285. Religiousness
286. Resilience
287. Resolution
288. Resolve
289. Resourcefulness
290. Respect
291. Rest
292. Restraint
293. Reverence
294. Richness
295. Rigor
296. Sacredness
297. Sacrifice
298. Sagacity
299. Saintliness
300. Sanguinity
301. Satisfaction
302. Security
303. Self-control
304. Selflessness
305. Self-reliance
306. Sensitivity
307. Sensuality
308. Serenity
309. Service
310. Sexuality
311. Sharing
312. Shrewdness
313. Significance
314. Silence
315. Silliness
316. Simplicity
317. Sincerity
318. Skillfulness
319. Solidarity
320. Solitude
321. Soundness
322. Speed
323. Spirit
324. Spirituality
325. Spontaneity
326. Spunk
327. Stability
328. Stealth
329. Stillness
330. Strength
331. Structure
332. Success
333. Support
334. Supremacy
335. Surprise
336. Sympathy
337. Synergy
338. Teamwork
339. Temperance
340. Thankfulness

341. Thoroughness
342. Thoughtfulness
343. Thrift
344. Tidiness
345. Timeliness
346. Traditionalism
347. Tranquility
348. Transcendence
349. Trust
350. Trustworthiness
351. Truth
352. Understanding
353. Unflappability
354. Uniqueness
355. Unity
356. Usefulness
357. Utility
358. Valor
359. Variety
360. Victory
361. Vigor
362. Virtue
363. Vision
364. Vitality
365. Vivacity
366. Warmth
367. Watchfulness
368. Wealth
369. Willfulness
370. Willingness
371. Winning
372. Wisdom
373. Wittiness
374. Wonder
375. X-Value
376. Youthfulness
377. Zeal

(b) Values identified by NCERT

1. Abstinence
2. Appreciation of cultural values
3. Anti-Untouchability
4. Citizenship
5. Consideration for others
6. Concern for others
7. Co-operation
8. Cleanliness
9. Compassion
10. Common Cause
11. Common good
12. Courage
13. Courtesy
14. Curiosity
15. Democratic decision making
16. Devotion
17. Dignity of the individual
18. Dignity of manual work

19. Duty
20. Discipline
21. Endurance
22. Equality
23. Friendship
24. Faithfulness
25. Fellow-feeling
26. Freedom
27. Forward look
28. Good manners
29. Gratitude
30. Gentlemanliness
31. Honesty
32. Helpfulness .
33. Humanism
34. Hygienic living
35. Initiative
36. Integrity .
37. justice
38. Kindness
39. Kindness to animals
40. Leadership
41. National Unity
42. Loyality to duty
43. National Consciousness
44. Non-Violence
45. National Integration
46. Obedience
47. Peace
48. Proper Utilisation of time
49. Punctuality
50. Patriotism
51. Quest for knowledge
52. Purity
53. Resourcefulness
54. Regularity
55. Respect for others
56. Reverence for old age
57. Sincerity
58. Simple living
59. Social justice
60. Self-discipline
61. Self-help
62. Self-respect
63. Self-confidence
64. Self-support
65. Self-study
66. Self-reliance
67. Self-control
68. Self-restraint
69. Social service
70. Solidarity of mankind
71. Sense of social responsibility
72. Sense of discrimination between good and bad
73. Socialism
74. Sympathy

75. Secularism and respect for all religions
76. Spirit of enquiry
77. Team work
78. Team spirit
79. Truthfulness
80. Tolerance
81. Universal truth
82. Universal love
83. Value for national and civic property

(c) Bill Gothard has informally specified a set of forty-nine virtues

1. Exhorting

1. Creativity vs. Underachievement
2. Discernment vs. Judgement
3. Discretion vs. Simple-mindedness
4. Enthusiasm vs. Apathy
5. Faith vs. Presumption
6. Love vs. Selfishness
7. Wisdom vs. Natural Inclinations

2. Giving

1. Cautiousness vs. Recklessness/Rashness
2. Frugality vs. Luxury
3. Fulfilment/Contentment vs. Covetousness
4. Gratitude/Gratefulness vs. Ungratefulness/ Unthankfulness
5. Promptness/Punctuality vs. Tardiness
6. Resourcefulness vs. Wastefulness
7. Tolerance vs. Intolerance/Prejudice

3. Mercy

1. Attentiveness vs. Unconcern
2. Compassion vs. Indifference
3. Deference vs. Rudeness
4. Fairness vs. Partiality

5. Gentleness vs. Harshness
6. Meekness vs. Anger
7. Sensitivity vs. Callousness

4. Organization

1. Ambition/Initiative vs. Unresponsiveness
2. Commitment vs. Untrustworthiness
3. Courage vs. Cowardice
4. Decisiveness vs. Vacillation/Double-mindedness
5. Determination vs. Faint-heartedness
6. Loyalty vs. Unfaithfulness
7. Orderliness vs. Confusion/Disorganization

5. Prophecy

1. Adventurousness/Boldness vs. Trepidation/Fearfulness
2. Compliance/Obedience vs. Obstinacy/Willfulness
3. Forgiveness vs. Disaffirmation/Rejection
4. Persuasiveness vs. Combativeness/Contentiousness
5. Sincerity vs. Two-facedness/Hypocrisy
6. Truthfulness vs. Duplicity/Deception
7. Uprightness vs. Impurity

6. Serving

1. Alertness vs. Unawareness
2. Availability vs. Self-centeredness
3. Endurance vs. Quitting/Giving up
4. Flexibility vs. Resistance
5. Generosity vs. Stinginess
6. Hospitality vs. Loneliness
7. Joyfulness vs. Self-pity

7. Teaching

1. Dependability vs. Inconsistency

2. Diligence vs. Slothfulness
3. Patience vs. Restlessness
4. Reverence vs. Disrespect
5. Security vs. Anxiety
6. Self-control vs. Self-indulgence
7. Thoroughness vs. Incompleteness

CLASSIFICATION OF VALUES

1. Gandhi's Classification

In order to create new social order Gandhiji introduced Nai Talim in the year 1937, which is popularly known as Basic Education.

- Truth
- Non-violence
- Freedom
- Democracy
- *Sarva Dharma Samabhava*
- Equality
- Self-realization
- Purity of ends and means
- Self-discipline
- *Suddhi*.

2. Gail M. Inlaw Classification

- Traditional and cultural values
- Economic values
- Political values
- Values in science and technology
- Philosophical values
- Values of the new left
- Values of the black community.

3. Plato's Classification

- Truth
- Beauty
- Goodness.

4. Parker's Classification of Values

- Biological values
- Economic values
- Affective values
- Social values
- Intellectual values
- Aesthetic values
- Moral Values
- Religious values.

5. Spranger's Classification

- Theoretical values
- Economic values
- Aesthetic values
- Social values
- Political values
- Religious values.

6. General Classification

In general, values may be classified as personal, social, moral, spiritual and behavioural values.

i. Personal Values

They refer to those, which are desired and cherished by the individual irrespective of his social relationship. The individual determines his own standards of achievement and attains these targets without explicit interaction with any other persons.

ii. Social Values

Social values refer to those, which are oriented and concerning to society. These values are practiced because of our association with others. Unlike personal values the practice of social values necessitates the interaction of two or more persons.

iii. Moral Values

Moral Values related to individual's character and personality conforming to what is right and virtuous. They reveal a person's self-control.

iv. Spiritual Values

Spiritual values refer to ethical value. It arises from the inner depth dimension of man. It bestows the capacity to see the false as the false and the true as the true. It is like a key to the integration of man. The ultimate ethical value is called spiritual value. Spiritual value is the awareness of itself.

v. Behavioural Values

Behavioural values refer to all good manners that are needed to make our life successful and joyous. These are the values, which are exhibited by our conduct and behaviour in our daily life. Behavioural values will adorn our life and spread cordially friendliness.

COMMITTEES AND COMMISSIONS TOWARDS VALUES

The importance of value education has been duly recognized by different education commissions and committees appointed by the government.

- The Hartog Committee (1929) felt that religious instruction can be given in common schools outside the school hours.
- The Central Advisory Board of Education felt in 1946 that religious and moral instruction was important and that it should be left to the community to which the pupils belong.
- The Radhakrishnan Commission (1948) felt that "if we exclude spiritual training in our institutions we would be untrue to our whole historical development".
- The Secondary Education Commission's report in 1953 favoured that religious and moral instruction should be given in schools outside the school hours on voluntary basis.
- The Sri Prakasa Commission of Religious and Moral instruction (1959) had recommended that moral education should be imparted in all educational institutions.
- Kothari Commission (1964-66) felt that "a serious defect in the school system is the absence of provision for education in social, moral and spiritual values. A national system of education that is related to life needs and aspirations of the people cannot afford to ignore this purposeful force."
- National Policy on Education (1986) felt that "the growing concern over the erosion of essential values and an increasing cynicism in society has brought to focus the need for readjustments in the curriculum in order to make education a forceful tool for the cultivation of social and Moral Values."
- Programme of Action (NPE, 1992) recommended that "the framework emphasized value education as an integral part of school curriculum. It highlighted the values drawn from national goals, universal perception, ethical considerations and character building. It stressed

the role of education in combating obscurantism, religious fanaticism, exploitation and injustice as well as the inculcation of values."

The main function of education is to produce citizens with sound character and a healthy personality. Good citizens are the only hope for the progress and prosperity of the country. Inspiring values, ideals, proper moral conduct, life based upon good principles is an essential requisite.

The ideals of virtue, goodness, truth and manliness form the very essence of real dignified living.

INCULCATION OF VALUES THROUGH CURRICULUM

"Today, it is no longer desirable to undertake educational reforms in piecemeal fashion, without a concept of the totality of the goals and modes of the educational process. To find out how to reshape its component parts, one must have a vision of the whole" (UNESCO, 1972).

The National Policy on Education has laid considerable emphasis on value education by highlighting the need to make education a powerful tool for cultivation of social and moral values. Keeping in view the pluralistic base of our society, the education system besides preserving our cultural heritage has also to nurture our youth to be more adaptable to life in the changing environment. An inter-linking of education and culture has also been emphasized in the Programme of Action for implementation of National Policy on Education.

People say that "Values cannot be taught but caught". Against this belief educationists strongly advocate that values could be taught with sufficient care and caution.

The National Council for Educational Research and Training (NCERT) in its publication documents on Social, Moral and Spiritual Values in Education (1979) has drawn up 84 values to be inculcated through education.

The cultural values need to be identified for standard curricula all over the country. Respect for the old, care for poor and up-privileged and tolerance should be some of the values. Value based inter-personal relations, importance of racial and religious harmony and concern for humanity should form the basis for friendship and cooperation amongst the people.

Fine arts, music, creative writing, puppetry and theatre are to be given due place in the curricula right from school to the university level.

The curriculum should strike a balance between theory and practice. Creative work in fields of music, dance, literature, drama, visual arts is essential to cultivate the inherent tolerance of children.

Value/moral education should be thought as a compulsory subject up to the high school level. It should be made an examinable subject at the school level. Evaluation of value education should be based on compassion, self-reliance, respect and honesty.

Language is an importance medium for inculcating, fostering and propagating of moral vales and national cultural heritage. Education through mother tongue needs to be ensured.

INCULCATION OF VALUES THROUGH CO-CURRICULAR ACTIVITIES

Co-curricular activities play a very significant role in inculcating different values in the students. For all-round development of personalities of the students co-curricular activities are considered to be very important now-a-days. Previously the term "extra-curricular activities" was used for outdoor activities and other cultural programmes organized in the school. But now-a-days this term has been discarded keeping in view the importance of these activities. In many progressive schools there is an allotment of certain periods for these co-curricular activities in their regular time table.

Through these activities, many values can be inculcated profitably. Co-curricular activities form an integral part of the modern school curriculum. They should be made more and more purposive and fruitful as well as value oriented with the democratic base and purposeful pursuit. This can be done, provided children have an opportunity of having living experience of moral life through these activities.

In programmes of outdoor activities, the children are taken out of the school to the areas of adventure, appreciation of art and culture and the places of historical values. They can be brought avenues in the training of initiative, team-work, self-discipline and learn much about our cultural heritage and historical details. Besides games and sports, there are several outdoor activities, namely, NCC, Scouting & Guiding, Mountaineering, Trekking, Excursion, Field trips etc., which may serve the purpose of inculcation of desired values among the students and formation of character.

Almost in all the schools and colleges various festivals are organized at different levels. Festivals may be classified into three heads:

1. National Festivals,
2. Religious Festivals and
3. Birth/Death anniversaries of great persons.

Besides these, there are so many occasions such as Sports Day, Teachers' Day, Parents' day, Annual Day, UNO Day, etc., in the school. Through these activities, the qualities of leadership, self-discipline, co-operation, team-work, etc., can be easily developed. Through these activities, new dimension can be given to the personalities of the students.

NEED FOR RESEARCH IN MORAL VALUES

Today there is lot of degradation of values in every walk of human life. Individuals are crazy for material wealth. Money making is the main motive of the majority of the individuals even through immoral ways. Proper foundation will be laid on moral values at the initial stages of the child. Schools and colleges are the institutions which can shoulder the responsibility of inculcating moral values among the people and students. Hence there is a need to take up research activities in the area of moral values.

RESUME OF SUCCEEDING CHAPTERS

Chapter 2 deals with a brief review of related research work done in the area of Moral Values/Judgement.

Chapter 3 deals with the present study, i.e., statement of the problem, need for the study, purpose of the study, scope of the study, definition of the terms, objectives of the study, hypotheses to be tested, variables studied and limitations of the study.

Chapter 4 deals with an account of methods employed in the investigation for collection of the data and the statistical techniques employed in the analysis of the data.

Chapter 5 deals with analysis of data and a detailed discussion of results of the present study.

Chapter 6 deals with summary of the investigation, major findings, conclusions, educational implications, recommendations and suggestions for further research.

2

REVIEW OF RELATED LITERATURE

"A good student is he who continuously uses his faculty of observation, puts two and two together and carves out for himself a path in life".

—Mahatma Gandhi

"Literature is not exhaustible, for the sufficient and simple reason that a single book is not. A book is not an isolated entity: it is a narration, an axis of innumerable narrations. One literature differs from another, either before or after it, not so much because of the text as for the manner in which it is read."

—Jorge Luis Borges

"Books are the carriers of civilization. Without books, history is silent, literature dumb, science crippled, thought and speculation at a standstill."

—Barbara W. Tuchman

This chapter deals with the internal review of the literature. It is an attempt to discover relevant materials published in the problem are under study. This covers the empirical research studies done previously in the problem area.

NEED TO KNOW ABOUT RELATED LITERATURE

"Practically all human knowledge can be found in books and libraries. Unlike other animals that must start a new with each generation, man builds upon the accumulated and recorded knowledge of the past" (Best, 1959).

For any worth while study in any field of knowledge, the research worker needs an adequate familiarity with the library and its many resources. Only then will an effective search for specialized knowledge be possible. The search for reference material is a time consuming, but very fruitful phase of a research programme. Every investigator must know what sources are available in his field of enquiry, which of them he is likely to use and where and how to find them (Sukhia *et al.*, 1980).

In the field of education, as in other fields too, the research worker needs to acquire up-to-date information about what has been thought and done in the particular area from which he intends to take up a problem for research. But it is found that generally the extent of important; up-to-date information regarding educational research and ideas possessed by educational workers is very limited (Sukhia *et al.*, 1980).

Availability of adequate information and possession of sufficient familiarity with it, however, is not one and the same thing. Availability of adequate information about educational thought and research does not by itself result in possession of its knowledge by the researcher. The researcher must apply himself keenly to the task. On the other hand a research worker may be very keen to possess up to date information regarding his field, and may try hard to be posted up to date, and yet fail to get enough information due to the non-existence of sources of such information. In India, the research worker quite often comes across the latter handicap (Sukhia *et al.*, 1980).

Survey of related literature, besides forming one of the early chapters in research report for orientating the researchers, serves some other purposes. Good, Barr and Scates (1941) analysed these purposes as given under:

1. To show whether the evidence already available solves the problem adequately without further investigation, and thus to avoid the risk of duplication;
2. To provide ideas, theories, explanations or hypotheses valuable in formulating the problem;
3. To suggest methods of research appropriate to the problem;
4. To locate comparative data useful in the interpretation of results; and
5. To contribute to the general scholarship of the investigator.

There are number of studies relating to the moral values done in the past. However, only the literature pertaining to the independent variables (sex, locality, caste, religion, study habits, self-concepts and personality etc.) used in the present study is referred in the succeeding pages.

MORAL VALUES – SOCIO-DEMOGRAPHIC VARIABLES

Boys and girls at the adolescent stage studying in urban and rural schools/colleges may be having different moral views. Because of the technological advancement in the urban environment may be more modern and sophisticated where as the rural environment may be more agriculture oriented. Therefore, this background itself might affect the moral values among the students. Not only locality but also other socio-demographic variables affect the moral values among the students. Hence, socio-demographic variables are treated as independent variables in the present study.

The term socio-demographic variables are broadly defined to include the social, educational, professional or occupational and economic status of the parents. The environment facilities also are taken into account.

Socio-economic status of the family plays an important role in boosting up the educational proficiency of children (Burt 1937, Jammur 1961, Chopra1966).

According to Mukharjee (1956), "values are socially approved desires and goals that are internalized through the process of conditioning, learning or socialization and that become subjective preferences, standards and aspirations."

According to Kane (1962), "values are the ideals, beliefs or norms which a society or the large majority members hold. They are responsible for the definition of a problem, they may help to create a problem and they may also interface with its solution."

According to Zale and Davig (1963), "values are the ideas in the minds of men comparable to norms in that they specify how people should behave. Values also such attach degrees of goodness to activities and prescribe how people should behave in certain relationship etc. We are expected to behave respectfully towards other persons."

Wright and Cox (1967) conducted a research on relationship between moral judgement and religious belief on a sample of 2276 pupils of whom 49.6% were boys and 50.4% girls from 6th forms of 96 maintained grammar schools in England. The major findings were as follows:

- ❖ On nearly all items, girls were more severe in their judgements than were boys.
- ❖ Age, subject of studies and experience of co-education were not found to be related to moral judgement.
- ❖ Consistency, indices of religiosity were found to be severity of moral judgement.

❖ The more ascetic the moral issue, the stronger the association with religious belief and practice.

Parikh (1968) conducted a study on development of moral judgement and its relation to family environmental factors in Indian and American families. The findings have indicated that the difference in the level of moral judgement development, between the mother and father suggest a possible sex difference but the results do not show any significant difference between boys and girls.

In terms of moral reasoning, proportionately more females remained at the conventional level than males and lesser percentage reached the post conventional level (Kohlberg and Turiel, 1971; Hunn, 1971; Hostein, 1973). One explanation for this difference was that limitations were imposed on female's growth by Social conventions and Behavioural expectations.

Chandrakumar and Arokiaswamy (1974) conducted the study to verify gender influence over the value orientation of the college students, findings of the study shows that:

(1) The female students had little better value orientation than the male students.

(2) Gender did not influence the value orientation of the college students.

(3) There was no consistency in the preferences and values in gender in all three years.

Freeman (1974) conducted a study to investigate individual differences in moral judgement in relation to age and sex. It was found that females more than males were influenced by the sex of the story model in their Judgements. Females showed more mature Judgements than males.

Mohundro (1976) attempted to determine a relationship between Kohlberg's stages of reasoning expressed in the justification of values with the value hierarchy sex and socio-economic and it was found that socio-economic status is related to the stages of moral reasoning and value positions.

Gupta (1977) studied individual differences in value pattern and personality type of the school going adolescents (400 boys and 400 girls were taken from the secondary schools of Eastern U.P.). The major findings of the study were boys and girls differed significantly in their values.

Dockstander (1979) made a comparative study of developmental sex differences in moral reasoning. The findings of this study showed no significant differences between males and females in the levels of moral development at the 7th and 11th grade. At the 7th grade level there was a significant difference at the 0.05 level between the moral reasoning of female experimental students and female control group students, and no such difference was shown at the 11th grade level.

Evans (1980), Gongre (1981) and Johnson (1979) were found that there was relationship regarding socio-economic status and the stages of moral development and moral judgement.

Evans (1980) conducted a study to investigate whether having knowledge of Kohlberg's theory of moral development was a factor in predicting stage development. The findings do not permit conclusions regarding the relationship of stages of development of knowledge of Kohlberg's theory and its multivariables – sex, academic achievement and socio-economic status.

Priya (1980) conducted a study on the relationship between feelings of security, insecurity, family attachment and values on educational achievement. It was concluded that the relationship between the security insecurity scores, the family attachment and values scores was positive.

Researches done by Siefering (1981), Fifis (1978), Benninga (1976) and Johnson (1981) findings indicated that there is no significant sex difference in moral judgement scores.

Bush (1981) investigated the validity of Kohlberg's measure of moral reasoning from a role-identification stand point. The findings revealed that males and females staged significantly higher on the Alternative Dilemma Questionnaire (ADQ) than on the Defining Issues Test (DIT).

Johnson (1981) conducted a study to determine whether selected children's stories can be utilized to increase on Kohlberg's moral development scale for 6th grade sample. The findings revealed no sex difference in moral growth. But there was a significant difference means gain score changes of the low socio-group and the middle socio-economic groups.

Lewis (1982) compared the moral development of gifted students with the moral development of regular ability students. The findings indicated that a positive correlation between cognitive and moral development and between cognitive development and socio-economic status. Gifted students were found to be significantly different from regular students in their socio-economic status.

Connor (1982) studied sex and leadership differences in moral perspective, field dependence and moral judgement. Female leaders were significantly more likely to be scored as demonstrating principled thinking in Defining Issues Test. It was suggested that the Defining Issues Test was possible tapping reasoning other than formal deductive logic. Examination of female protocols indicated; support for the idea that female reason inductively about moral problems rather than deductively applying the rules to fairness.

Bannon (1982) conducted a study on sex differences in parental press at several socio-economic levels. The study was conducted to know the parental involvement and their contribution to the education of the child.

The major findings of the study were:

(1) The distribution of scores of boys and girls in all the five areas (educational, social, physical, emotional and moral) of parental press showed lack of symmetry.

(2) The girls secured better points in educational and physical

areas whereas boys exhibited better scores in the emotional and moral areas.

(3) Sex, locality and Socio-economic Status did not affect the parental press scores.

(4) The emotional, educational and moral areas of parental press appeared to make major contribution in the prediction of academic achievement of boys whereas in the case of girls, moral, social and educational areas of parental press seemed to contribute much in the predication of academic achievement.

(5) For both the groups' moral press played a dominating role among the five areas of parental press.

Sipaur (1983) compared educated boys and girls of 9th and 11th grade. For moral development and self-concept, he found that the moral development scores of the girls were significantly higher than those of boys for overall sample and for 9th grade level. But no significant difference was found at the 11th grade.

Marrie and Elliot (1984) conducted a study to know the children's (90 subjects, ages 6, 8 and 10 years) concepts of moral and prudential rules were assessed in this study. Moral and prudential events are similar in that they may involve consequences to persons, but also differ in that morality bears upon social relations and prudence does not. The findings showed that most subjects regard moral and prudential rules as useful their violation as wrong, the validity of the actions as non-contingent on rules or authority, and as generalisable; these effect were stronger for the moral than the prudential rules, with older children distinguishing the 2 male types. However, the reasons given in justification of moral rules focused on both consequences. Moral rules were attributed more importance than the prudential rules. The pattern of findings indicated that children differentiate between consequences and regulations of social were no significant difference on emotional maturity. Residence did not link with emotional maturity. Intelligence and value of superior boys was higher than that of superior girls.

Verma and Tyagi (1988) made an attempt to find out whether the sex differences exist in the values of senior secondary school teachers. The findings indicated that male teachers were significantly higher on economic and political values and lower on social values as compared to female teachers.

Zupanic and Horvat (1990) studied the relation of moral development, disciplinary methods, and emergence of guilt feelings. The results were evaluated according to group, identification of character, emotional recognition, character Judgement in conditions of intentional and accidental damage, and conceptions of guilt. Results indicate that age but not social group is associated with guilt conceptions.

Chand (1992) conducted study to examine the personal values of adolescent boys and girls in relation to socio-economic status and academic achievement. Findings revealed that there was no significant correlation between socio-economic status and religious, democratic, economic, knowledge, hedonistic, power and family and prestige values.

Sati (1992) compared the needs, values, aspirations and adjustments of SC and non-SC secondary schools in relation to their academic achievement. Sample of the study consisted of 200 students from each group. The findings of the study revealed that the SC boys and girls did not differ in their values and educational aspirations. SC students had higher theoretical, political, order autonomous, affiliation nurturance and endurance needs than non-SC students.

Wark and Krebs (1996) investigated the effects of gender, gender role, and type of moral dilemma on moral maturity and moral orientation on 55 female and 55 male university students. Moral state, moral orientation and the relation between them varied across dilemmas. Females were more consistent than males in moral stage; males were consistent in moral orientation. Females made higher stage and more care-based moral judgement than males made on personal real-life dilemmas. The observed variations occurred primarily because males reported more State 2, justice pulling anti-social dilemmas than females, and females reported more State 3, care-pulling pro-social dilemmas than males.

Elbedour *et al*., (1997) examined the moral development of three groups of children, who had been subjected to varying degrees of political violence and economic advantage, in an attempt to determine if group membership or gender influenced the level of moral reasoning or orientation. Ninety-three students (8-13 years old Israel Jewish and Bedouin school children, and Palestine west bank school children) were asked various moral reasoning questions based on an animal fable involving a moral dilemma fewer than 3 (hypothetical, role-taking, political) conditions. Results indicate that mutually solutions to moral dilemmas were given more frequently by Israel Jewish children than Israeli Bedouin or Palestinian children as the questions shifted from abstract to real life situations. No significant gender differences were found between Jewish children and Bedouin children in hypothetical issues; however, violence and limited resources were found to affect moral judgement in real life situations for boys, but not for girls.

Lagerspetz (1998) administered a Moral Approval of Aggression (MAA) inventory and the Bem Sex-Role Inventory to 48 Military Officer Trainers (OTs), 35 conscientious objectors (COs) to armed service, and 32 women of comparable age. Aggression was mostly approved of among the OTs and least among the COs, with the women scoring in the middle somewhat closer to OTs. Differences in sex role identity emerged, so that OTs often chose a masculine sex role, whereas for COs, the choice of an androgynous roles with equal frequency. The MAA count not be explained on the basis of sex role identification.

Mahamoodali (1998) examined the relationship among personal values career aspirations, socio-economic status, academic achievements and educational choice. Researcher conducted the study on 500 samples (250 male and 250 female). The finding of the study reveals that the academic achievement correlated significantly and positively with socio-economic status, knowledge value and occupational aspirations and negatively with power value.

Humphrics *et al* (2000) examined the ways in such gender, empathy and cultural orientation (communalism and competitive individualism) influence the Moral Judgements of urban 5th and 8th grade African American children. Pencil and paper measures of these constructs were completed by 44 - 5th, 56 - 8th graders. Results revealed separate correlation matrices and path analysis models were computed for girls and boys. Communalism, empathy, and grade emerged as significant correlations and predictors' moral reasoning and moral reasoning for boys. Grade was the only significant correlate and predictor of moral reasoning for girls.

Deguchi and Ohkawa (2000) examined that characteristics of empathy with age and the relationship between empathy and moral jedgement on 1148 male and 170 female juvenile delinquents (14-19 years) in Japan.

The main results:

(1) The female Ss (subjects) showed higher empathy rates and moral judgement rates than male Ss, but females' in-group B showed a lower empathy rate than any other group.

(2) The male Ss; empathy rate and moral judgement rate increased with age.

(3) The female Ss; empathy rate and moral judgement rate did not show significant differences between ages, but females in group B showed the lowest rate among the 3 groups.

Koexing (2001) explained the limited knowledge on moral development in abused, neglected and non maltreated children from low socio-economic backgrounds. Findings showed that, contrary to prediction, neglected children engaged in significantly less rule-compatible behaviour compared to non-maltreated children. In addition, maltreatment status differences interacted with gender on several of the moral paradigms. Abused girls displayed significantly less guilt and fewer dónation behaviours than neglected girls, finally results revealed that both abusive and neglectful mothers are more likely to depict a power assertive discipline style, whereas comparison mothers are likely to employee an inductive style of discipline. However, no evidence was found that maternal discipline styles act as a moderator in relation between maltreatment and moral development.

Yadava *et al*. (2001) investigated on a sample of 200 male/female students (aged 15-17) of IX and X classes and sub-cultural difference in aggression and moral values. Results indicated that the aggression was not influenced by gender or areas. However, moral disengagement was found to be higher in males and in rural subjects as compared to their female and urban be an important mediator of aggression, at least in rural and female subjects.

Dawson (2002) examined the four sets of data, collected by four different teams over a period of 30 years. Common item equating, which yielded correlations from 94 to 97 across data sets, was employed to justify the data for a new analysis. Probabilistic conjoint measurement was used to model the results. The detailed analysis of these pooled data confirms results reported in previous research about the ordered acquisition of moral stages and the relationship between moral stages and age, education, and sex. The major findings are:

(1) Empirical evidence that transitions between childhood and adult stages of development involve similar mechanisms.

(2) Support for the notion of stages as qualitatively distinct modes of reasoning that display properties consistent with a notion structured ensemble.

(3) Evidence of a stage between Kohlberg's stage 3 and 4 consist with reports from earlier research, the relationship between educational attainment and moral development is linear, suggesting that educational

environments have an equivalent impact across the course of development. Older males have slightly higher score than older females after age and education are taken into account.

MORAL VALUES – PERSONALITY

Maslow (1938) considered "values as a psychological need".

Woodruff (1952) defines "values as an object, condition or activity which the individual feels, has an effect on his well being". According to him "values are conceptualized in terms of personal happiness, security and existence of behaving organism".

Hardold Falding (1965) says "a value is a generalized end that guides behaviour towards uniformity in the varieties of situation with the object of repeating a particular self-sufficient satisfaction. Thus, the values are organizing ends, organizing precisely because many other satisfaction and actions are subordinate to them".

Hall and Lindzey (1966) opine the amount of psychic energy invested in an element of the personality is called value of that element. Value is a measure of intensity. When we spear of placing a high value upon a particular idea as fouling be mean that the idea as fouling exerts a considerable force instigating and directing behaviour.

According to Jones and Gerad (1967), value is a motivation which sustains an individual's efforts to achieve a particular goal. "This suggests that the person makes his persistent efforts to achieve a goal because it is a value for him".

Varma (1972) had undertaken a study of 'Relationship between the parents of interpersonal relation and the value of teachers and students in secondary schools'. The major findings were:

i) The value system of the teachers and students were found to be quite different from each other and teachers were found to be more concerned with their status and power and less with knowledge and social virtue.

ii) Friendly interpersonal relation between the pairs of individuals was found to be unrelated to the value systems of the paired members.

iii) The unfriendly interpersonal relation between the pairs of individuals was not found to be related to the value systems of paired members.

iv) The role of a value, in its individual capacity as a correlates of interpersonal relations, was found to be depend on its own native such as affiliate or competitive, and on its position in the value system of the group.

v) A competitive value was found to be a correlate of paired friendly relations when it was low, average and not high. An affiliate value was found to be correlate of paired friendly relations when it was high or average and not low.

vi) Dominant values did not differentiate between high and low SES groups and vii) The popular teachers were found to be helpful and cooperative in achieving the students goals and making their school life a pleasant experience, while the unpopular teachers were likely to produce the reverse effect.

Ravan Hushim Rowahan (1974) conducted a study to find the relationship between moral judgement and age, sex, intelligence and social class. It was found that age, sex, social class, and intelligence had no effect on moral judgement.

Gaur (1975) conducted a study on 'A study of values and perceptions of high school students of the state of Rajastan and their relation to learning'. The major findings of the study were:

i) On theoretical values, boys and girls of either rural or urban origin did not differ but urban differed from rural girls.

ii) On economic values, rural boys and girls, and rural and urban girls did not differ but urban boys were significantly higher than urban girls.

iii) Rural boys and girls did not differ in aesthetic values, political and religious values.

iv) Urban boys and girls did not differ significantly on perception of self-confidence.

v) Rural boys and girls, and urban boys and girls did not differ significantly on perception of self-confidence.

vi) In case of urban girls, learning was related positively to theoretical and social values but negatively to economic and religions values.

vii) In case of rural girls, social and theoretical values were related to learning significantly.

viii) In case of urban boys, theoretical values were related significantly.

Bhagavathy (1977) did an analytical study of personality, intelligence, values and problems of adolescent girls. The investigator had given the following findings: Significant differences were seen in the personality variable and intelligence (both verbal and non-verbal) between the four deviant and one normal group studied and the five groups could be differentiated on the number and nature of problems in the areas of health, family, personality, social, educational, vocational, financial and religion.

Dolres (1977) conducted a study on the effect of two methods of training upon the development of moral judgement in young children. The result revealed that moral judgement as developed in a cognitive conflict model was not distinguishable from a cognitive model among seven years old children as predicted. The lack of change in classroom climate scores may have been functions of the constancy of children's preconceived perceptual view of teach attitude and behaviour. The age of seven is perhaps too early for measurable growth to be expected.

Hilton (1978) conducted a study to examine the relationship between the criterion variable of moral judgement and 3 independent variables of interpersonal trust socio-economic status and intelligence quotient of 195, 11th grade students from an urban Denver High School. There was also a correlation between moral judgement and socio-economic status. A combination of IQ and socio-economic status proved to be the best predictor of level of moral judgement and were significant at 0.01 levels.

Fifis, Daniel Francis (1978) investigated the relationship between predictive ability, empathy, intelligence and sex to moral judgement in adolescents. The subjects were 39 high school students, aged 17 years and above, reading in ninth grade level. Correlations between predictive ability, empathy, intelligence, sex and moral judgement scales did not reach a statistically significant level. When classified by sex, it was fund that the correlation, 0.64 for empathy and moral judgement was significant for males at the 0.05 level.

An investigation into the values, aspirations and personality traits of adolescents of Rajasthan was attempted by Bhatnagar (1979). The major findings of the study were:

i) Student leaders and conformists gave highest preference to power values followed by hedonistic and economic values whereas religious, aesthetic, social and knowledge values marked lowest; delinquents preferred hedonistic value, while power value was given second place.

ii) Most adolescents gave top priority to scientific fields, student leaders and conformists gave second priority to the study of arts subjects whereas, delinquents ranked commerce as second choice.

iii) All the adolescents wanted to see their country free from poverty and preferred peace and morality to material prosperity.

iv) All the adolescents aspired for friendship with other nations and for world peace.

v) The overall adjustments of student learners were significantly better than the adjustment of conformists had the healthiest attitude towards parents but delinquents did not see their parents as sources of affection and protection.

vii) All adolescents expressed unfavourable attitude towards other generation.

viii) Students leaders had a favourable attitude towards their peers, including girls.

In a study by Kenney *et al.*(1980) the relationship between cognitive, role-taking and moral judgement abilities of adolescents was examined. Results of this study indicated no difference between the two samples for mental and chronological ages or for intellectual abilities. A significant difference was found between the role-taking abilities of each sample and only a slight difference noted between the moral judgement skills of both groups with the emotionally disturbed adolescents being the weaker in each category.

Siefering (1981) investigated the relationship between moral reasoning and intelligence. In addition, sex and behaviour correlates impulse control and social conformity were also explored. It indicated that both social conformity and impulse control were significantly related to moral reasoning. Sex was not a factor in moral reasoning.

Wiron, Donglar (1982) made an attempt to study the teaching of values in the college classrooms; faculty and students perception at three contrasting institutions. The objective of the study was whether institutions of higher education had a responsibility to teach values in the college classrooms as distinct from teaching only the information necessary to master content are obtained employment. This research was based on 161 personal interviews with freshmen, seniors and professors at three institutions of higher learning in the State of Utah. Students and faculty were presented for distanced models for dealing with values in the college class rooms. They were asked to identify the model they believed were in use at each institution. The major findings were:

i) The responses or the selected freshman, seniors and faculty to those questions were remarkably similar on almost all questions.

ii) Students and faculty were satisfied with the teaching of values taking place at appropriate level at all institutions.

iii) No congruence between what was taking place and what they believed ought to be lacking place.

iv) At each institution the value advocacy model was prepared by a majority of the respondents.

Zamen (1982) conducted a study on religious, moral and social values of class IX students and to find out their relationship with character traits and personality adjustment. Findings of the study revealed that there were differences in the values held between urban and rural students, between students of two sexes, and among the three communities, viz., Hindu, Muslim and Christian. All the three values had greatest influence on character traits and lowest on personality adjustment. It was found that social and moral values influenced the personality traits much more than religions values, whereas all the character traits (Congeniality, Helpfulness, Kind-heartedness Truthfulness and Dutifulness) appeared to be significantly influenced by values. The study suggested that the development and strengthening of health, social, moral and religious value system among students should be a very important function of the secondary schools, which help in solving problem of student unrest and discipline.

Begum Shahina (1983) studied on the effect of personality traits on the moral judgement of 300 Xth standard students of Bangalore district. The study has revealed the following findings:

- Boys and girls did not significantly differ in all the five dimensions of moral judgement.

- Rural students are having better moral judgement than the urban students in the honest, non-violence dimensions and *in toto*.
- Rural boys and rural girls did not significantly differ in their moral judgement.
- Rural boys are having better moral judgement than the urban boys in the dimensions of honesty, obedience, and justice and *in toto*.
- Rural boys and urban girls did not significantly differ in their moral judgement.
- Rural girls are having better moral judgement than the urban boys in the dimensions of honesty, obedience, justice and *in toto*.
- Rural girls and urban girls did not significantly differ in their moral judgement than urban girls.
- Urban boys have got better moral judgement than urban girls.

Annamma (1985) carried out a study on 'values, aspirations and adjustment of college students'. The main objective of this study was to gain an understanding of students through a study of their values, aspirations, adjustments, opinions and practices.

Sibia Sukhvinder (1990) attempted to study the value pattern of children at Piagetian concrete and formal stages of development. Age was found to be very important factor influencing the value pattern of the children. Academic achievement was related to value pattern.

Kalamani (1991) made an attempt to study the adolescent's problems in the personnel, family, socio-emotional and educational areas as well as to see their value systems. Findings of the study revealed that the Adolescent boys and girls had more problems in personnel, family, socio-emotional and educational areas. All the adolescent students in higher secondary schools were low in potential and religious values and high in social values.

Shama and Kaur (1992) investigated the effect of intelligence, birth order, and age of the children on the moral judgement of 150 boys. The factorial design of the study was 2 × 2 × 2; with two levels of intelligence (higher/lower), two birth orders (first born/last born in the family) and age were important factors in influencing moral judgement. None of the interactions were significant.

Arokiasamy (1993) attempted to study the value perception of the first degree students in colleges affiliated to the Madurai Kamaraj University in relation to certain personality and environmental factors.

The findings were:

i. The value perception was dominant with loving, honest, ambitious and instrumental value.

ii. As terminal value was concerned, students' value perception was dominant with freedom, happiness and equality.

iii. Male students were dominant with loving, ambitious, honest, freedom, happiness and equality.

iv. Female students were dominant with honest, loving, helpful, happiness, freedom and world at peace.

v. Arts students are dominant with loving, honest, ambitious, freedom, happiness and equality.

vi. Science students are dominant with loving, honest, ambitious, freedom, happiness and equality.

vii. Students of very low family income were dominant with loving, ambitious, helpful, freedom, happiness and a comfortable life.

viii. Students of very high family income were dominant with loving, self controlled, honest, happiness, wisdom and freedom.

Chaya (1993) investigated moral judgement in its five dimensions among students of eighth standard in relation to their sex, intelligence, religiosity and socio-economic status. The findings of the study were:

- ❖ Boys were significantly higher than girls in the 'non-violence' dimension of moral judgement.
- ❖ Higher the religiosity, higher was the moral judgement in all its dimensions.
- ❖ Socio-economic status was not found a significant factor contributing for moral judgement among students.
- ❖ Boys having high religiosity had the highest 'honest', 'obedience' dimensions of moral judgement.

Ranu, Sarbjit Kaur (1995) studied the value dimensions as related to level of aspiration and intelligence of post graduate students of three universities. The findings revealed that there were minor deviations in the ranking order of the two most preferred values, while students at Panjab and Punjabi universities gave first preference to political and second to theoretical with GNDV students gave first preference to theoretical and second to political. Males were significantly higher on theoretical value, but lower on the aesthetic and social value than the females. Art students were significantly higher on aesthetic, social and political values than the science students. In order of ranking values, of high level of aspiration and intelligence group were theoretical, political, economic, social, religious and aesthetic while for the low group were political, theoretical, aesthetic, economic, social and religious. High and low aspiration female groups were nearly homogenous in their value patterns. Multiple correlation results indicate that level of aspiration and intelligence could be established in predicting theoretical, economic and aesthetic values.

An exploratory, descriptive investigation into the relationship between college students' critical thinking ability and their development with in the academic, personal and moral domains was done by Hill (1966). Results of this study indicate that students' critical thinking ability levels are positively associated with their measured levels of academic, personal and moral development. Students' critical thinking ability levels were also found to be positive.

A comparative study of value perceptions and normative rule compliance of Malaysian and American secondary school students was conducted by Barone, Thomas Nicholas (1998). American and Malaysian education are increasingly concerned with the moral orientation of young people. The purpose of this study was to examine the norm conformity and value acceptance of Malaysian secondary school students. It was hypothesized that with in each country female students would be characterized by greater norm conformity and value acceptance when compared with male students. Norm conformity and value acceptance of students were measured by the responsibility, socialization, self control and norm favouring scales of California psychological inventory. Further, a value/behaviour questionnaire was administered to students in both countries which measured the adherence to value based social norms. Further, to understand the nature of rule compliance and value perceptions of secondary school students and teachers in both countries are interviewed. It was found that Malaysian students had higher norm conformity and value acceptance for American students (significant for all scales). For gender, significant differences were found in these scales measured collectively in Malaysia but no gender differences were found for American students. The results of the values/behaviour questionnaire showed that although they were differences by country, most students reported adherence to positive social norms. There was a gender differences in social norms. Finally, some data obtained from the rule/behaviour questionnaire triangulated with the results of the students and teacher interviews which focus as value perceptions and the role of the teacher as a moral agent. Unlike Malaysian students, American students were not sure if teachers should teach values. Students in both countries also felt that the teacher/student relationship was governed by implicit values of justice, fairness and respect. Student also felt that good teachers could teach positive values and American students felt they could go to the good teacher for advice with moral dilemmas.

Debruin and Van-Lange (1999) studied few studies and showed how behavioural information about the morality or intelligence of another person influences impressions, exceptions of cooperative behaviour, and own cooperation in a mixed motive interdependence situation. Results revealed morality and intelligence had more impact on impressions and interactions relevant measures than positive information.

Aleixo and Norris (2000) examined personality, moral reasoning maturity, intellectual capacity, and family back ground in 101 convicted male young offenders (aged 16-21 years). Results suggested that both official and self-reported measures of offending were related to high extraversion. While lower levels of moral reasoning maturity were found, no relationship to self-reported offending was apparent.

Chaturvedi, Archana (2001) made an attempt to find out personality traits-normal values and national awakening among the students studying in different culturally bases schools. The findings of the study revealed that the leadership ability of the students studying in western oriented schools was highest, whereas the Hindu, Christian and Muslim school students were at the second and third position respectively. The students of Saraswathi Shishu Mandirs scored higher on moral values. Students of Western culture and Christian culture schools were in second and third position. In national awakening programme students of Hindu, Western Christian and Muslim culture obtained the first, second, third and fourth position respectively.

Mehta (2000) carried out a study on 'Social Values and Futuristic Perceptions of College Girls in Delhi: A Study of Sociology of Youth Culture'. The objectives of the study were:

i) To understand the perceptions of the college girls of Delhi about the future of the Indian nation and society.

ii) To discover what the girls of the various colleges of India's metropolis during 1999 were believing, thinking, feeling and preferring in regard to the whole of complex social cultural values, traditional as well as modern values.

The questionnaire was administered to over 600 college girls randomly throughout Delhi during 1999. Social survey method was used and both quantitative and qualitative data were collected. The major findings of the study were:

i) The girls appear to be progressive, rational, bold in their orientations towards economic independence, self-dependence, and equality of education and social opportunities, career freedom and decision making.

ii) Their social values have in recent years changed a lot due the fact of their living in the India's metropolis and receiving high education. Education is making them confident, broad minded and progressive.

iii) They are conscious of the importance of higher education, especially professional and vocational education, which serves as an important instrument of upwards social mobility and progress in life.

iv) Regarding perception of personal future, most girls were not able to look ahead seriously and imaginatively beyond 2005.

Mathur, S.L. (2003) studied on 'A study of Effectiveness of Science of Living in Developing Human Values on School Children of Ladnun'. The main objective of the study was to analyse the impact of Science of Living (SOL):

- On the cognitive domain which constitutes emotional stability, altruism, moral values, moral judgement and intellectual achievement.
- On the behavioural component which comprises of tolerance, self-discipline, co-operation, life style and obedience.

The study was conducted on a sample of 90 students of age group of 11-14 years of two schools of Ladnun. The tests used in the study included emotional stability test for children by Sengupta and Singh; Altruism scale (ALTS) by Rai and Sanwat Singh; Moral Value Scale (MVS) by Alpana Sen Gupta and Arun and Meera Verma and teacher made tests for half yearly exams of students. A pre-post experimental design with control groups was followed. The statistical analysis of the data was made under two steps; inter group and intra group comparison. The data processing involved comparison in terms of EST, ALTS, MVS, MJT, Achievement test and Parent's Response Test for intra group statistic 't' was used.

The findings of the study were given below:

i) The pre-experimental stage of the subjects of both the groups was found to be homogenous in all the four types of values namely; emotional stability, moral values, altruism and moral judgement, but their level of these values was not significant.

ii) The students of the experimental group after the intervention were found to be more stable in their emotions and proved more altruistic. Their level of moral judgement and moral values also increased significantly.

iii) With respect to inter group comparison, the achievement of the subjects of experimental group comparison, the achievement of the subjects of experimental group increased significantly in both half yearly and annual exams. This shows that learning of Science of Living supports the level of overall achievement.

iv) In the case of intra-group comparison, the students of experimental group found significant impact of using Science of Living. Three values namely, emotional stability, moral values and altruism were found significant.

Dhull and Mahashweta (2005) carried out a study on 'Value Patterns of B.Ed. Pupil Teachers in relation to their Sex, Intelligence and Socioeconomic Status'.

The main objectives were:

(i) To compare the value patterns of male and female B.Ed. students.

(ii) To compare the value patterns of B. Ed. Students belonging to high and low intelligence groups.

(iii) to compare the value patterns of B. Ed. Students belonging to high and low socio-economic status. A sample of 200 students was selected from Colleges of Education of Rohtak city through random sampling technique.

The tools used were: *Samoohik Mansik Yogyata Pariksha* by Tandon, Socio-economic Status Scale by Bhardwaj, Gupta and Chauhan and PVQ by Ojha. The obtained data was analysed using t-test. The main findings of the study were:

(1) The males scored significantly higher than the females on theoretical and political values.

(2) The females scored significantly higher than the males on aesthetic and religious values.

(3) No significant difference was found between high and low intelligence groups with respect to value patterns.

(4) The students belonging to high socio-economic status were found to be significantly higher on theoretical values when compared to those belonging to low socio-economic status.

MORAL VLAUES - SELF-CONCEPTS

Self-concept refers to the experience or one's own being. It includes what people come to know about them through experience, reflection, and feed-back from others. The self-concept is an organized cognitive structure comprised of a set of attitudes, beliefs and values that cut across all facets of experience and action, organizing and typing together the variety of specific habits, abilities, out looks, ideas, and feelings that a person displays.

Self-concept is operationally defined as a measure of the evaluation, which the individual makes and customarily maintains with regards to himself; it expresses an attitude of approval or disapproval and indicates the extent to which the individual believes himself to be capable, significant, successful and worthy (Cooper Smith 1959, 1967). Despite controversy regarding the meaning of self as a unitary trait or an integrated system of situationally specific traits, all are agreed that self is a life space on life force for the individual and particularly for the adolescent (Gergen, 1971). The awareness of self comes through the gradual process of adaptation to the environment (Piaget, 1969). It begins when an individual becomes aware of being a separate entity. This is when the individual can differentiate those events emanating from or involving one knows just as other environmental events can be objects of one's knowledge (Turner 1973).

Manar (1981) compared the attitudes, values, and self-concepts of the professional college students with non-professional college students. Hypothesis was that there would be significant difference in self-concepts of professional and non professional college students. It was found that professional students perceived themselves as more confident and suffering from the feeling of emotional instability than the non-professional students.

Saraswat (1982) made an attempt to examine the relationship of self-concept measures with adjustment, values, academic achievement and socio-economic status of boys and girls. It was found that boys and girls differed significantly with regard possession of values and significantly influenced the achievement of students.

Kulshreshtha (1983) studied the 'Value orientation, interests and attitudes as correlates of self-concept among male and female adolescents'. The researcher had framed the following objectives:

i) To determine and study the impact of value orientation, interests, peer relations upon the concept of self in both male and female adolescents.

ii) To obtain interactions among as well as between value orientation, interests and peer relations on bi-variable and tri-variable levels of operation while affecting the concept of self so that the dynamics of the concepts of self could understood.

iii) To determine difference in the dynamics of the concept of self between both the sexes.

iv) To determine the growth of self-concept of the students in the Indian Social cultural setting.

The main findings were:

i) Values orientation affected the concept of self in adolescents.

ii) Value orientation has positive affinity with self-concept among male as well as female adolescents under different levels of interests.

iii) Interest played an important role in the growth of self-concept. It promoted the concept and also demoted the concept of self in various associations with value orientations and peer relations.

iv) Interests were shaping and forming the male adolescents' concept of self.

v) Growth of self-concept during the period of adolescence in both the sexes depends upon the variations promoted the concept of self also but only when value orientation of interests was operating.

vi) Promotion or demotion of the concept of self by peer relations in cases of both males and females remained different.

Bani (1992) attempted to find out the personal value pattern and self-concept of Nagaland College students and also to see its relationship existed between the values. Results indicated that there have no significant differences in the values scores of arts, science and commerce students with respect to social, aesthetic, economic, knowledge, hedonistic, family prestige and health values. There was a significant difference between scores of tribal and non-tribal students on religions, social, aesthetic and democratic values, whereas boys and girls differed significantly in their scores on social, aesthetic knowledge, power and family prestige values. There was positive correlation between self-concept and social as well as democratic values and negative correlations between self-concept and power as well as family prestige values, but there was no relationship between self-concept and religious, aesthetic, economic, knowledge and health values.

MORAL VALUES - STUDY HABITS

Every parent wants their child to do well in school and to learn as much as they possibly can. To be good students children need to develop good study habits at home and at school. The outcome of education determines the level of life, progress and status of the people, living anywhere in the world and it is the vital force for the development of human life and the society at large. No education is worth its name unless it helps the students to feel at home in the world of books. With the explosion of knowledge no

Educationist can acquire or impart all the information pertaining to a subject. The best any one can do is to make the students cultivate a taste for reading and this can be done only helping students to build up study habits. Through these habits he gets good character and other values. Onubugwu (1990) defines study habits as the techniques a student employ to go about his or her studies, which are consistent, and have become stereotyped as a result of long application or practice.

The study of Humanities (History, Literature, Communications, and Social Science), students can develop their moral reasoning.

Bishop Young articulates ways in which lecturers can help students to further their feelings of empathy for others. He argues that the development of moral feeling is the responsibility of all tertiary institutions and especially a Catholic one.

Humanities

The Humanities, dealing as they do with people in relationships, has an important role to play in the development of moral feeling. Science (dealing also with relationships) can also do this.

In any moral problem, a multidisciplinary approach, drawing on a range of resources, seems the most useful. In the humanities, we can consider the feelings of others, real and fictional. It would seem to be the aim of art to generate an affective response in the audience. Some have gone as far as to suggest that if the response is revulsion, it is still good art for having generated such a strong response! We can also objectify cases and dilemmas to explore very personal problems from a literary distance. We are able to examine our myths, stereotypes, prejudices and biases. Any serious study of the world can generate a love for the beauty beyond goodness and a hatred for the evil beyond vice, as the philosopher Hannah Arendt has argued. This way of presenting the idea that good is more than doing something good and that Evil is more than the sum of all bad things, speaks to the modern mind, especially in the face of the holocaust.

History

History units can expose student to indigenous, black and feminist history - history from the underside - and they are empowered to reclaim and to write their own histories. This process can result in several important insights.

The study of history further develops a feeling for truth. Truth and reconciliation commissions in several countries plagued by civil war have shown that even if reconciliation is not in fact achieved, at least lies can no longer be told.

'All that a truth commission can achieve is to reduce the number of lies that can be circulated unchallenged in public discourse. In Argentina its work has made it impossible to claim, that the military did not throw half dead victims in the sea from helicopters. In Chile it is no longer permissible to assert in public that the Pinochet regime did not dispatch thousands of entirely innocent people'. (Michael Ignatieff, cited by Boraine 1998)

Literature and Communication

Literature and Communications must provide students with a vocabulary for moral thinking and talking. Will that language be 'philosophical', esoteric or abstract? Or will it be in plain language, part of common discourse and concrete? Even the term 'morality' requires urgent deconstruction as it has come to mean for many people a pre-packaged set of instructions - the opposite of what it should mean. It can thus obscure the issues and processes of real decision-making faced by people in the modern world.

Creative writing, especially poetry, enables students to explore their feelings and give expression to them. This can be a healthy and non-violent outlet for anti-authority feelings. Students' participation in conceiving, writing and performing drama and role-plays enables them to enter into other people's worlds, other people's concerns. This is a form of 'empathy', the capacity to 'feel with' other people.

Social Sciences

Social Sciences enable students to engage methodically and critically with the same human, social, political and economic concerns that they are meeting in history and literature. Contemporary trends in the study of the human or social sciences (psychology, sociology, anthropology, culture studies and religious studies) allow for more room for passion, for advocacy, for the pursuit of justice, rather than a purely (or supposedly) objective, detached, investigation of facts. Information, which in itself is morally neutral, is actually used to either oppress or liberate.

Wojcicki and Convey (1982) offer a list of social science topics (with American students in mind), which have a social justice dimension: Culture, population, poverty, decolonisation, causes of war, limits of national sovereignty, United nations, world law, immigration history, labour movements ... liberation movements, developing nations, terrorism, capital punishment, economic imperialism, family values, welfare, work ethic, unemployment, racism, sexism, violence, alienation, consumerism, sexual identity, social engineering lobbying, suffrage.

After review of literature, the investigator has not found any empirical study in this field.

STUDIES RELATED TO MORAL INSTRUCTION/ ACTIVITIES IN SCHOOLS/COLLEGES

Sarangi (1944) studied the implications of moral education in schools. His objective was to study the extent of utilization of moral education and the interest of children in moral education.

Ammanamma (1984) in her *Values aspiration and adjustment of college students in Kerala*, studied moral instruction and values of college students according to sex, age, curriculum, religion, residential background, family background, socio-economic status and academic achievement. She found moral instruction is beneficial and majority college students are conformists with a stable system without religious tendencies.

Prabḥavathi Kumari (1987), in her study, "Personality needs, moral judgment and value patterns of secondary school teachers – a correlational study", studied the impact of moral instruction and mean scores differences on value, personality needs and moral judgments according to sex, locality and generations and found that moral instruction had a good impact on male, urban and older generation and they had positive value patterns with the other groups.

One of the early studies by Raths *et al.* (1996), they considered how to work with values in the classroom.

Singh (1961) conducted a critical survey of the opportunities provided in the secondary schools for developing democratic values in students.

Mohamood Keiser (1974), made an appraisal of the provision of moral instruction in the secondary schools.

Mallaradhya (1975) appraised the study of moral and religious instruction in the higher primary schools.

Roychowdhary (1979) investigated upon the religious education impact on the secular concepts of pupils in schools of Bombay.

Anand Bhushan (1977) studied the impact of dogmatization and secular schools on attitudes and eighteen instrumental values of adolescents.

"School boards will be encouraged to design and develop course which will make value transmission an integral part of an integrated personality", (NCERT).

Singh (1999) carried out a study on 'Values in School-based Curricula'. The main objective of the study was 'to investigate how the basic values of democracy, egalitarianism and secularism, which Indian Society aspires to achieve, are placed in school-based curriculum. For the purpose, school curriculum was examined on four levels as:

(a) analsysis of textual material,
(b) interview to know teachers perceptions of curricula,
(c) non-participant semi-structured observation of the classroom on the application of curricula, and

(d) observation on Institutional climate. The collected data was analysed descriptively.

The main findings of the study were:

i) The hidden curricula as translated in the textual materials continue to emphasize authoritarian and hierarchical social values of the past. The revelation of democratic, egalitarian and secular values more objectively is yet to happen.

ii) Teachers' perceptions were limited to the face value of the written texts and not their import.

iii) Evaluation of students' performance was confined to the memorization of information.

iv) It was also found that school environment with traditional methods and activities remains non-participatory for individual students.

Dwivedi, Om Prakash (2002) carried out a study on 'A Study of Character Traits of Junior High School Boys and their Educational implications'. The main objectives of the study were:

i) To study the specific pattern of development of moral character of Junior High School Students (stuuents of 6th, 7th and 8th Classes).

ii) To study the effect of high and low deprivation on the aspects of character mainly attitudinal, cognitive and behavioural.

iii) To study the effect of residential background, rural and urban on the development of moral character.

iv) To determine degree of relationship between moral development and academic achievement of the selected students.

v) To study the degree of relationship between moral development and general intelligence.

The sample consisted of 360 students of Classes 6th, 7th and 8th selected with the help of district situated in eastern

U.P. from 431 senior basic schools and 173 high schools and intermediate colleges selected through lottery method from the urban area and rural area respectively. The study was carried out by using the descriptive survey method. Tools used included Moral Judgement Test, Adjustment Inventory, *Samoohik Mansik Yogyata Pariksha*, Prolonged Deprivation Scale, Measure of Character Structure and Situational tests of moral character. Out of these tests, the researcher developed Measure of Character Structure and Situational Test of moral character. The data collected were analysed with the help of mean, standard deviation, product moment correlation, t-test and analysis of variance.

The major findings of the study were:

i) The urban students had consistently scored higher marks in all the five aspects of character such as moral knowledge, moral judgement, socialization empathy and autonomy, than the rural students.

ii) Deprivation had some influence on behaioural aspects of character. Low deprived students appeared to be scoring high on cheating. Rural students had scored considerably high on these dimensions than their urban counterparts.

iii) The urban students had consistently scored high marks in moral judgement test. The low deprived children evidence more mature level of moral judgement than highly deprived children. Urban boys enjoy facility of Tele- vision, News papers and magazine besides meeting people of different walks of life, whereas rural students do not get much of these facilities.

iv) Residential background had remarkable effect on the moral judgement of the student's grade and deprivation had also remarkable effect on moral ground increases with the advancement of age and experience.

v) Moral judgement had significant correlation with general intelligence. Various components of character structure also showed significant positive correlation with general intelligence.

Devi (2002) carried a study on 'An Evaluation of the Realisation of Moral, Secular and Democratic Values in the Textbook Content in Telugu Language at Primary and Secondary School levels in Andhra Pradesh'. The objectives of the study were:

i) To examine the extent to which moral, secular and democratic values are being given importance in the current school level textbooks of mother tongue.

ii) To study the extent to which these values are being realized in prose lessons.

iii) To study the extent to which the poetry lessons are realizing these values.

iv) To study the extent to which these values being realized in Non-Detailed textbook.

v) To examine the content with reference to value manifestations, explicit, implicit and eclectic expression used, simple or narrative procedure followed and the use of contemporary or historical approach.

For the purpose of the study, document analysis method was used. It included analysing, classifying and quantifying the written material from a given source into certain pre-determined categories and criterion measures. This methodology is more concerned with the ideas and concepts presentation. The documents considered for study are prescribed in the schools.

The finds of the study were:

i) Of the three values, there is more emphasis on moral values especially at secondary level than at primary level.

ii) The emphasis given to democratic value is found to be little more than the average.

iii) Comparatively there is less emphasis on secular value with almost a negligible emphasis at primary level.

iv) Standard-wise, even emphasis was not given to the three values.

Srivastava (2004) carried a study on 'A study of School Activities Promoting Values Inherent in Fundamental Duties mentioned in the Indian Consitittution'. The main objectives of the study were given below:

i) To find the educational activities offered by different types of educational institutes for including and developing values inherent in fundamental duties.
ii) To find out level of awareness about fundamental duties among the students studying in different types of schools.
iii) To find out gender difference in the level of awareness among the students.
iv) To find out the difference in awareness among students studying in similar types of schools situated in Hindi speaking States.

The population of the study includes secondary school students in different typical institutions of capital cities of seven Hindi speaking states. The sample consisted of 7000 students of government aided schools, missionary schools, public schools and Vidya Bharati institutions. These students were tested with two tools namely Fundamental Duty Awareness Inventory (FDAI) and Fundamental Duty Adherence Questionnaire (FDAQ). Teachers of these schools were also administered Fundamental Duties Development Programme Inventory (FDDPI).

The findings of the study were:

i) Morning assembly, games and sports, celebration of national days, debate and cultural programmes are activities common to all the schools.
ii) The greatest amount of duty awareness is obtained by missionary schools of Raipur, Chhattisgarh while government aided schools of Lucknow find their place at the bottom.

iii) Irrespective of type of institution, taking the entire sample together the total duty awareness is found to be highest for Chhattisgarh State and lowest for Delhi State.

iv) Boys indicated significantly lower level of duty awareness than the entire group of girls.

v) With respect to duty awareness, schools were ranked as follows: Missionary schools, Vidya Bharathi, Government aided schools, Public schools and Government schools. States also fall in the following rank order, Chhattisgarh (Raipur), Rajasthan (Jaipur), Bihar (Patna), Jharkhand (Ranchi), Madhya Pradesh (Bhopal), Uttar Pradesh (Lucknow) and Delhi.

vi) With respect to duty adherence, government schools of Delhi ranked first and public schools of Delhi were at the lowest.

vii) The overall rank for the types of institutions combined for different state capitals on the duty adherence dimension emerge in the following order: Vidya Bharati, Missionary schools, Government schools, Government aided and Public schools.

viii) If the duty adherence is considered State-wise irrespective of school type, the rank order is Raipur, Jaipur, Ranchi, Lucknow, Bhopal, Delhi and Patna.

STUDIES RELATED TO CONCEPT OF VALUE-ORIENTED EDUCATION

Pande (1959) studied the place of philosophical and practical values in education. He find out, for recognition of the system of education with certain basic values for restoring harmony and poison into human life.

Cremin (1961) refers to the effective education, as originated in the late 1800's which is known under different names such as 'psychological education', 'confluent education', 'student directed learning', 'open classrooms' and 'value education'.

Nagarjuna Rao (1968) takes insight into the values he sees two views, the ideals of military process and industrial enterprise and the ideal for swadharma as means of universal peace and happiness.

Bhushan studies value, values system of value preferences (1979) by male and female groups belonging to service and non-service class and find out possessing value preferences more by service class rather than non-service class families.

NCERT, document (1979) of social, moral and spiritual values in education has enlisted eighty-four values, which have neither inter-relationship nor hierarchy (Rdhidekar *et al.*, 1987). Five basic values supported in all eight major religions of the world identified by Gokark and they are truth, right conduct, love, peace and non-violence.

Swami Vivekananda said "Each soul is potentially divine. The goal (of human life) is to manifest this divinity within". This divinity within, the self, is the source of all perfection, power, bliss and glory. The purpose of our value education programme with therefore is to help people become aware of their innate divinity and how to make its perfection and happiness manifest in every movement of life.

Patel (1981) compared value systems of men and women, hostlers, day scholars and students belonging to different streams such as arts, sciences and commerce and found women, hostlers and students in sciences possess positive value system when compared to others.

Sinha (1981) measured value oriented and value patterns of students and their parents and found some significant results in favour of parents.

Raj (1981) studied theoretical and socio-cultural values in between Indian teachers and Indian teachers at Ethiopian counterpart and find Indian teachers of Ethiopian counterpart possess a positive and higher attitude rather than other.

Indrani (1981) made an analysis of the place of moral education in a secular society. She identifies social values, values pertaining to self, values pertaining to the country and the world process as important values to be cultivated.

Stella Annelobo (1983) studied principles, concepts of values and pupils concept of principle values and found principles whose value system manifested coreness achieved a relatively higher degree of institutional efficiency.

Shrique (1984) studied educational view point in relation to their values, attitudes and preferences for political ideologies. He found most teachers had a progressive outlook on different aspects of education like aims, methods, pupil control, and policy of promotions need for in-service education.

Dahler (1985) analyses the literature concerned with the study of global problems and concludes that the crisis in human values and in ethics is the outcome of a crisis in the inner or ethical life of mankind.

Oad (1986) traces the evolution of humanism in the independent India and its impact on educational values. He puts forth a mate of hope that our future will promote values of co-operation and congruence between means and ends.

Bhagia (1986) identifies the new emerging values as "values of constraints" which include concern for emigrant tolerance and integration all leading to one major value good life. She implies with oath in advocating for co-operation through field community participation.

NCERT, resource material-1 (1987) for in-service training of school teachers puts in simple words, every society wants to inculcate in its children knowledge, skills and certain qualities which may help them to become good citizens, which is value education. It includes Rashtriya Panchasheela namely:

- Cleanliness
- Truthfulness

- Hard work
- Equality
- Co-operation.

Raychowdery (1988), Reddy and Reddy (1992), Blet (1996), Sridhar Babu (2000), Dhanalakshmi (2001) elaborate the concept of value education relevant to the elementary, secondary, college and university levels.

Sharma (1990) advocates for a deeper understanding of the fundamental values of love, freedom, truth and justice citing the impact of saints from history and from more contemporary times (Ramakrishna, Vivekananda, Gandhi).

Sheshadri (1992) explains that value education is referred to a planned educational action aimed at the development of proper attitudes, values, emotions and character in the learners.

Further Sharma (1995) concludes that values are permeated through the conduct of the elders and imbedded by among the youngster.

Indian Council of Philosophical Research (ICPR): Education is intrinsically and by definition value-oriented. To speak, therefore, of value-oriented education are, in a sense, tautologies. In fact, education is a subset of a larger setting of culture, and culture consists of cultivation of faculties and powers pertaining to reason, ethics and aesthetics in the light of the pursuit of values of Truth, Beauty and Goodness (Satyam, Sivam and Sundaram).

According to Perry, a neo-realist regards values as an object of interest. An object, real as imaginary, acquires values, if some one is interested in it.

According to some contemporary realists, values don't exist in time and space; they subsist in themselves above space and time. They regard God as totality of values.

Pragmatists regard truth, good and beauty as relatives to human needs. Truth is workability, practical efficiency or utility.

It is not distinct from good health, education, business and other cultural and social values. Values are good because of their valuable consequences. Belief in God and immortality, two important articles of religion, has a healthy influence on life and so have pragmatic utility. The will to belief is the cause of many beliefs. Faith is justified as practical utility.

According to Rokeach "values are beliefs about how one ought not to behave, as about some state of existence worth or not worth attaining. Values are abstract ideals, positive or negative, that represent a person's beliefs about ideal modes of conduct and ideal terminal goals.

Frisancho (1996) studied the Efficiency of an educational programme in improving moral reasoning and cognitive complexity levels in 18 male and female high school students (aged 15-16 years) in Peru. Results showed that no structural advances in terms of moral reasoning level but do demonstrate an increase in reasoning complexity and in the number of elements of social situations students were able to identify.

Bawa and Chahal (2003) studied on 'Changing Value System through Women-oriented TV Programme'. The main objectives of the study were:

i) To know the impact of women-oriented TV programmes on values of the adults of Punjab.

ii) To find out the gender differences in the impact of women-oriented TV programmes on values.

iii) To reveal the impact of women-oriented TV programmes on values in relation to socio-economic status of adults of Punjab.

iv) To explore the impact of women-oriented TV programmes on values with respect to the age of the adults of Punjab.

The sample for the study was collected from Patiala district of Punjab. 158 adults (85 males and 73 females) in the age group 21 to 60 years constituted the sample. Eighty-eight adults (46 males and 42 females) belonged to 21-35 years and 70 adults (39 males and 31 females) were above 35 years of age. The tools used were: A test to measure the impact of women-oriented TV programmes on values prepared by the investigator and modified form of Socio-economic Status Test by S.P. Kulshrestha. 't' test and ANOVA were applied to find out the significant differences between and among the groups under study.

The findings of the study were:

i) Only 25.3 per cent respondents had felt very strong impact on their values through women-oriented TV programmes and more or less the same number of respondents had felt very less impact on their values through such programmes.

ii) The impact of women-oriented TV programmes on values was similar on the respondents belonging to higher socio-economic status, average or low socio-economic status.

iii) Younger group was compared on the basis of sex; the results revealed that there is a significant difference in the impact of women-oriented TV programmes on values in male and female adults of less than 35 years age.

iv) Most of the younger females are less emotionally mature than their counterparts and may be less exposed to the external environment.

v) The impact of women-oriented TV programmes on their values is more on the younger females than male adults who are more aware of the realities of life and are more emotionally mature.

Sah (2003) studied on 'Orientation of Value Patterns of the Santal Tribal and Non-Santal College Students'. The objective of the study is 'to study the orientation of value patterns of the Santal and non-Santal college students. The sample of the study was 200 (100 Santal college students and 100 non-Santal college students). A life value pattern scale developed by Sah & Singh (2001) was used to collect data which were treated with 't'-test to be analysed. The findings of the study were:

i) Santal tribals and non-Santal did not differ significantly in terms of any of the behavioural value patterns, except that of the religious and political ones, as also the total value pattern.

ii) It was recorded that Santal tribals too had higher levels in the entire behavioural value pattern, except political and economic ones.

Reddy, V.D. (2004) made an attempt to study on 'Attitude towards Value-oriented Education in Primary School Children in Chittoor District'. The major objectives of the study were:

i) To find out the significant difference between urban and rural teachers on value-oriented education.

ii) To study the difference between government teachers and private teachers on value-oriented education.

Random sampling technique was used to select a sample of 300 primary school teachers from the Chittoor District. The tool for the study was adopted, which was developed, standardized and administered for the same purpose. The data relating to the scores of primary school teachers regarding attitude towards value-orientated education has been summarized in a data sheet for 300 teachers according to Locality and Management. Appropriate coding was given to facilitate statistical calculation.

Major findings of the study were:

i) The urban primary school teachers had higher mean scores than the rural primary school teachers. On the other hand the private primary school teachers were showing higher mean scores when compared with their counter-parts.

ii) The moral and value-oriented education with the inclusion of common ethical teachings of all great religions highlights the nation unity.

iii) Value-oriented education strengthens national integration by accelerating the process of modernization and development of scientific temper and outlook.

iv) Value-based education system cultivates the basic values of humanism, democracy, socialism and secularism.

STUDIES RELATED TO MORAL VALUES

Ushasri (1966) traces the process of value development and internalization of values by individuals; she explains the hierarchical sequence of internalization and the influencing factors on value attainment. She suggests that conflicts between values cherished by an individual and values practiced in the society can be resolved by autonomous functioning with inter control and wholesome consciousness.

Srivastava (1981) measured the moral ideals and values of PUC, BA class students. The findings are:

- For every increase in the educational ladder there is a corresponding decrease in moral values.
- After high school education, a decrease in the magnitude of moral values are observed corresponding with the increase in age.

NATIONAL MORAL EDUCATION CONFERENCE (1981)

It was organized in India and the resolutions of the conference were:

❖ A course on moral education in all classes up to the university stage in all colleges should be run inculcating moral and human values in students to make them better and more useful members of society.

- Moral education should be a separate subject.
- The content of moral education should include common ethical teaching of all great religions highlighting their unity.
- The syllabus for moral education should include stories, illustrations and event mainly from India and its literature from various religions. So that it leads to national integration.
- In higher classes, a course in comparative religion should be introduced as it will promote social harmony a liberal attitude and less financial approach to religion.

"Religion is a significant area of human experience. This is true in history and in the contemporary world. As such, it is worthy of study by pupils so that they can have some understanding of one of the prime motivating factors behind human behaviour, both individual and social. The importance of religious education is not confined to appreciating the historical and social role of religion. There is also a personal dimension, linked to the individual's search for answers to questions about meaning, value and purpose in life. "Moral education in schools has traditionally been associated with religious education. One reason for this is that all religions stress the importance of morality and give guidance in the form of general principles, codes or rules". "Traditional ideas about right and wrong are continually challenged by new circumstances and new technology. This gives rise to two complementary aspects of moral education: appreciation of common values such as honesty, liberty, justice, fairness, respect for others; and a personal process of clarification of values and decision-making to enable the individual to cope with change." (Scottish Executive, Religious and Moral Education, 5-14 National guidelines, 1992).

Garg (1983) reported that personal attitudes and prolonged derivational level had significant influence of value development.

Singh (1983) found that prolonged deprivation had a negative impact on development of values.

De (1984) found that the mean scores of dutifulness, sincerity and co-operation, conformity to school rules, honesty, loyalty and respect to seniors among boys of classes V to X were high and varied among classes. There was no significant difference between the means of boys of classes V, VII and IX in respect of sincerity.

Annamma (1984) found that family size was positively related to value development in college students but no significant relation was seen between father's education and occupation and value development of their children.

Lewis (1984) studied the academic and socio-cultural influences on the development of values, among students in two years colleges, females rated school environment higher in respect of its influence on the development of orderliness and friendliness along with moral and religions values. Private college students reported greater influence of values than did public school students.

Sharma (1985) reported that values are the outcomes of culture and are responsible for creating sub-culture at college level.

Roy (1986) found that family and friends were influencing factors of the development of moral and social values in young boys and girls.

Bhargava (1986) analyzed the development of values in the concrete and formal operational periods and related it to home and educational environment.

Rani (1986) found that increase in age correspond with an increase in the knowledge of moral values. A very similar pattern of moral values was found in the children of all age groups. As the children matured, their mental ability influenced their knowledge of moral value. The religion of family did not contribute to the knowledge of moral values in children.

The Programme of Action (POA) Document, 1992

It dealt with value education; it has widely interpreted value education broad cultural education leading to removal of superstition, obscurantism, religious fanaticism and all other narrow loyalties. It has stressed the importance of positive approach in which the roots of Indian culture have to be highlighted along with the development of scientific temper and unity and national integrity having a specific focus.

National Resource Centre for Value Education

A National Resource Centre for Value Education (NRCVE) has been recently set up. The activities of NRCVE preparation and production of supplementary reading material for students for inculcation of different values using stories, parables, anecdotes from literature on different faiths.

Dhull and Khatri (2002) attempted to study the 'Effect of Value Clarification on Moral Reasoning of Children in Relation to Parental Attitude'. The main objectives of the study were:

i) To study the effect of value clarification on moral reasoning of children.

ii) To compare the effect of value clarification on the development of moral reasoning of children in relation to accepting attitude of parents.

iii) To compare the effect of value clarification on the development of moral reasoning of children in relation to avoiding attitude of parents.

iv) To compare the effect of value clarification on the development of moral reasoning of children in relation to avoiding attitude of parents.

The sample consisted of 100 students studying in Class IX in different schools located at Bahadurgarh and surrounding rural areas. The entire section from a particular class was taken as a cluster in sample schools. Test-retest method was used.

Tools used included family relationship inventory by Shery and Standardised Moral Dilemmas developed by Raths, Kohlberg and others were adopted by the investigators. Statistical techniques like Mean, Standard Deviation and 't'-values were computed for testing the significant difference between students' performance in Pre and Post-test mean gain scores of subjects.

The major findings of the study were:

i) Value clarification technique has a positive significant effect on the development of moral reasoning of children.

ii) Accepting attitude of parents has a positive significant effect on the development of moral reasoning of children as a result of value clarification.

iii) Concentrating attitude of parents does not have significant influence on the development of moral reasoning of children as a result of value clarification.

iv) Avoiding attitude of parents does not have a significant effect on the development of moral reasoning of children as a result of value clarification.

Reddy and Reddy (2004) carried a study on 'Life Values: A Study on M.B.A. Students'. The main aim of the study is to study the relative importance of the students attached to different value domains. The sample comprised 104 students pursuing M.B.A. programme in the University of Madras and they were administered a questionnaire consisting of 23 value items. The collected data was treated with Z-test. The major findings of the study were given below.

i) There is no significant difference in mean importance ratings between any of the pairs of value domains.

ii) There is significant difference in mean importance ratings between each value domain in first layer and each domain in second layer.

iii) With the value domain in the first layer having significantly higher importance ratings compared to the value domain in the second layer.

Talesara (2004) made a study on 'Development of Values through Jeevan Vigyan: An Experimental Study'. The main objectives of the study were:

i) To study different values in middle class students studying in Class VIII.

ii) To compare the development of values between general students and students gone thorough Jeevan Vigyan.

iii) To compare values of urban and rural areas students and to identify differences in respect of values of government school and non-government school students.

Sample consisted of Class VIII students of Udaipur District. A pilot study was for collection data. Statistical techniques like questionnaire were used efficient of correlation were computed. The main finding of the study is students could not only be benefited from Jeevan Vigan Programme but also teachers, curriculum and surrounding would be conductive facilitating the teaching-learning process.

Shamshuddin (2005) carried out a study on 'Values and Academic Achievement'. The main objectives of the study were:

i. To study the existing value pattern of DIET students.

ii. To study the influence of personal variables namely, college, gender, region, religion, locality, subject of study, fathers' education, mothers' education, basic entry qualification, parents occupation and parents income on academic achievement of DIET students.

iii. To study the influence of values on the academic achievement of DIET students.

iv. To estimate the percent of contribution of different independent variables to academic achievement of DIET students.

The total sample of the study was 960 DIET students in three regions of Andhra Pradesh namely; Coastal Region, Rayalaseema Region and Telangana Region. Personal Value

Questionnaire, Objective Achievement Test and Personal Information Sheet were used.

The major findings of the study were:

i) Male students belonging to Costal region have obtained high value pattern scores on social and health values whereas male students representing Rayalaseema region have scored high value pattern scores on social, economic and health values, whereas male students representing Telangana regions have scored average value pattern scores on all values.

ii) As for region wise distribution is concerned, female students belonging to Coastal region have obtained high scores on economic and hedonistic values, female students of Telangana region have secured high scores on health value and female students belonging to Rayalaseema region have secured high scores on economic, knowledge and hedonistic values.

iii) In case of male students whose parents were in the higher income group, male students have secured high score on health value.

iv) The achievement scores of students are more or less normally distributed. The mean, median, and mode of the distribution are 343.43, 342.56 and 334.56. The maximum score is 500 and the mean scores obtained by the students are more than average.

Vijayalakshmi (2006) studied on 'Prioritisation of Secondary School Children's Values by their Parents and Teachers'. She said that values are very important for all human beings, mainly for students and teachers. The main objectives of the study are: To find out the difference in prioritising values by the parents (whose children studying at secondary level) and teachers (who are handling the classes at the secondary level).

A sample of 40 teachers (20 male and 20 female) and 40 parents (20 male 20 female) from both rural and urban areas were selected at random. The survey method was used. The subjects were provided a list of 40 values in three alternatives, viz. most important, important and less important, and were asked to mark their preferences. The data provided by the parents and teachers were analysed.

The main findings were:

(1) All categories of teachers and parents gave more importance to only five values, namely worthiness, sympathies, discipline, equality and caring.

(2) Hundred per cent of teachers gave priority to open mindedness, practicality, and academic bent of mind, self-reliance, forgiveness, obedience and creativity.

(3) Hundred per cent of parents gave priority to the values namely honesty, truthfulness, cleanliness, duty mindedness, love, kindness, spirituality, humanity, aesthetics, morality, punctuality, cooperation and objectivity.

(4) There was light difference ranging from eighty one per cent to ninety seven per cent in the preference of values of teachers and parents, viz. empathy, food, organisational capacity, leadership, appreciation, optimism, friendliness, tolerance, being fair and frank, protest against wrongs, loyalty, patriotism, sociability, intellectual efficiency, self-control, self-awareness, self-esteem, self-confidence, justice, dependability, purity of thought, civic scene, charity, accountability and rationality.

(5) The difference in the values was observed between rural and urban teachers as well as parents, male and female teachers as well as parents, educated and uneducated parents, above 40 years and up to 40 years age group of parents and teachers, rich and poor parents, parents having small and big families and teachers teaching arts and science subjects.

Rangaswamy (2006) carried a work on 'A study on Moral Judgement of High School Pupils in Relation to certain Factors'. The objectives of the study were:

A) Moral Stages

1. Does the sex of the students have any influence in reasoning of each moral stage?
2. Does the class of study of the students influence the reasoning of each moral stage?
3. Does the locality of the students have any influence in reasoning of each moral stage?

B) Moral Levels

1. Does the sex of the students have any influence in reasoning of each moral level?
2. Does the class of study of the students influence the reasoning each moral level?
3. Does the locality of the students have any influence in reasoning of each moral level?

C) Moral Judgement

1. Does the sex of the students have any influence on moral judgement made?
2. Does the class of study of the students have any influence on moral judgement made?
3. Does the locality of the students have nay influence on moral judgement made?
4. Does the personality of the students have any influence on the moral judgement?
5. Does the size of the family of the students have any influence on moral judgement?

Nine hundred samples (450 boys and 450 girls) were taken for this study. Appropriate statistical techniques like 't' test,

Pearson's correlation co-efficient, one-way analysis of variance, 2 × 3 × 2 analysis of factorial design were employed in this study. Moral Judgment Questionnaire (MJQ), Raven's Standard Progressive Matrices (RPM), 14 Personality Factor Questionnaire (14 PF) and Socio-Economic Status Scale (SES) were used.

The major findings of the study were:

1. Sex has no relationship on subjects as regard to moral stage-I reasoning.
2. There is a significant relationship between the subjects studying in different classes of study with regard to their moral stage-I reasoning.
3. Locality has no relationship on subjects as regard to moral stage-I reasoning.
4. Sex has influence on subjects as regard to conventional level reasoning.
5. Locality has no influence on subjects as regard to conventional level reasoning.
6. Sex has influence on subjects as regard to moral judgement score.
7. There is significant relationship between the subjects studying in different classes of study with regard to their moral judgement score.
8. Locality has no influence on subjects as regard to moral judgement score.
9. There is significant relationship between intelligence (R.P.M.) and moral judgement score of the students.
10. There is no significant relationship between the personality factors A, B, C, D, E, F, H, I, J, O, Q_2, Q_3 and Q_4 with moral judgement score.
11. There is no significant difference between socio-economic status of the student (low, middle and high) and moral judgement score.

Somnath Chatterjee (2009) in his convocation address; 30th convocation, Acharya Nagarjuna University, Guntur, Andhra Pradesh; gave a call to the student community to be more vigilant against all declining values in all walks of life.

> "Criminalisation of politics has led to immense pressure on functioning of political institutions and there is considerable cynicism among citizens of the country."—Mr. Somnath Chatterjee opined.

STUDIES RELATED TO THEORIES OF MORAL DEVELOPMENT

Piaget's stages of moral judgement and Kohlberg's theory of Moral Development, Domain Theory: Distinguishing Morality and Convention and Carol Gilligan-Morality of Care are discussed hereunder.

Piaget's Stages of Moral Judgment

Jean Piaget (1965) is among the first psychologists whose work remains directly relevant to contemporary theories of moral development. In his early writing, he focused specifically on the moral lives of children, studying the way children play games in order to learn more about children's beliefs about right and wrong. According to Piaget, all development emerges from action; that is to say, individuals construct and reconstruct their knowledge of the world as a result of interactions with the environment. Based on his observations of children's application of rules when playing, Piaget determined that morality, too, can be considered a developmental process. For example, Ben, a ten year old studied by Piaget, provided the following critique of a rule made-up by a child playing marbles: "it isn't a rule! It's a wrong rule because it's outside of the rules. A fair rule is one that is in the game". Ben believed in the absolute and intrinsic truth of the rules, characteristic of early moral reasoning. In contrast, Vua, aged thirteen, illustrates an understanding of the reasoning behind the application of rules, characteristic of later moral thinking. When asked to consider the fairness of a made-up rule compared to a traditional rule, Vua replied "It is just as fair because the marbles are far apart"(making the game equally difficult).

In addition to examining children's understanding of rules about games, Piaget interviewed children regarding acts such as stealing and lying. When asked what a lie is, younger children consistently answered that they are "naughty words". When asked why they should not lie, younger children could rarely explain beyond the forbidden nature of the act: "because it is a naughty word". However, older children were able to explain "because it isn't right", and "it wasn't true". Even older children indicated an awareness of intention as relevant to the meaning of an act: "A lie is when you deceive someone else. To make a mistake is when you make a mistake". From his observations, Piaget concluded that children begin in a "heteronomous" stage of moral reasoning, characterized by a strict adherence to rules and duties, and obedience to authority.

This heteronomy results from two factors. The first factor is the young child's cognitive structure. According to Piaget, the thinking of young children is characterized by egocentrism. That is to say those young children are unable to simultaneously take into account their own view of things with the perspective of someone else. This egocentrism leads children to project their own thoughts and wishes onto others. It is also associated with the uni-directional view of rules and power associated with heteronomous moral thought, and various forms of "moral realism". Moral realism is associated with "objective responsibility", which is valuing the letter of the law above the purpose of the law. This is why young children are more concerned about the outcomes of actions rather than the intentions of the person doing the act. Moral realism is also associated with the young child's belief in "immanent justice." This is the expectation that punishments automatically follow acts of wrong-doing. One of the most famous cases of such childhood thinking was that of the young boy who believed that his hitting a power pole with his baseball bat caused a major power blackout in the New York City area.

The second major contributor to heteronomous moral thinking in young children is their relative social relationship with adults. In the natural authority relationship between adults and children, power is handed down from above. The relative powerlessness of young children, coupled with childhood egocentrism feeds into a heteronomous moral orientation.

However, through interactions with other children in which the group seeks to play together in a way all find fair, children find this strict heteronomous adherence to rules sometimes problematic. As children consider these situations, they develop towards an "autonomous" stage of moral reasoning, characterized by the ability to consider rules critically, and selectively apply these rules based on a goal of mutual respect and cooperation. The ability to act from a sense of reciprocity and mutual respect is associated with a shift in the child's cognitive structure from egocentrism to perspective taking. Coordinating one's own perspective with that of others means that what are right needs to be based on solutions that meet the requirements of fair reciprocity. Thus, Piaget viewed moral development as the result of interpersonal interactions through which individuals work out resolutions which all deem fair. Paradoxically, this autonomous view of morality as fairness is more compelling and leads to more consistent behaviour than the heteronomous orientation held by younger children.

Piaget concluded from this work that schools should emphasize cooperative decision-making and problem solving, nurturing moral development by requiring students to work out common rules based on fairness. This is a direct rejection of sociologists Emile Durkheim's (1961) view of proper moral education. Durkheim, similar to Piaget, believed that morality resulted from social interaction or immersion in a group. However, Durkheim believed moral development was a natural result of attachment to the group, an attachment which manifests itself in a respect for the symbols, rules, and authority of that group. Piaget rejected this belief that children simply learn and internalize the norms for a group; he believed individuals define morality individually through their struggles to arrive at fair solutions. Given this view, Piaget suggested that a classroom teacher perform a difficult task: the educator must provide students with opportunities for personal discovery through problem solving, rather than indoctrinating students with norms.

An excellent contemporary adaptation of Piaget's theory for moral development of young children may be found in DeVries and Zan (1994). "Moral Children: Constructing a Constructivist Atmosphere in Early Education." New York: Teachers College Press.

Piaget studied many aspects of moral judgment, but most of his findings fit into a two-stage theory. Children younger than 10 or 11 years think about moral dilemmas one way; older children consider them differently. As we have seen, younger children regard rules as fixed and absolute. They believe that rules are handed down by adults or by God and that one cannot change them. The older child's view is more relativistic. He or she understands that it is permissible to change rules if everyone agrees. Rules are not sacred and absolute but are devices which humans use to get along cooperatively.

At approximately the same time 10 or 11 years children's moral thinking undergoes other shifts. In particular, younger children base their moral judgments more on consequences, whereas older children base their judgments on intentions. When, for example, the young child hears about one boy who broke 15 cups trying to help his mother and another boy who broke only one cup trying to steal cookies, the young child thinks that the first boy did worse. The child primarily considers the amount of damage the consequences whereas the older child is more likely to judge wrongness in terms of the motives underlying the act (Piaget, 1932).

There are many more details to Piaget's work on moral judgment, but he essentially found a series of changes that occur between the ages of 10 and 12, just when the child begins to enter the general stage of formal operations.

Intellectual development, however, does not stop at this point. This is just the beginning of formal operations, which continue to develop at least until age 16. Accordingly, one might expect thinking about moral issues to continue to develop throughout adolescence. Kohlberg therefore interviewed both children and adolescents about moral dilemmas, and he did find stages that go well beyond Piaget's. He uncovered six stages, only the first three of which share many features with Piaget's stages.

Kohlberg's Theory of Moral Development

Lawrence Kohlberg (1969) modified and elaborated Piaget's work, and laid the groundwork for the current debate within psychology on moral development. Consistent with Piaget, he proposed that children form ways of thinking through their experiences which include understandings of moral concepts such as justice, rights, equality and human welfare. Kohlberg followed the development of moral judgment beyond the ages studied by Piaget, and determined that the process of attaining moral maturity took longer and was more gradual than Piaget had proposed.

KOHLBERG'S METHOD

Kohlberg's (1958) a core sample was comprised of 72 boys, from both middle- and lower-class families in Chicago. They were ages 10, 13, and 16. He later added to his sample younger children, delinquents, and boys and girls from other American cities and from other countries (1963, 1970).

KOHLBERG'S SIX STAGES

Level-1: Pre-conventional Morality

Stage-1: Obedience and Punishment Orientation

Kohlberg's stage 1 is similar to Piaget's first stage of moral thought. The child assumes that powerful authorities hand down a fixed set of rules which he or she must unquestioningly obey. To the Heinz dilemma, the child typically says that Heinz was wrong to steal the drug because "It's against the law," or "It's bad to steal," as if this were all there were to it. When asked to elaborate, the child usually responds in terms of the consequences involved, explaining that stealing is bad "because you'll get punished" (Kohlberg, 1958).

Although the vast majority of children at stage 1 oppose Heinz's theft, it is still possible for a child to support the action and still employ stage 1 reasoning. For example, a child might say, "Heinz can steal it because he asked first and it's not like he stole something big; he won't get punished". Even though the child agrees with Heinz's action, the reasoning is still stage 1; the concern is with what authorities permit and punish.

Kohlberg calls stage 1 thinking "pre-conventional" because children do not yet speak as members of society. Instead, they see morality as something external to themselves, as that which the big people say they must do.

Stage-2: Individualism and Exchange

At this stage children recognize that there is not just one right view that is handed down by the authorities. Different individuals have different viewpoints. "Heinz," they might point out, "might think its right to take the drug, the druggist would not." Since everything is *relative,* each person is free to pursue his or her *individual* interests. One boy said that Heinz might steal the drug if he wanted his wife to live, but that he doesn't have to if he wants to marry someone younger and better-looking (Kohlberg, 1963). Another boy said Heinz might steal it because may be they had children and he might need someone at home to look after them. But may be he shouldn't steal it because they might put him in prison for more years than he could stand. (Colby and Kauffman. 1983). What is right for Heinz, then, is what meets his own self-interests.

It is noticed that children at both stages 1 and 2 talk about punishment. However, they perceive it differently. At stage 1 punishment is tied up in the child's mind with wrongness; punishment "proves" that disobedience is wrong. At stage 2, in contrast, punishment is simply a risk that one naturally wants to avoid.

Although stage 2 respondents sometimes sound amoral, they do have some sense of right action. This is a notion of *fair exchange* or fair deals. The philosophy is one of returning favours—"If you scratch my back, I'll scratch yours." To the Heinz story, subjects often say that Heinz was right to steal the drug because the druggist was unwilling to make a fair deal; he was "trying to rip Heinz off," Or they might say that he should steal for his wife "because she might return the favor some day" (Gibbs *et al.*, 1983).

Respondents at stage 2 are still said to reason at the pre-conventional level because they speak as isolated individuals rather than as members of society. They see individuals exchanging favors, but there is still no identification with the values of the family or community.

Level-II: Conventional Morality

Stage-3: Good Interpersonal Relationships

At this stage children who are by now usually entering their teens see morality as more than simple deals. They believe that people should live up to the expectations of the family and community and behave in "good" ways. Good behaviour means having good motives and interpersonal feelings such as love, empathy, trust, and concern for others. Heinz, they typically argue, was right to steal the drug because "He was a good man for wanting to save her," and "His intentions were good, that of saving the life of someone he loves." Even if Heinz doesn't love his wife, these subjects often say, he should steal the drug because "I don't think any husband should sit back and watch his wife die" (Gibbs *et al.*, 1983 and Kohlberg, 1958b).

If Heinz's motives were good, the druggist's were bad. The druggist, stage 3 subjects emphasize, was "selfish," "greedy," and "only interested in him, not another life." Sometimes the respondents become so angry with the druggist that they say that he ought to be put in jail (Gibbs *et al.*, 1983). A typical stage 3 response is that of Don, age 13.

It was really the druggist's fault, he was unfair, trying to overcharge and letting someone die. Heinz loved his wife and wanted to save her. I think anyone would. I don't think they would put him in jail. The judge would look at all sides, and see that the druggist was charging too much. (Kohlberg, 1963)

Don defines the issue in terms of the actors' character traits and motives. He talks about the loving husband, the unfair druggist, and the understanding judge. His answer deserves the label "conventional "morality" because it assumes that the attitude expressed would be shared by the entire community—"anyone" would be right to do what Heinz did (Kohlberg, 1963).

As mentioned earlier, there are similarities between Kohlberg's first three stages and Piaget's two stages. In both sequences there is a shift from unquestioning obedience to a relativistic outlook and to a concern for good motives. For Kohlberg, however, these shifts occur in three stages rather than two.

Stage-4: Maintaining the Social Order

Stage 3 reasoning works best in two-person relationships with family members or close friends, where one can make a real effort to get to know the other's feelings and needs and try to help. At stage 4, in contrast, the respondent becomes more broadly concerned with *society as a whole.* Now the emphasis is on obeying laws, respecting authority, and performing one's duties so that the social order is maintained. In response to the Heinz story, many subjects say they understand that Heinz's motives were good, but they cannot condone the theft. What would happen if we all started breaking the laws whenever we felt we had a good reason? The result would be chaos; society couldn't function. As one subject explained,

I don't want to sound like Spiro Agnew, law and order and wave the flag, but if everybody did as he wanted to do, set up his own beliefs as to right and wrong, then I think you would have chaos. The only thing I think we have in civilization nowadays is some sort of legal structure which people are sort of bound to follow.

Because stage 4, subjects make moral decisions from the perspective of society as a whole, they think from a full-fledged member-of-society perspective (Colby and Kohlberg, 1983).

You will recall that stage 1 children also generally oppose stealing because it breaks the law. Superficially, stage 1 and stage 4 subjects are giving the same response, so we see here why Kohlberg insists that we must probe into the reasoning behind the overt response. Stage 1 children say, "It's wrong to steal" and "It's against the law," but they cannot elaborate any further, except to say that stealing can get a person jailed. Stage 4 respondents, in contrast, have a conception of the function of laws for society as a whole a conception which far exceeds the grasp of the younger child.

Level-III: Post-conventional Morality

Stage-5: Social Contract and Individual Rights

At stage 4, people want to keep society functioning. However, a smoothly functioning society is not necessarily a good one. A totalitarian society might be well-organized, but it is hardly the moral ideal. At stage 5, people begin to ask, "What makes for a good society?" They begin to think about society in a very theoretical way, stepping back from their own society and considering the rights and values that a society ought to uphold. They then evaluate existing societies in terms of these prior considerations. They are said to take a "prior-to-society" perspective (Colby and Kohlberg, 1983).

Stage 5 respondents basically believe that a good society is best conceived as a social contract into which people freely enter to work toward the benefit of all. They recognize that different social groups within a society will have different values, but they believe that all rational people would agree on two points. First they would all want certain basic *rights*, such as liberty and life, to be protected. Second, they would want some *democratic* procedures for changing unfair law and for improving society.

In response to the Heinz dilemma, stage 5 respondents make it clear that they do not generally favor breaking laws; laws are social contracts that we agree to uphold until we can change them by democratic means. Nevertheless, the wife's right to live is a moral right that must be protected. Thus, stage 5 respondent sometimes defend Heinz's theft in strong language:

It is the husband's duty to save his wife. The fact that her life is in danger transcends every other standard you might use to judge his action. Life is more important than property.

This young man went on to say that "from a moral standpoint" Heinz should save the life of even a stranger, since to be consistent; the value of a life means any life. When asked if the judge should punish Heinz, he replied:

Usually the moral and legal standpoints coincide. Here they conflict. The judge should weight the moral standpoint more heavily but preserve the legal law in punishing Heinz lightly. (Kohlberg, 1976)

Stage 5 subjects, - then, talk about "morality" and "rights" that take some priority over particular laws. Kohlberg insists, however, that we do not judge people to be at stage 5 merely from their verbal labels. We need to look at their social perspective and mode of reasoning. At stage 4, too, subjects frequently talk about the "right to life," but for them this right is legitimized by the authority of their social or religious group (e.g., by the Bible). Presumably, if their group valued property over life, they would too. At stage 5, in contrast, people are making more of an independent effort to think out what any society ought to value. They often reason, for example, that property has little meaning without life. They are trying to determine logically what a society ought to be like (Kohlberg, 1981 and Gibbs *et al.*, 1983).

Stage -6: Universal Principles

Stage 5 respondents are working toward a conception of the good society. They suggest that we need to (a) protect certain individual rights and (b) settle disputes through democratic processes. However, democratic processes alone do not always result in outcomes that we intuitively sense are just. A majority, for example, may vote for a law that hinders a minority. Thus, Kohlberg believes that there must be a higher stage—stage 6 —which defines the principles by which we achieve justice.

Kohlberg's conception of justice follows that of the philosophers Kant and Rawls, as well as great moral leaders such as Gandhi and Martin Luther King. According to these people, the principles of justice require us to treat the claims of all parties in an impartial manner, respecting the basic dignity, of all people as individuals. The principles of justice are therefore universal; they apply to all. Thus, for example, we would not vote for a law that aids some people but hurts others. The principles of justice guide us toward decisions based on an equal respect for all.

In actual practice, Kohlberg says, we can reach just decisions by looking at a situation through one another's eyes. In the Heinz dilemma, this would mean that all parties the druggist, Heinz, and his wife—take the roles of the others. To do this in an impartial manner, people can assume a "veil of ignorance" (Rawls, 1971), acting as if they do not know which role they will eventually occupy. If the druggist did this, even he would recognize that life must take priority over property; for he wouldn't want to risk finding himself in the wife's shoes with property valued over life. Thus, they would all agree that the wife must be saved—this would be the fair solution. Such a solution, we must note, requires not only impartiality, but the principle that everyone is given full and equal respect. If the wife was considered of less value than the others, a just solution could not be reached.

Until recently, Kohlberg had been scoring some of his subjects at stage 6, but he has temporarily stopped doing so, For one thing, he and other researchers had not been finding subjects who consistently reasoned at this stage. Also, Kohlberg has concluded that his interview dilemmas are not useful for distinguishing between stage 5 and stage 6 thinking. He believes that stage 6 has a clearer and broader conception of universal principles (which include justice as well as individual rights), but feels that his interview fails to draw out this broader understanding. Consequently, he has temporarily dropped stage 6 from his scoring manual, calling it a "theoretical stage" and scoring all post-conventional responses as stage 5 (Colby and Kohlberg, 1983).

Theoretically, one issue that distinguishes stage 5 from stage 6 is civil disobedience. Stage 5 would be more hesitant to endorse civil disobedience because of its commitment to the social contract and to changing laws through democratic agreements. Only when an individual right is clearly at stake does violating the law seem justified. At stage 6, in contrast, a commitment to justice makes the rationale for civil disobedience stronger and broader. Martin Luther King, for example, argued that laws are only valid insofar as they are grounded in justice, and that a commitment to justice carries with it an obligation to disobey unjust laws. King also recognized, of course, the general need for laws and democratic processes (stages 4 and 5), and he was therefore willing to accept the penalties for his actions. Nevertheless, he believed that the higher principle of justice required for civil disobedience (Kohlberg, 1981).

Moral Thought and Moral Behaviour

Kohlberg's scale has to do with moral thinking, not moral action. As everyone knows, people who can talk at a high moral level may not behave accordingly. Consequently, we would not expect perfect correlations between moral judgment and moral action. Still, Kohlberg thinks that there should be some relationship.

As a general hypothesis, he proposes that moral behaviour is more consistent, predictable and responsible at the higher stages (Kohlberg *et al.*, 1975), because the stages themselves increasingly employ more stable and general standards. For example, whereas stage 3 bases decisions on others' feelings, which can vary, stage 4 refers to set rules and laws. Thus, we can expect that moral behaviour, too, will become more consistent as people move up the sequence. Generally speaking, there is some research support for this hypothesis (e.g., with respect to cheating), but the evidence is not clear-cut (Blasi, 1980; Brown and Herrnstein, 1975).

Some research has focused on the relationships between particular stages and specific kinds of behaviour. For example, one might expect that juvenile delinquents or criminals would typically reason at stages 1 or 2, viewing morality as something imposed from without (stage 1) or as a matter of self-interest (stage 2), rather than identifying with society's conventional expectations (stages 3 and 4). Again, some research supports this hypothesis, but there also are some ambiguous results (Blasi, 1980).

Several studies have examined the relationship between post-conventional thinking and student protest. In a landmark study, Haan *et al*. (1968) examined the moral reasoning of those who participated in the Berkeley Free Speech Movement in 1964. Haan found that their thinking was more strongly post-conventional than that of a matched sample of non-participants, but this finding was not replicated for some other protests, apparently because moral principles were not at stake (Keniston, 1971).

Blasi (1980), after reviewing 75 studies, concludes that overall there is a relationship between moral thought and action, but he suggests that we need to introduce other variables to clarify this relationship. One variable may simply be the extent to which individuals themselves feel the need to maintain consistency between their moral thoughts and actions (Blasi, 1980, Kohlberg and Candee, 1981).

Moral Thought and Other Forms of Cognition

Kohlberg has also tried to relate his moral stages to other forms of cognition. He has first analyzed his stages in terms of their underlying cognitive structures and has then looked for parallels in purely logical and social thought. For this purpose, he has analyzed his own stages in terms of implicit *role-taking capacities,* capacities to consider others' viewpoints (Kohlberg, 1976; Selman, 1976 and Rest, 1983).

At first, at stage 1, children hardly seem to recognize that viewpoints differ. They assume that there is only one right view, that of authorities. At stage 2, in contrast, they recognize that people have different interests and viewpoints. They seem to be overcoming egocentrism; they see that perspectives are relative to the individual. They also begin to consider how individuals might coordinate their interests in terms of mutually beneficial deals.

At stage 3, people conceptualize role-taking as a deeper, more empathic process; one becomes concerned with the other's feelings. Stage 4, in turn, has a broader, society-wide conception of how people coordinate their roles through the legal system.

Stages 5 and 6, finally, take a more idealized look at how people might coordinate their interests. Stage 5 emphasizes democratic processes, and stage 6 considers how all parties take one another's perspectives according to the principles of justice.

The moral stages, then, reflect expanded insights into how perspectives differ and might be coordinated. As such, the moral stages might be related to stages of logical and social thought which contain similar insights. So far, the empirical evidence suggests that advances in moral thinking may rest upon prior achievements in these other realms (Kohlberg, 1976; Kuhn *et al.*, 1977). For example, children seem to advance to stage 2, overcoming their egocentrism in the moral sphere, only after they have made equivalent progress in their logical and social thought. If this pattern is correct, we can expect to find many individuals who are logical and even socially insightful but still underdeveloped in their moral judgment.

DOMAIN THEORY: DISTINGUISHING MORALITY AND CONVENTION

In the early 1970s, longitudinal studies conducted by the Kohlberg research group began to reveal anomalies in the stage sequence. Researchers committed to the basic Kohlberg framework attempted to resolve those anomalies through adjustments in the stage descriptions. Other theorists, however, found that a comprehensive resolution to the anomalous data required substantial adjustments in the theory itself. One of the most productive lines of research to come out of that period has been the domain theory advanced by Elliot Turiel and his colleagues.

Within domain theory a distinction is drawn between the child's developing concepts of morality, and other domains of social knowledge, such as social convention. According to domain theory, the child's concepts of morality and social convention emerge out of the child's attempts to account for qualitatively differing forms of social experience associated with these two classes of social events. Actions within the moral domain, such as unprovoked hitting of someone, have intrinsic effects (i.e., the harm that is caused) on the welfare of another person. Such intrinsic effects occur irregardless of the nature of social rules that may or may not be in place regarding the action. Because of this, the core features of moral cognition are centered on considerations of the effects which actions have upon the well-being of persons. Morality is structured by concepts of harm, welfare, and fairness.

In contrast, actions that are matters of social convention have no intrinsic interpersonal consequences. For example, there is nothing intrinsic to the forms of address we employ that makes calling a college teacher "professor" better or worse than calling the person Mr. or Ms., or simply using their given names. What makes one form of address better than another is the existence of socially agreed upon rules. These conventions, while arbitrary in the sense that they have no intrinsic status, are nonetheless important to the smooth functioning of any social group. Conventions provide a way for members of the group to coordinate their social exchanges through a set of agreed upon and predictable modes of conduct. Concepts of convention then are structured by the child's understandings of social organization.

These hypothesized distinctions have been sustained through studies over the past 20 years. These studies have included interviews with children, adolescents and adults; observations of child-child and adult-child social interactions; cross-cultural studies; and longitudinal studies examining the changes in children's thinking as they grow older. An example of the distinction between morality and convention is given in the following excerpt from an interview with a four-year-old girl regarding her perceptions of spontaneously occurring transgressions at her preschool.

CAROL GILLIGAN - MORALITY OF CARE

Second major critique of Kohlberg's work was put forth by Carol Gilligan, in her popular book, "In a Different Voice: Psychological Theory and Women's Development" (1982). She suggested that Kohlberg's theories were biased against women, as only males were used in his studies. By listening to women's experiences, Gilligan offered that a morality of care can serve in the place of the morality of justice and rights espoused by Kohlberg. In her view, the morality of caring and responsibility is premised in nonviolence, while the morality of justice and rights is based on equality. Another way to look at these differences is to view these two moralities as providing two distinct injunctions - the injunction not to treat others unfairly (justice) and the injunction not to turn away from someone in need (care). She presents these moralities as distinct, although potentially connected.

In her initial work, Gilligan emphasized the gender differences thought to be associated with these two orientations. The morality of care emphasizes interconnectedness and presumably emerges to a greater degree in girls owing to their early connection in identity formation with their mothers. The morality of justice, on the other hand, is said to emerge within the context of coordinating the interactions of autonomous individuals. A moral orientation based on justice was proposed as more prevalent among boys because their attachment relations with the mother, and subsequent masculine identity formation entailed that boys separate from that relationship and individuate from the mother. For boys, this separation also heightens their awareness of the difference in power relations between themselves and the adult, and hence engenders an intense set of concerns over inequalities. Girls, however, because of their continued attachment to their mothers, are not as keenly aware of such inequalities, and are, hence, less concerned with fairness as an issue. Further research has suggested, however, that moral reasoning does not follow the distinct gender lines which Gilligan originally reported. The preponderance of evidence is that both males and females reason based on justice and care. While this gender debate is unsettled, Gilligan's work has contributed to an increased awareness that care is an integral component of moral reasoning.

Educational approaches based on Gilligan's work have emphasized efforts to foster empathy and care responses in students. Perhaps the most comprehensive treatment of these issues may be found in Nel Noddings (1992) book, "The challenge to care in schools".

APPRAISAL

It may be seen from the brief review of literature presented in the forgoing pages that a very few studies have been carried out in the area of moral values/judgement. For right conduct and better society, moral values are so important. It is almost a neglected area of research. The area (moral values) under investigation is a novel and unexplored one with to Intermediate Students.

Another interesting feature is that the studies in the area of moral values/judgement confined to single correlational analysis between predictors and the criterion variables. Individual and commutative effects of several independent variables on moral values could be assessed more accurately by employing step-wise multiple regression analysis. Therefore, the main aim of the study is to predict the multiple effects of independent variables on Moral Values of Intermediate Students and further to suggest suitable regression equation in the prediction of Moral Values of Intermediate Students.

By and large except on a few variables, the results obtained in the area of moral values/judgement are not coinciding and hence warranting further explorations. Further, studies on the relative impact of each of the several independent variables that affect moral values/judgement are rare to find. The need for research on the area of moral values/judgement of Intermediate Students is warranting.

The above crucial conditions led the investigation to make an attempt in this area of Moral Values of Intermediate Students in relation with certain psycho-sociological variables. Keeping all these observations in view the problem is stated clearly with its objectives and suitable hypotheses are formulated in the succeeding chapters.

3

THE PRESENT STUDY

This chapter deals with statement of the problem, title of the problem, need for the study, purpose of the study, scope of the study, definitions of the terms, objectives and hypotheses of the study, variables included in the study and limitations of the study.

INTRODUCTION

The word 'Moral' comes from the Latin word '*mores*' which means custom, practice, a way of accomplishing things. Therefore, it has come to mean "belonging to manners and conduct of men" or "Pertaining to right and wrong, good and bad

Morality: Three Principal Meanings

In its first, descriptive usage, morality means a code of conduct held to be authoritative in matters of right and wrong. Morals are created and defined by society, philosophy, religion, or individual conscience.

In its second, normative and universal sense, morality refers to an ideal code of conduct, one which would be espoused in preference to alternatives by all rational people, under specified conditions. To define 'morality' in this sense is a position known as moral skepticism.

In its third usage, 'morality' is synonymous with ethics, the systematic philosophical study of the moral domain.

Ethics seeks to address questions such as how a moral outcome can be achieved in a specific situation (applied ethics), how moral values should be determined (normative ethics), what morals people actually abide by (descriptive ethics), what the fundamental nature of ethics or morality is, including whether it has any objective justification (meta-ethics), and how moral capacity or moral agency develops and what its nature is (moral psychology). In applied ethics, for example, the prohibition against taking human life is controversial with respect to capital punishment, abortion and wars of invasion. In normative ethics, a typical question might be whether a lie told for the sake of protecting someone from harm is justified. In meta-ethics, a key issue is the meaning of the terms "right" or "wrong". Moral realism would hold that there are true moral statements which report objective moral facts, whereas moral anti-realism would hold that morality is derived from any one of the norms prevalent in society (cultural relativism); the edicts of a god (divine command theory); is merely an expression of the speakers' sentiments (emotivism); an implied imperative (prescriptive); falsely presupposes that there are objective moral facts (error theory). Some thinkers hold that there is no correct definition of right behaviour, that morality can only be judged with respect to particular situations, within the standards of particular belief systems and socio-historical contexts. This position, known as moral relativism, often cites empirical evidence from anthropology as evidence to support its claims. The opposite view, that there are universal, eternal moral truths is known as moral absolutism. Moral absolutists might concede that forces of social conformity significantly shape moral decisions, but deny that cultural norms and customs define morally right behaviour.

We came together because of our moral values: care and responsibility, fairness and equality, freedom and courage, fulfillment in life, opportunity and community, cooperation and trust, honesty and openness. We united behind political principles: equality, equity and government for the people-all the people. The nature of an understanding depends upon its founding values, which makes morality (the actual values adopted) the vital concern for parents, with the early experiences of infancy the most critical for the formation of understanding in a child. This means that the lessons taught to the infant during the first weeks or months of its existence are the most important, as every subsequent value must reflect those values already adopted by the maturing mind of the person. For once the foundation of values is set; it is for life, with the values taught during child rearing becoming a permanent part of the adult's understanding.

STATEMENT OF THE PROBLEM

The present study is concerned with the 'Attitude of Intermediate Students towards moral values in relation with certain variables'. It examines the differences in the attitudes of Intermediate Students towards moral values residing in the rural and urban; private, aided and government colleges. The study is designed to make an in depth study of moral values in relation with certain Socio-Demographic variables, Study Habits, Self-concepts and Personality factors of students.

NEED FOR THE STUDY

'No great moralist was made so in a day.
Nor any one of them was a born moralist'.

It is time for us all to take the first step to become weak and gentle so that we see the necessity to come together and acquire a collective voice. As Lao-Tze so wisely put it:

A man is born gentle and weak
At his death he is hard and stiff

Green plants are tender and filled with sap
At their death they are withered and dry
The stiff and unbending is the disciple of death
The gentle and yielding is the disciple of life
An army without flexibility never wins a war
A tree that is unbending is easily felled
The hard and the strong will fall
The soft and weak will overcome
Yes, India needs to restore its moral voice.

Many of us, particularly parents, worry about the morals and ethics of today's society and wonder how to safeguard our children from the temptations of drugs, crime, promiscuity, etc. There is, of course, no foolproof way of doing so, but it is true one of the strongest forces working in favour of virtue is every human being's intense desire to be good. At the basic level, thanks to the conditioning we receive from our earliest age, this translates into a need for society's approbation, to be seen as desirable role models. Maybe it encourages hypocrisy and the projection of appearances; on the other hand, how many times it must have stopped us from giving in to our lawless desires? Society's disapproval is a powerful deterrent to bad behaviour.

No society has ever respected cowardice over courage. Fairness, kindness, dignity, charity, integrity, honesty, concern for others, patience, empathy, compassion, justice, integrity and commitment are among the desirable primary values that have been accepted universally in every age. Values may be subjective, but not the principles of Nature.

Breaking up of joint families into nuclear families, most homes do not have a value-giver today. Homes have turned into mere houses where family members come to eat, watch TV and sleep. "Values are inculcated by the mother, who is usually not available to the child for the major part of the day.

When the mother arrives home after the day's work, she is already too tired and has other things to look after. At the most she manages to help them in doing the homework often not even that. Then, usually the whole family sits before the TV till bedtime. Where are the values going to come from?"

Mahatma Gandhi used to say that there is enough in this world to satisfy man's need, but not his greed. Gogate, an Indian interior designer-turned-corporate trainer, feels that "conversion of needs into greed prevents right values from prevailing in our society". Greed manifests itself as absence of trust in the Big Plan, belief in scarcity and a general feeling of insecurity.

The greatest tragedy of the modern world is that it has given us enough to live with but nothing to live for. Today, our purpose of life has become hazy. Existence has become more important than living. People today do not ask themselves what they feel concerned about and what they would like to dedicate their lives to; they ask which field has better 'scope'. They seek to take decisions on the basis of what lies in the external world, instead of being driven from within. But unless we find a cause to live for, we are not fit to live.

Today, there is a powerful image of people, who seem to be leading happy and respectable lives even without ethics. Respect is proportional to money and external achievements, not to the quality of means employed to get them. Impressionable young minds choose unhealthy role models for themselves early in their lives.

Our school textbooks talk more about wars than about the lives of people with exemplary values. The students look for role models from the contemporary world, as they can relate to them. However, textbooks imply that such people lived only in *Sat Yuga* (the spiritually evolved era according to Hinduism) or centuries ago. The media also underplays reports of exemplary people as it assumes that good deeds are uninteresting, hence un-saleable.

Today's children are tomorrows' citizens. So, it is necessary to take care about present generation students. Values are very important for all human beings. A life with peace and tranquility of mind is what every individual would aspire for. Any human society has continued its existence only so far as there has been peace in it free from internal squabbles among its own members and from external onslaught. Even wars or civil wars are fought with the object of establishing a longer context alone that the ancient Indians always called for peace through the several santi mantras (hymns praying for peace) such as:

Sahanâvavatu sahanaubhunaktu

sahavîryam karavâvahai

tejaswinâvadhitamastu

mâvidvishâvahai

Om shantih shantih shantih.

(May He protect both of us; may we share our experiences; may we strive together vigorously; may our study bring enlightenment; may we not hate each other. Peace, peace, peace.)

Through following this kind of life the ancient Indians desired to be led from darkness to light, from untruth towards truth and from immorality to morality:

Asato mâ sadgamayâ

tamasomâ jyotirgamayâ

mruthyormâ amritamgamayâ

Om shântih shântih shântih.

Since, society continues to exist though the individual perishes the social heritage needs to be preserved, protected and improved through education and training. How can we expect good education, harmony or peace in any society without its members being moral? It is always the acts of immorality that have sown the seeds of unhappiness, hatred, jealousy, enmity etc., in any human society. The first and foremost requisite therefore for any society is that its members must be moral.

Moral education is imperative for two reasons. It prevents individuals from getting into the undesirable company of immoral persons. It preserves and cherishes our social heritage which includes the fundamental moral principles. In the absence of such education whatever progress is already achieved may be arrested and the society may stagnate or even degenerate.

So, moral values are important in the day to day life of human beings. It is necessary to investigate into its nature and also to know whether it is related to factors like personality, study habits, self-concepts and socio-demographic etc.

PURPOSE OF THE STUDY

The present study aims at investigating the pattern of the moral values prevailing in the Intermediate Students in relation with certain variables. The purpose of the study is an attempt to answer the following aspects:

1. What is the position of values in the present scenario?
2. Whether there is any relationship between personality factors and moral values of the students?
3. Whether there is any relationship between study habits and moral values of the students?
4. Whether there is any relationship between self-concepts and moral values of the students?
5. Whether there the socio-demographic variables have any impact on moral values of the students?

SCOPE OF THE STUDY

The main intention of the study is to make a survey of moral values of intermediate students in Rural and Urban; Government, Aided and Private; Residential and Non-residential; Boys and Girls; Group Subjects and Medium of Study.

The study attempted to identify the type of relation between the dependent variable (moral values) and independent variables viz., Personality Factors, Study Habits, Self-concepts and Socio-Demographic variables.

DEFINITIONS OF THE CERTAIN TERMS

Moral

A moral is a message conveyed or a lesson to be learned from a story or event. The moral may be left to the hearer, reader or viewer to determine for themselves, or may be explicitly encapsulated in a maxim. As an example of the latter, at the end of Aesop's fable of the Tortoise and the Hare, in which the plodding and determined tortoise wins a race against the much-faster yet extremely arrogant hare, the moral is "slow and steady wins the race."

Value

- Value (ethics): The degree of importance, including the value independent on subjective valuations by any individual
- Value (personal and cultural): The principles, standards, or quality which guides human actions
- Value (mathematics): The value of a variable in mathematics.
- Value (economics): The market worth or estimated worth of commodities, services, assets, or work.

Morality

Morality may be defined as "The quality of being in accord with standards of right or good conduct".

"*Morality is a private and costly luxury.*"

—**Henry Brooks Adams**

"The only immorality is not to do what one has to do when one has to do it."

—Jean Anouilh

"Moral excellence comes about as a result of habit. We become just by doing just acts, temperate by doing temperate acts, brave by doing brave acts."

—Aristotle

"The moral virtues, then, are produced in us neither by nature nor against nature. Nature, indeed, prepares in us the ground for their reception, but their complete formation is the product of habit."

—Aristotle

"Never let your sense of morals get in the way of doing what's right."

—Isaac Asimov

"While moral rules may be propounded by authority the fact that these were so propounded would not validate them."

—Sir Alfred Jules Ayer

Pupil/Student

"A person studying under relatively close supervision and tutelage of a teacher"

—Good (1959)

"Refers to those enrolled in a school, college or university to follow a particular course of study".

Religion

Defined portion of the earth's surface now especially as distinguished by certain natural features, climatic conditions a special fauna or flora, or the like. A separate part or division of the world or Universe, as the air, Heaven etc.

—Vivan Ridler (1961)

Caste

"Caste is a system of stratification in which mobility up and down the status ladder, at least ideally may not occur."

—Green

Locality

'A place considered with reference to some particular events or circumstances connected with it, a quarter in which certain things are done or which chosen for particular operations.'

—Vivan Ridler (1961)

Moral Absolutism

Moral absolutism is the belief that there are absolute standards against which moral questions can be judged, and that certain actions are right or wrong, devoid of the context of the act. "Absolutism" is often philosophically contrasted with moral relativism, which is a belief that moral truths are relative to social, cultural, historical or personal references, and to situational ethics, which holds that the morality of an act depends on the context of the act.

Moral Agency

Moral agency is a person's capacity for making moral judgments and taking actions that comport with morality.

Moral Codes

Teachers and parents should confront the child with their own moral codes in a very clear and definite manner so that, whether he accepts or rejects a code, at least he knows what he is accepting or rejecting (Wilson in Wilson *et al.*, 1967, p.132).

Codified morality is generally distinguished from custom, another way for a community to define appropriate activity, by the former's derivation from natural or universal principles. In certain religious communities, the Divine is said to provide these principles through revelation, sometimes in great detail. Such codes may be called laws, as in the Law of Moses, or community morality may be defined through commentary on the texts of revelation, as in Islamic law. Such codes are distinguished from legal or judicial right, including civil rights, which are based on the accumulated traditions, decrees and legislation of a political authority, though these latter often invoke the authority of the moral law.

Moral Development

Moral development is the process through which children develop proper attitudes and behaviors toward other people in society, based on social and cultural norms, rules, and laws.

Moral Education

Bull in his book *Moral Education* (1969) explains that:

'The child is not born with a built-in moral conscience. But he is born with those natural, biologically purposive capacities that make him potentially a moral being.'

The content of the moral curriculum, its pedagogy and pacing, the academic subjects to be involved and the school organization needed are all clearly related to the total social structure within which any school is set. Very rarely does a school attempt to change the moral code of a society (Musgrove, 1978).

If we want to be able to show that certain types of education produce 'morally educated' people, we must first identify a 'morally educated' person so that we know what types of education to look for (Musgrove, 1967).

Only a handful of educational theorists hold the view that if only the adult world would get out of the way, children would ripen into fully realized people. Most thinkers, educational practitioners, and parents acknowledge that children are born helpless and need the care and guidance of adults into their teens and often beyond. More specifically, children need to learn how to live harmoniously in society. Historically, the mission of schools has been to develop in the young both the intellectual and the moral virtues. Concern for the moral virtues, such as honesty, responsibility, and respect for others, is the domain of moral education.

Moral Particularism

The view owing its ancestry to Aristotle, and defended by the contemporary British philosopher Jonathan Dancy, that in deciding the rights and wrongs of action general principles are of little value: the devil lies in the details. It thus stands opposed to ethics relying on highly general and abstract principles, particularly those associated with the Kantian categorical imperative. The view may go so far as to say that taken on its own, no consideration points in any particular way, but taken to this extreme the view seems to threaten any kind of reasoning about what to do, since that can only proceed by identifying salient features of a situation that weigh on one side or another.

Moral Relativism

In philosophy, moral relativism is the position that *moral* or *ethical* propositions do not reflect objective and/or universal moral truths, but instead make claims *relative* to social, cultural, historical or *personal* circumstances. Moral relativists hold that no universal standard exists by which to assess an ethical proposition's truth; it is the opposite of moral absolutism. Relativistic positions often see moral values as applicable only within certain cultural boundaries or in the context of individual preferences. An extreme relativist position might suggest that judging the moral or ethical judgments or acts of another person or group has no meaning, though most relativists propound a more limited version of the theory.

Moral Universalism

Moral universalism is the meta-ethical position that some system of ethics, or a universal ethic, applies universally, that is to all people regardless of culture, race, sex, religion, nationality, sexuality, or other distinguishing feature. The source or justification of this system may be thought to be, for instance, human nature, shared vulnerability to suffering, the demands of universal reason, what is common among existing moral codes, or the commands of a God. It is the opposing position to various forms of moral relativism.

Moral Zeitgeist

The Moral Zeitgeist is a term used by some atheists to describe the evolution of morality. Proponents of a moral *Zeitgeist* believe that morality evolved to help our ape-like ancestors survive in large groups as social animals. This theory suggests that moral acceptability is chosen by the masses. As the people's view of what is a morally acceptable change, the moral Zeitgeist is said to "shift."

Words Related to Moral

The words related to 'Moral' are given below:

- Moral Absolutism
- Moral Acceptance
- Moral Action
- Moral Agency
- Moral Argument
- Moral Argument
- Moral Asynchrony
- Moral Authority
- Moral Awareness
- Moral Battle
- Moral Behaviour
- Moral Certainty
- Moral Character
- Moral Chat
- Moral Clarity
- Moral Code
- Moral Cognition
- Moral Community
- Moral Concept
- Moral Conscience
- Moral Consciousness
- Moral Crisis
- Moral Deadline
- Moral Debate
- Moral Decay
- Moral Decline
- Moral Determinism
- Moral Development
- Moral Dialogue
- Moral Dilemma
- Moral Economy
- Moral Education
- Moral Emblems
- Moral Entitlement
- Moral Entrepreneur
- Moral Equivalence
- Moral Equivalent
- Moral Essay
- Moral Fabric
- Moral Fashions
- Moral Formation
- Moral Geographies
- Moral Good
- Moral Graph
- Moral Hazard
- Moral Idiocy
- Moral Imagination
- Moral Imperative
- Moral Instinct
- Moral Instruction
- Moral Intelligence
- Moral Intensity
- Moral Inventory
- Moral Issue

- Moral Judgement
- Moral Justification
- Moral Law
- Moral Lepers
- Moral Lesson
- Moral Life
- Moral Limits
- Moral Luck
- Moral Mafia
- Moral Majority
- Moral Masochism
- Moral Mazes
- Moral Measures
- Moral Message
- Moral Minds
- Moral Motivation
- Moral Nihilism
- Moral Obligation
- Moral Opposite
- Moral Orientation
- Moral Panic
- Moral Particularism
- Moral Philosopher
- Moral Philosophy
- Moral Pluralism
- Moral Practices
- Moral Principle
- Moral Problems
- Moral Properties
- Moral Psychology
- Moral Purity
- Moral Realism
- Moral Reasoning
- Moral Reasons
- Moral Relativism
- Moral Responsibility
- Moral Responsiveness
- Moral Schizophrenia
- Moral Sense
- Moral Sentiments
- Moral Sinner
- Moral Skepticism
- Moral Societies
- Moral Skepticism
- Moral Spots
- Moral Standards
- Moral Status
- Moral Stories
- Moral Superiority
- Moral Support
- Moral Tales
- Moral Teaching
- Moral Theology
- Moral Theory
- Moral Therapy
- Moral Treatment
- Moral Universalism
- Moral Values
- Moral Victory
- Moral Views
- Moral Violence
- Moral Vision
- Moral World
- Moral Zeitgeist

OBJECTIVES OF THE STUDY

The study is designed with the following specific objectives:

1. To study the attitude of Intermediate Students towards Moral Values.
2. To study the influence of Personality Factors on the attitude of students towards Moral Values.
3. To study the impact of Study Habits on the attitude of students towards Moral Values.
4. To study the impact of Self-concepts on the attitude of students towards Moral Values.
5. To know the influence of Socio-Demographic variables on the attitude of students towards Moral Values.
6. To predict the Moral Values with the help of different sets of independent variables namely
   (i) Socio-Demographic variables,
   (ii) Personality Factors,
   (iii) Self-concepts,
   (iv) Study Habits and
   (v) All the independent variables in the study.

HYPOTHESES OF THE STUDY

Based on the above objectives, the following hypotheses were formulated for the purpose of the study.

1. In general there would not be good moral values among Intermediate Students.
2. There would be no significant influence of the main effects namely sex and college on the moral values.
3. There would be no significant interaction effect of sex × college on moral values.
4. There would be no significant influence of the main effects of community and caste on moral values.

5. There would be no significant interaction effect of community × caste on the *Moral Values*.
6. There is no significant influence of Personality Factors on the attitude of students towards *Moral Values*.
7. There is no significant impact of Self-concepts on the attitude of students towards *Moral Values*.
8. There wouldn't be significant influence of Study Habits on the attitude of students towards *Moral Values*.
9. There is no significant influence of Socio-Demographic variables on the attitude of students towards *Moral Values*.
10. Socio-Demographic variables, Personality Factors, Self-concepts and Study Habits would not turnout to be the predictors of *Moral Values*.
11. No independent variable out of 55 turnout to be significant predictor of *Moral Values*.

VARIABLES STUDIED

The review of literature in the field of Moral Values reveals the fact that the Moral Values of the students have been influenced by a number of psycho-sociological variables collectively. Hence the following psycho-sociological variables are included in the study. Out of total variables 55 are independent variables and one is dependent variable. 22 are Socio-Demographic variables for which information is gathered through a personal data sheet.

A. Independent Variables

1. Socio-Demographic Variables

1. College
2. Age
3. Family Annual Income
4. Educational Qualification of Father

5. Educational Qualification of Mother
6. Father Occupation
7. Mother Occupation
8. Birth Order
9. Total Members in the Family
10. Residence
11. Sex
12. Community
13. Caste
14. Native Place
15. Economic Position
16. Medium of the Study
17. Religious Festivals
18. Religious Discourses
19. Visiting Temple
20. When you go wrong who corrects you,
21. Type of Family
22. Group Subjects

2. Psychological Variables

i) HSPQ consisting of 14 personality factors.

1. Factor A (Reserved Vs Outgoing)
2. Factor B (Less Intelligent Vs More Intelligent)
3. Factor C (Emotionally less stable Vs More Intelligent)
4. Factor D (Phlegmatic Vs Excitable)
5. Factor E (Obedient Vs Assertive)
6. Factor F (Sober Vs Happy go lucky)
7. Factor G (Moral Standards Vs Super ego strength)
8. Factor H (Shy Vs Venturesome)
9. Factor I (Though minded Vs Tense minded)

10. Factor J (Vigorous Vs Doubting)
11. Factor O (Placid Vs Apprehensive)
12. Factor Q_2 (Group Dependent Vs Controlled)
13. Factor Q_3 (Undisciplined Vs Controlled)
14. Factor Q_4 (Relaxed Vs Tense)

ii) Self Concept questionnaire consisting of 10 areas.

1) Health and Sex Appropriateness
2) Abilities
3) Self-confidence
4) Self-acceptance
5) Worthiness
6) Present, Past and Future
7) Beliefs and Convictions
8) Feeling of Shame and Guilt
9) Sociability
10) Emotional Maturity
11) Self-concepts Total Score (Total of all the 10 areas)

iii) Study Habits questionnaire consisting of 7 areas.

1. Home environment and planning of work
2. Reading and note-taking
3. Planning of subject
4. Habits of concentration
5. Preparation for examinations
6. General habits and attitudes
7. School environment
8. Study Habits Total Score (Total of all the 7 areas)

B. Dependent Variable

Attitude scores of Intermediate Students towards Moral Values are taken as the dependent variable.

LIMITATIONS OF THE STUDY

The following limitations are observed in this investigation.

1. The study is limited to the students of Senior Intermediate only.
2. The attitude of students is measured through the Moral Values Attitude Inventory constructed by the investigator.
3. Attitude of students towards Moral Values depend on Psychological, Sociological, Economic and Environmental factors. No factor can be studied in isolation.
4. Due to laborious calculations, only certain variables are studied in this investigation.
5. The study is confined to 16 intermediate colleges in Chittoor District of Andhra Pradesh.
6. This is only a presage study in the area of Moral Behaviour.

4

METHODS OF INVESTIGATION

This chapter deals with the various procedures followed for the construction and standardization of data-gathering instruments on selected variables for the present study; the methods adopted in selection of sample, collection of the data, scoring, analysis, and statistical techniques employed.

The flowchart showing the procedures followed in the present investigation is given in Fig. 4.1.

Prerequisites of a Good Test

The aims of a sound and strategic achievement measurement are best met by a test which:

a) Covers all the major dimensions of factors, which analytically demonstrate, in any attempt to describe, individual differences comprehensively.
b) Is conveniently applied, either an individual test or a group test in the classroom.

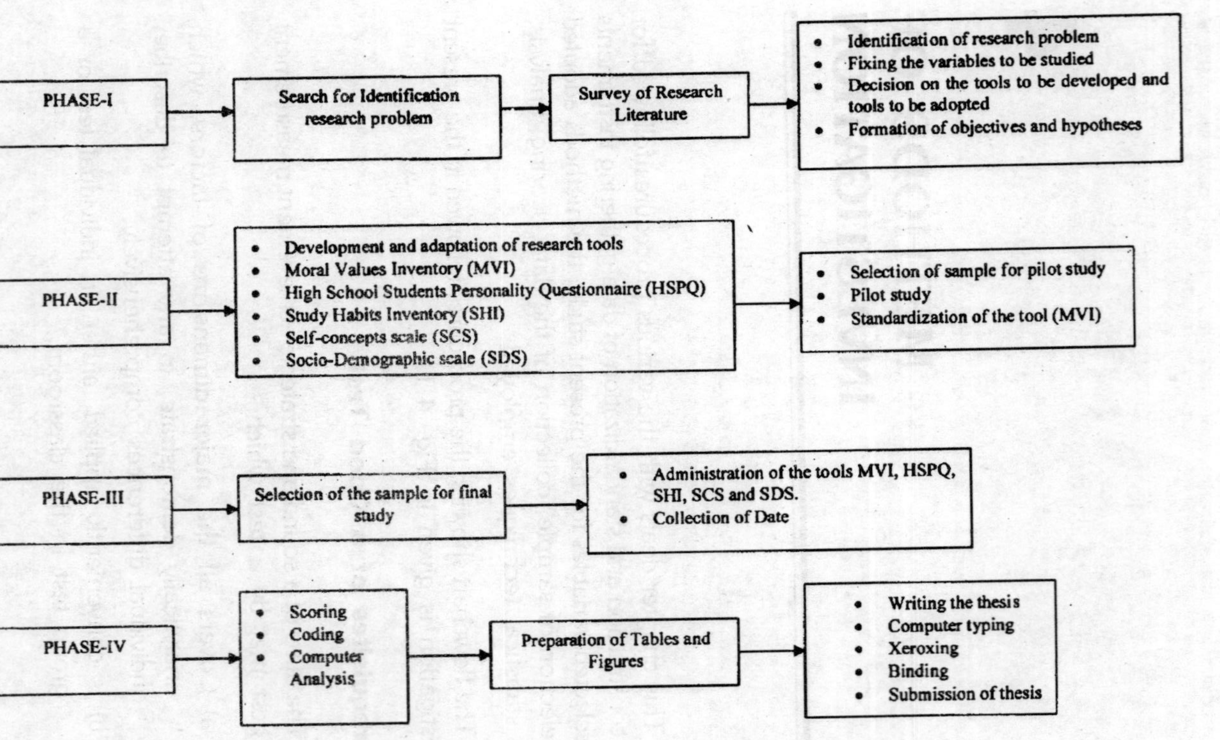

Fig. 4.1: The procedures followed in the present investigation

TOOLS USED FOR THE STUDY

1) Moral Values Inventory (MV).
2) High School Student Personality Questionnaire (HSPQ)
3) Study Habits Inventory (SHI)
4) Self-concepts Scale (SCI)
5) Socio-Demographic Scale (SDS)

CONSTRUCTION OF THE MORAL VALUES INVENTORY

The investigator searched for the tools for measuring Moral Values. The investigator has not found suitable tool for measuring the Moral Values of Intermediate Students. Hence, the investigator planned to develop a tool for measuring the Moral Values of the Intermediate Students.

On the basis of review of literature, a list of 100 attitude items on Moral Values was prepared. These items were given to some experts. The experts had checked the suitability and vocabulary used in the items. 13 items were deleted on the advice of the experts and 87 items retained were suitable to measure the Moral Values of Intermediate college students. Each item of the inventory was arranged on a unipolar 5 point scale with responses: Strongly Agree, Agree, Doubtful, Disagree and Strongly Disagree.

A separate answer sheet is used. The student is asked to write any one of the appropriate letter namely A, B, C, D and E in the bracket given against the respective moral attitude statement number.

It was translated into Telugu version, the regional language of the subjects on whom it had to be used. Five judges who were well versed with psychological testing checked the translation. Terms, which were ambiguous, were discussed and resolved. The Telugu version thus prepared was administered to a small group of students of Intermediate Second Year. They were asked to answer the items and also check those words, which they could not understand. Such of those terms, which the students marked were modified or substituted with simple words. Thus the constructed Moral Values Inventory was used to measure the attitude of moral values of the students.

Pilot Study

The Telugu version of the Moral Values Inventory was administered on a representative sample of 370 students studying Intermediate Second Year selected at random from the 16 Colleges representing in Chittoor District covering all the four Revenue Divisions and also considering the sex and the locality. The inventory was administered in small groups; sufficient time was given to the students in order to respond properly. For the purpose of scoring numerical values were assigned to each of the five categories of responses: Strongly Agree, Agree, Doubtful, Disagree and Strongly Disagree. The numerical values for the positive and negative items are shown in Table 4.1.

TABLE 4.1:Numerical values for different alternatives of the positive and negative items

Item	Alternatives				
	Strongly Agree	Agree	Doubtful	Disagree	Strongly Disagree
Positive	5	4	3	2	1
Negative	1	2	3	4	5

The total score of the each student on Moral Values Inventory was indicated on the top of the answer sheet.

Selection of the Items

The selection of the items was based on the results of item analysis, which provides an index of item difficulty. Since, the discrimination of the each item was to be determined; students were classified into High group and Low group.

First the total answer scripts (370) were arranged in an ascending order on the basis of the total score obtained by the students. The upper 27% of the papers (i.e., 100 papers) were placed in the High group and the lower 27% of the papers (i.e., 100 papers) were placed in the Low group. The rest were excluded from the analysis. These two groups provide criterion groups from which to evaluate the individual items.

The calculation of 't' value for the item number 1 of the pilot study inventory is shown in Table 4.2.

For the calculation of the 't' values the procedure suggested by Edward (1957) was followed:

The items with 't' values less than 1.97 (0.05 level of significance) were deleted. In this investigation 8 items were deleted and 79 items were retained for the final study.

Out of 79 items in the final study, there are 41 positive items. The item numbers 1, 2, 3, 4, 11, 13, 21, 22, 25, 28, 29, 30, 31, 35, 39, 40, 41, 43, 44, 45, 48, 50, 51, 52, 53, 54, 55, 56, 57, 60, 64, 66, 69, 71, 72, 73, 74, 76, 77, 78 and 79 are positive. The remaining items (38 items) are negative. The 't' values for all the items of the pilot study of Moral Values Inventory are presented in Table 4.3.

Validity of the Inventory

The definition suggests that to determine how valid the test is, one must compare the reality of what it does measure with some ideal construction what it ought to measure. The validity of the test is an estimate of the correlation between the raw test scores and true criterion scores. Although a test is developed to serve a defined purpose, it is often used for other purposes also. For example, a cognitive test or test of intelligence developed to measure the mental ability of children can serve

TABLE 4.2: The calculation of 't' value for evaluating the difference in the mean response to the Item No.1 of the pilot study of Moral Values Inventory for the High group and Low group.

Response Categories	High group				Low group			
	x	f	fx	$f(x)^2$	x	f	fx	$f(x)^2$
Strongly Agree	5	66	330	1650	5	14	70	350
Agree	4	28	112	448	4	64	256	1024
Doubtful	3	2	6	18	3	6	18	54
Disagree	2	2	4	8	2	10	20	40
StronglyDisagree	1	2	2	2	1	6	6	6
		100	454	2126		100	370	1474

t = 6.41

other useful purposes; predict college performance, serve as a basis of classification in vocational selection, identify moral values, study habits and learning difficulties, etc.

TABLE 4.3: The 't' values for all the items of the pilot study of Moral Values Inventory

Item No.	't' Value	Remarks
1	6.41	Retained
2	4.32	Retained
3	5.41	Retained
4	3.22	Retained
5	4.54	Retained
6	2.32	Retained
7	10.12	Retained
8	3.14	Retained
9	5.75	Retained
10	4.32	Retained
11	3.35	Retained
12	1.42	Deleted
13	2.54	Retained
14	4.26	Retained
15	3.31	Retained
16	4.27	Retained
17	3.71	Retained
18	3.11	Retained
19	5.34	Retained
20	2.98	Retained
21	0.88	Deleted
22	12.54	Retained
23	2.98	Retained
24	7.97	Retained
25	5.62	Retained
26	6.22	Retained

(contd.)

Item No.	't' Value	Remarks
27	4.13	Retained
28	9.37	Retained
29	5.32	Retained
30	12.91	Retained
31	5.37	Retained
32	4.42	Retained
33	2.23	Retained
34	8.21	Retained
35	10.94	Retained
36	7.15	Retained
37	6.69	Retained
38	-0.85	Deleted
39	7.78	Retained
40	9.12	Retained
41	5.28	Retained
42	6.12	Retained
43	3.19	Retained
44	3.31	Retained
45	-1.25	Deleted
46	5.32	Retained
47	4.38	Retained
48	7.34	Retained
49	1.42	Deleted
50	6.63	Retained
51	0.96	Deleted
52	4.35	Retained
53	4.14	Retained
54	3.57	Retained
55	9.32	Retained
56	4.32	Retained
57	4.15	Retained
58	5.21	Retained

Item No.	't' Value	Remarks
59	3.39	Retained
60	3.65	Retained
61	0.84	Deleted
62	7.31	Retained
63	4.39	Retained
64	5.31	Retained
65	4.21	Retained
66	1.26	Deleted
67	5.32	Retained
68	4.12	Retained
69	2.97	Retained
70	5.32	Retained
71	3.94	Retained
72	4.76	Retained
73	9.72	Retained
74	5.33	Retained
75	4.31	Retained
76	2.99	Retained
77	5.11	Retained
78	4.16	Retained
79	5.19	Retained
80	7.91	Retained
81	3.37	Retained
82	6.96	Retained
83	5.32	Retained
84	4.25	Retained
85	2.65	Retained
86	4.75	Retained
87	8.34	Retained

Content Validity

"Content Validity is estimated by evaluating the relevance of the test items, individually and as a whole. Each item should be a sampling of the knowledge or performance, which the test purports to measure. Taken collectively, the items should constitute a representative sample of the variable to be tested. At the same time, it is essential that the content not be compounded by introducing irrelevant problems and materials" (Freeman, 1965).

"Validity is demonstrated by showing how well the content of the test samples the class situations or subject matter about which conclusions are to be drawn; the test user wishes to determine how an individual performs at present in a universe of situations that the test situation is claimed to represent". (Good, 1973)

Validity of content should not depend upon the subjective judgement of only one specialist. In the construction of the inventory, related literature, empirical findings, views of several specialists and actual subject matter were considered for the selection of the items.

Thus content validation rested first upon the expert analysis of the materials to be sampled and second upon the use of available statistical procedures to refine the original selection of items. Thus, it can be reasonably assumed that the Moral Values Inventory has content validity.

Item Validity

There are many indices and procedures for determining item validity. One of which stresses the number of discriminations of the desired sort that the item is capable of making. It emphasizes the content to which the item predicts segregation of examinees into those with high criterion versus low criterion scores. The discriminative power (Validity Index) of each item was established before including them in the final form. The Validity Index calculated for each of the item is a measure of the extent to which a given statement differentiates the high and low groups. So, there is item validity in Moral Values Inventory.

Intrinsic Validity

Guilford (1954) defined intrinsic validity as "the degree to which a test measures what it measures". It is "testing a type of evidence of validity, based upon the fact that the items in a test are selected so as to simulate the criterion items that the test is used to predict" (Good, 1973). This can also be stated in terms of how well the obtained scores measure the test's true score component. This validity is given by the square root of its reliability. Hence, the intrinsic validity of the Moral Values Inventory was "0.95 = 0.98.

Face Validity

"A term which indicates a validity referring not to what a test actually measure but to what it appears, on the basis of a subjective evaluation, to measure, of all the concepts of validity, the least justifiable, valuable in the original writing of test items" (Good, 1973).

It is a "measure of the degree to which a test appears to be valid, while this is the most superficial kind of validity, it may contribute significantly to the legitimacy of the test in the eyes of the candidates" (Madhu Raj, 1996)

If a common thread of achievement runs through all the items of the test, the resultant test has "face validity". All the items in the Moral Values Inventory have a common thread of measuring Moral Values. So there is face validity in Moral Values Inventory.

Construct Validity

Construct Validity of test measures particular characteristics of an individual. If a test can indicate the individual's actual achievement of instructional objectives, it is valid from the construct point of view.

Construct validity is "validity evaluated by investigating what qualities a test measures, that is, by determining the degree to which certain explanatory concepts or constructs account for performance on a test". (Good, 1973)

Hence there is construct validity for Moral Values Inventory.

Concurrent Validity

In a situation of some observable criterion, the scale's validity can be investigated by seeing how good an indicator it is. This approach leads to two categories of validity, i.e. 'predictive validity' and 'concurrent validity'.

Concurrent validity is a 'validity based upon correlation with a criterion variable, that is, by determining the degree to which certain explaining concepts or constructs account for performance on the test'. (Good, 1973)

Predictive Validity

Predictive validity is concerned with how the scale forecast a future criterion and concurrent validity with how well it can describe a present one. Good defined it as 'validity based upon correlation with a criterion variable that is not available until sometime after testing (as, for example, school grades)'. Predictive validity can be 'obtained by giving a test to a group of subjects and then comparing the test results with the job performance of those tested. Predictive validity is the type of validity most strongly advocated by the EEOC, because Predictivity Valid Tests are excellent indicators of future performance' (Madhu Raj, 1996).

The results in the succeeding chapter show that Moral Values Inventory has both concurrent validity and predictive validity.

Criterion Validity

Validity demonstrated by comparing the test scores with one or more external variables considered to provide a direct measure of the characteristic or behaviour in question; may take the form of an expectancy table or, most commonly, a correlation relating to the test score to a criterion measure; the test user wishes to forecast an individual's present standing on some variable of particular significance that is different from the test.

It is 'an examination for which an individual's score indicates the relationship of the individual's performance to a specified criterion' (Madhu Raj, 1996).

Reliability

Next to validity, reliability is the most indispensable characteristic of any measuring instrument. It refers to the consistency of scores obtained by the same individuals at different occasions or with different sets of equivalent items.

"Traditionally, the text books have told us that there are three fundamental types of approach to the estimation of reliability. All of these were designed to answer the question, what is the self-correction of this test. There have been three standard procedures, known as the 'split-half', 'alternative forms', and 'test-retest methods'" (Guilford, 1954).

A tool is said to be reliable if it reveals similar results in various situations. The test-retest and parallel form methods of estimating reliability may be common and legitimate for both power and speed tests. In the power test, each student has enough time to respond to correct answer. Speed test usually yields spuriously high reliability co-efficient when split-half and internal consistency methods are employed. (Stanley *et al.*, 1978).

Split-Half Reliability

"By means of this technique, which is used to find internal consistency the items in a whole test were divided into two halves which should be equivalent or very nearly so. Thus the two scores, one for each half, one obtained for each individual by administering the test only once and each score is treated as though it is represented a separate form" (Freeman, 1965).

It is sometimes called co-efficient of equivalence. The test is split into two equivalent halves usually by pooling the odd numbered items for one half, where as the even numbered items form the second half of the test. This usually makes the two scores obtained from a single test reasonably equivalent. By applying the Spearman-Brown prophecy formula the calculated correlation co-efficient for the half test is 0.902. The correlation co-efficient for the full test is also calculated and it is equal to 0.948. It shows that the reliability of the instrument is very high.

Test-Retest Reliability

The reliability of the Moral Values Inventory is also computed using Test-Retest Method on a sample of 360 with a gap of 15 days for retest. The Test-Retest Reliability of the Moral Values Inventory is 0.936.

SOCIO-DEMOGRAPHIC SCALE (SDS)

Socio-Demographic Scale is defined as the ranking of an individual in terms his/her material belongings and cultural possessions along with the degree of respect, power and influence she/he derives.

The investigator prepared a Socio-Demographic Scale and is used in the present study.

Organisation of Items

The number of items were collected and selected to obtain information regarding the Socio-Demographic variables selected for this study. A panel of judges consisting of experienced lecturers and experts persuade all the items. They were requested to examine the items carefully and to comment on clarity of expression and adequacy of information to be collected for the study. The comments and suggestions were carefully examined and the questionnaire was accordingly modified and improved.

Some items were provided with a number of alternative responses to restrict the responses strictly to the point required. In this questionnaire: 1) Type of College, Age, Birth order, Residence, Educational qualifications, Sex, Community, Caste, Native place, Medium of study of the Student, 2) Annual Income, Economic position, Religious festivals, Religious discourses, Members go to temple and Type of family of the student and 3) Educational qualifications and Occupations of the student's Mother and Father etc., are covered. Adequate number of copies were printed and used in the study.

The investigator used the English version of SDS to gather the information about the socio-demographic variables of the students in the study.

Scoring of the Items

The items with quantitative measurement were considered separately. The numerical values were assigned according to their weightage for the statistical purpose.

Validity

If any measurement exactly measures what it is purported to measure, it is said to be valid. Adequacy of information is also important for the questionnaires. Hence there was adequacy of information and the questionnaire was highly valid.

Reliability

The questionnaire for pupils was administered on a sample of 200 pupils twice with a gap of fifteen days between the first and the second administrations. The responses were compared. They were found to be highly correlated. Thus the test-retest reliability of the tool was established.

HIGH SCHOOL PERSONALITY QUESTIONNAIRE (HSPQ)

Personality of an individual plays an important role in his/her Moral Values. The review of related literature revealed that there are a number of studies showing the relationship of personality and Moral Values at both school and college levels. The investigator searched for the theories of the personality and the means of measuring the totality behaviour. Cattell's theory, of all the numerous theories, is the only theory based on the principle of totality of behaviour of the individual.

Nature of Personality

Personality is defined by many in many ways. Some define it as 'one's social stimulus. Others define it as 'the some total of innate dispositions, impulses, appetites, instincts, tendencies and habits'.

Allpport (1937) asserted that, "Traits are discovered not by deductive reasoning, not by faith, not by naming and are themselves never directly observed. They are discovered only through an inference made necessary by the demonstrable consistency of the separate observable acts of behaviour".

According to Cattell (1950), "Personality is that which permits a prediction of what a person will do in a given situation".

"Personality is a dynamic organization with in the individual of those psycho-physical systems that determined his unique adjustment to his environment" (Allport, 1949).

The total psychological and social reactions of an individual; the synthesis of his subjective, emotional and mental life, his behaviour, and his reactions to the environment; the unique or individual traits of a person are connoted to a seller degree by "personality" than by the term "character". (Good, 1973)

For the individual all the aspects of behaviour, thought and feeling that make the person unique for psychologists a major area of theory and research. (Derek Rowntree, 1981)

i) A psychological term that refers to the predictable and unique indicator of the way an individual might respond to the environment. ii) A personal reference that usually connects acceptability and liability. (Madhu Raj, 1996), (John Bellingham, 2004).

Selection of the Tool HSPQ

By observing one's physical feature and sociability, one cannot judge one's personality. It will be possible when one study carefully in all the aspects like biological as well as social, he can have an idea about his personality.

The HSPQ handles the multiplicity of predictions from the test. It helps to obtain scores on 14 dimensions of personality, so that insightful understanding of the individual and his development as well as statistical predictions is possible. Hence the investigator selected the HSPQ for assuming the personality traits of the students.

Every factor will be found here and on score and profile records to be provided with two labels; the exact bi-polar title as used throughout the technical psychological literature, and a more popular dictionary phrase to use in communicating with parents, employees, and laymen generally.

The HSPQ has factorial validity. Further, applied research carried out over the years with the factors has produced constant and substantial correlation of these primary factor scales to a wide array of criteria in educational, clinical, occupational and other areas, establishing its criterion validity. (Cattell, 1969)

Keeping this in mind, the personality of the students was assessed in the study, using Cattell's Junior Senior High School Personality Questionnaire (HSPQ) Form-A. It is applicable to the age group of students 12 to 18 years. The Form-A of HSPQ was translated into Telugu, the regional language of the respondents, for the present study. The translation was corrected and modified after having verified by five judges who were well versed in testing of psychological traits of the pupils. Then the translated HSPQ was administered to a small group of 200 pupils of class XII. The investigator carefully modified such terms; those pupils felt any ambiguity with simple and understandable words.

Characteristic Expressions of the Personality Factors in HSPQ

"For purposes of cross-reference to research studies, the factors are named, first by their technical, psychological titles, but also by more popular but looser descriptive labels suitable for explaining results in the discussion of cases with the laymen". (Cattell, 1969)

Factor A

Low Score	Versus	High Score
SIZOTHYMIA		AFFECTOTHYMIA
Reserved, Detached, Critical, Aloof, Stiff	Vs	Warm-hearted, Outgoing, Easygoing, Participating
Critical	Vs	Good Natured, Easygoing
Stands by his own ideas	Vs	Ready to Cooperate, Likes to Participate
Cool, Aloof	Vs	Attentive to People

Low Score	Versus	High Score
Precise, Objective	Vs	Softhearted, Casual
Distrustful, Skeptical	Vs	Trustful
Rigid	Vs	Adaptable, Careless, "Goes Along"
Cold	Vs	Warmhearted,
Prone to Sulk	Vs	Laughs Readily

A low scorer on Factor A tends to be more uncompromising and earnest, prefers words or things to people, likes working alone, favours a thinking quality in companionship, and is introspective. A low scorer is more penetrating in their evaluations of people and things, more dependable in long term undertakings and requiring exactness.

A high scorer on Factor A tends to be permeation of all thinking by affect (feeling), a warm, easygoing relaxation, accessible emotions and interest in people. In the questionnaire responses a high scorer student expresses marked preference for occupations dealing with people, enjoys social recognition, is more tolerant of "difficult" people and is generally willing to "go along" with expediency. A high scorer more readily forms active groups, more impulsively generous in personal relationships, less disturbed by criticism, better able to remember names of people and shows superior social adjustments.

Factor B

Low Score	Versus	High Score
LOW INTELLIGENCE	Vs	HIGH INTELLIGENCE
Crystallized, Power Measure	Vs	Crystallized, Power Measure
Dull		Bright
Low Mental Capacity	Vs	High General Mental Capacity
Unable to Handle Abstract Problems	Vs	Insightful, Fast Learning, Intellectually Adaptable

Low Score	Versus	High Score
Apt to Be Less Well Organized	Vs	Inclined to Have More Intellectual Interests

It measures "crystallized" rather than "fluid" general ability. A low scorer on Factor B tends to be slow to learn and grasp things, dull, sluggish. He tends to have little capacity for the higher forms of knowledge, which is a reflection of low intelligence.

A high scorer on Factor B tends to be more intelligent child to show better morale, more persistent and greater school interest. He tends to be popular with peers as a work partner, well adjusted to school, a leader and less likely to be found in institutionalized delinquent groups.

Factor C

Low Score	Versus	High Score
EMOTIONAL INSTABILITY or EGO WEAKNESS	Vs	HIGHER EGO STRENGTH
Affected by Feelings, Emotionally Less Stable, Easily Upset, Changeable	Vs	Emotionally Stable, Mature, Faces Reality, Calm
Gets Emotional when Frustrated	Vs	Emotionally Mature
Changeable to Attitudes and Interests	Vs	Stable, Constant in Interests
Easily Perturbed	Vs	Calm
Evasive of Responsibilities Tending to Give Up	Vs	Does not Let Emotional Needs, Obscure Realities of Situation, Adjusts to facts
Worrying	Vs	Unruffled
Gets into Fights and Problem Situations	Vs	Shows Restraint in Avoiding Difficulties

A low scorer on Factor C tends to be easily annoyed by things and people, is more often dissatisfied with his family and his school, has emotional difficulty in keeping quite and restraining himself, and is discouraged by his inability to meet good standards of behaviour. He tends to be high in frustration, low in tolerance for unsatisfactory conditions, changeable, avoiding necessary reality demands, neurotically fatigued, worrying, easily annoyed, usually dissatisfied. Low score on Factor C is common to almost all forms of neurotic and mental disorders.

A high scorer on Factor C tends to be emotionally matured, stable, calm, realistic about life, unruffled, possessing ego strength, having an integrated philosophy of life, better able to maintain high group morale.

Factor D

Low Score	Versus	High Score
PHLEGMATIC TEMPERAMENT	Vs	EXCITABILITY
Undemonstrative, Deliberate, Inactive, Stodgy	Vs	*Excitable, Impatient, Demanding, Overactive, Unrestrained*
Stoical	Vs	Demanding, Impatient
Complacent	Vs	Attention-getting, Showing off
Deliberate	Vs	Excitable
Not Easily Jealous	Vs	Prone to Jealousy
Self-effecting	Vs	Self-assertive, Egotistical
Constant	Vs	Distractible
Not Restless	Vs	Shows Many Nervous Symptoms

A low scorer on Factor D is more temperamental, excitable than a low scorer on Factor C. Though he seems likable and affectionate in quieter moods, he is apt to be regarded as a considerable nuisance in restrictive situations, since he is so "impulsive".

A high scorer tends to be a restless sleeper, easily distracted from work by noise or intrinsic difficulty, is hurt and angry if not given important positions, or whenever he is restrained or punished, and so on. This factor shows substantial dimension in children.

Factor E

Low Score	Versus	High Score
SUBMISSIVENESS	Vs	DOMINANCE
Obedient, Mild, Easily Led, Docile, Accommodating	Vs	*Assertive, Aggressive, Competitive, Stubborn*
Submissive	Vs	Assertive, Self-assured
Dependent	Vs	Independent-minded
Considerate, Diplomatic	Vs	Stern, Hostile
Expressive	Vs	Solemn
Conventional, conforming	Vs	Unconventional, Rebellious
Easily Upset by Authority	Vs	Headstrong
Humble	Vs	Admiration Demanding

A low-scorer on Factor E tends to be dependent and a follower. He is often soft hearted, expressive and easily upset. This positivity is part of many neurotic syndromes.

A high-scorer on Factor E tends to be assertive, self-assumed, independent-minded and bold in his approach to situations. He may at times be hard, a law to himself, hostile, tough-minded, authoritarian and disregards authority.

Factor F

Low Score	Versus	High Score
DESURGENCY	Vs	SURGENCY
Sober, Taciturn, Serious	Vs	*Enthusiastic, Headless,* Happy-go-lucky
Silent, Introspective	Vs	Talkative

Low Score	Versus	High Score
Full of Cares	Vs	Cheerful
Concerned, Reflective	Vs	Happy-go-lucky
Incommunicative, Sticks to Inner Volumes	Vs	Frank, Expressive, Reflects the Group
Slow, Cautious	Vs	Quick and Alert

A low-scorer on Factor F tends to be restrained and introspective. He is sometimes incommunicative, pessimistic, anxious and considered to be swung. He tends to be a sober, dependable person.

A high-scorer on this trait tends to be active, frank, cheerful, quick, expressive, talkative, alter and unperturbable. He is often chosen as an elected leader, he may be impulsive and mercurial.

Factor G

Low Score	Versus	High Score
LOW SUPEREGO STRENGTH	Vs	SUPEREGO STRENGTH
Disregards Rules, Expedient	Vs	*Conscientious, Persistent, Moralistic, Staid*
Quitting, Fickle	Vs	Persevering, Determined
Frivolous	Vs	Responsible
Self-indulgent	Vs	Emotionally Disciplined
Slack, Indolent	Vs	Consistently ordered
Undependable	Vs	Conscientious, Dominated by Sense of Duty
Disregards Obligations to People	Vs	Concerned about Moral Standards and Rules

A low-scorer on this trait tends to be unsteady in purpose. He is often casual and lacking in effort for group understandings and cultural demands. His freedom from group influence may lead to antisocial acts, but at times make him more effective, while his refusal to be bound by rules causes him to have less somatic upset from stress.

A high-scorer on this trait tends to be strong in character, preserving, responsible, determined, consistent, playful, energetic, cautious and well organized. He is usually conscientious or moralistic and he prefers hard working people to witty companions.

Factor H

Low Score	Versus	High Score
THRECTIA	Vs	PARMIA
Shy, Timid, Restrained, Threat-sensitive	Vs	*Adventurous, Thick-skinned, Socially Bold*
Shy, Withdrawn	Vs	Adventurous, Likes Meeting People Active, Overt Interest in Opposite Sex
.Retiring in Face of Opposite Sex	Vs	Responsive, Genial
Emotionally Cautious	Vs	Friendly
Apt to be Embittered	Vs	Impulsive
Restrained, Rule-bound	Vs	Emotional and Artistic Interests
Restricted Interests	Vs	Carefree, Does not See Danger
Careful, Considerate, Quick to See Dangers	Vs	Signals

A low-scorer on Factor H shows the shy, withdrawn, careful, "well-behaved" syndrome, which may be one condition in schizoid pre-psychotics. He reports himself to be slow and impeded in expressing himself. He dislikes occupations with personal contacts, prefers one or two close friends to crows, avoids large parties or open competition, is fearful of situations, easily resentful and distrustful, but very considerate of others' sensitivities, and not given to keeping contact with all that goes on around him. A high-scorer on Factor H feels free to participate, but are privately voted to be long-winded, insensitive speakers. He is bold, ready to try new things, spontaneous and abundant in emotional response. He tends to be pushy and actively interested in opposite sex.

Factor I

Low Score	Versus	High Score
HARRIA	Vs	PREMSIA
Tough-minded, Rejects Illusions	Vs	Tender-minded, Sensitive, Dependent, Overprotected
Unsentimental, Expects Little	Vs	Fidgety, Expecting Affection, and Attention
Self-reliant, Taking Responsibility	Vs	Clinging, Insecure, Seeking Help and Sympathy
Hard (to point of cynicism)	Vs	Kindly, Gentle, Indulgent, to Self and Others
Few Artistic Responses (but not lacking in taste)	Vs	Artistically Fastidious, Affected Theatrical
Unaffected by "Fancies"	Vs	Imaginative in Inner Life and in Conversation
Acts on Practical, Logical Evidence	Vs	Acts on Sensitive Intuition
Keeps to the Point	Vs	Attention-seeking, Flighty
Does not Dwell on Physical Disabilities	Vs	Hypochondriacal, Anxious about Self

A low-scorer on Factor I shows a definite fastidious dislike of "crude" people and rough occupations, a recreational taste for "romantic" travel and new experiences, an imaginative, esthetic mind, a love of dramatics, and certain impracticality in general affairs. He tends to be practical, realistic, masculine, independent, responsible but skeptical of subjective and 'uncultured'. He is sometimes unmoved, hard, cynical and smug. He tends to keep a group operating on a practical and realistic 'no nonsense' basis.

A high-scorer on this trait receives significantly more descriptions as fussing, slowing up group performance in arriving at decisions, and making social-emotional, negative remarks. He is tender-minded, daydreaming, and artistically fastidious. He is sometimes demanding of attention and help, impatient, dependent and impractical. He dislikes crude people and rough occupations.

Factor J

Low Score	Versus	High Score
ZEPPIA	Vs	COASTHENIA
Zestful, Liking Group Action	Vs	*Circumspect Individualism, Reflective, Internally Restrained*
Likes to Go with the Group	Vs	Acts Individualistically
Likes Attention	Vs	Guarded, Wrapped Up in Self
Sinks Personality into Group Enterprise	Vs	Fastidiously Obstructive
Vigorous	Vs	Neurasthenically Fatigued
Accepts Common Standards	Vs	Evaluates Coldly

A low-scorer on Factor J likes to go with the group rather than acting individually. He is zestful, vigorous. He is ready to accept common standards.

A person who scores high on Factor J tends to prefer to do things on his own. He is physically and intellectually fastidious. He thinks over his mistakes and how to avoid them. He does not forget if he is unfairly treated. He has private views, differing from the group, but prefers to keep in the background to avoid argument. He has fewer friends.

Factor O

A low-scorer on this trait tends to be placid, calm, with unshakable stability. He has a mature, unanxious, confidence in himself and has capacity to deal with things.

Low Score	Versus	High Score
UNTROUBLED ADEQUACY	Vs	GUILT PRONENESS
Self-assured, Placid, Secure, Complacent, Serene	Vs	*Apprehensive, Self-reproaching, Insecure, Worrying, Troubled*
Self-confident	Vs	Worrying, Anxious
Cheerful, Resilient	Vs	Depressed, Cries Easily
Impenitent, Placid	Vs	Easily Touched, Overcome by Moods
Expedient, Insensitive to people's Approval or Disapproval	Vs	Strong Sense of Obligation, Sensitive to People's Approval and Disapproval
Does Not Care	Vs	Scrupulous, Fussy
Rudely Vigorous	Vs	Hypochondrical and Inadequate
No Fears	Vs	Phobia Symptoms
Given to Simple Action	Vs	Lonely, Brooding

A high-scorer on this trait feels over fatigued by exciting situations, and has a sense of inferiority and inadequacy in meeting the rough daily demands of life. He is unable to sleep through worrying, is easily downhearted, and remorseful and guilty. He gets emotionally upset by pressure from authority, prefers books, and quite interests to people and noise. Definite fears, central feeling of inadequacy and loneliness are prominent. He is tend to be rated as hinderer and is unpopular with peers, socially maladjusted.

Factor Q_2

Low Score	Versus	High Score
GROUP DEPENDENCY	Vs	SELF-SUFFICIENCY
Sociably Group Dependent, A "Joiner" and Sound Follower	Vs	*Self-sufficient, Resourceful, Prefers Own Decisions*

A low-scorer on this trait tends to go with the group, who strongly values social approval and is conventional and fashionable. He prefers to work and make decisions with other people and depends on social approval and admiration. He needs group support as he may be lacking in individual resolution.

A high-scorer on this factor is significantly more dissatisfied with group integration, makes remarks which are more frequently solutions than questions and tends to be rejected. He is a confident and resourceful self-sufficiency, with some apparent disdain of the "mob", which is often mistaken for shyness, sizothemia and other components of introversion.

Factor Q_3

Low Score	Versus	High Score
LOW SELF-SENTIMENT INTEGRATION	Vs	HIGH STRENGTH OF SELF-SENTIMENT
Uncontrolled, Lax, Follows Own Urges, Careless of Social Rules	Vs	*Controlled, Exacting Will Power, Socially Precise, Compulsive, Following Self-image*

A low-scorer on this factor does not bother about will-control and regard for social demands. He is not over considerable, careful or pains-taking. He may show maladjustment.

A high-scorer on this trait tends to have strong control over his emotions. He proves to be chosen as a leader. He makes more group remarks than others do. He is associated with success in mechanical, mathematical and productive organizational activities. He is associated with all kinds of occupational and scholastic success.

Factor Q_4

A low-scorer on this trait tends to be excitable, tense, restless, impatient, ego-weakness and guilt proneness.

Low Score	Versus	High Score
LOW ERGIC TENSION *Relaxed, Tranquil, Torpid, Unfrustrated, Composed*	Vs	HIGH ERGIC TENSION *Tense, Frustrated, Driven, Overwrought, Fretful*

A high-scorer on this trait tends to be irrationally worried, tense, irritable and is turmoil. He feels frustrated and is sensitively aware of being criticized by parents for untidiness, fantasy and neglect of good goals.

One of the unique features of the HSPQ and other personality scales developed by Cattell is that each of the items in any factor is selected on the basis of their known correlation with the pure factors. In other words, the HSPQ has factorial validity. Further applied research carried out over the years with the factors has produced constant and substantial correlation of their primary factor scales to a wide array of criteria in educational, clinical, occupational and other areas establishing its criterion validity (Cattell, 1969).

Five judges who were well versed with psychological testing checked the translation. The ambiguous terms were discussed and changed with suitable ones. The Telugu version of the HSPQ thus prepared was administered on a sample of 200 students. They were asked to answer the items and point out if they found any ambiguity in understanding the terms or statements. Such of those terms or statements were modified and substituted with simpler words or statements.

Adoption of the Instrument HSPQ

Junior-Senior High School Personality Questionnaire (HSPQ) Form A prepared and standardized by Cattell (1950) was adopted for the present study.

Scoring Procedure for HSPQ

There are 142 items in the personality inventory HSPQ with three alternative answers for each question. The first item is to know whether the student has understood the instructions and the last question is to make sure if the student has answered all the questions. So the remaining 140 questions are related to personality of the student.

Pupils were motivated to give only one answer for each question. The answers were scored according to the weightages given by the author. The scoring was done for each student and for each factor.

Validity and Reliability of HSPQ

For calculating validity and reliability, the procedure suggested by Garret (1973) was followed. Reliability of the two sub-tests of each factor (based on raw scores) as obtained by Split-Half technique, and validity, which is the square root of reliability is presented in Table 4.4 and Table 4.5. The Split-Half Reliability was calculated on a sample of 200.

TABLE 4.4: Reliability and Validity of HSPQ Form-A using Split-Half Technique

Factor	A	B	C	D	E	F	G
0	1	2	3	4	5	6	7
Reliability	0.62	0.72	0.75	0.67	0.79	0.81	0.77
Validity	0.79	0.85	0.87	0.82	0.89	0.9	0.88

Factor	H	I	J	O	Q_2	Q_3	Q_4
0	8	9	10	11	12	13	14
Reliability	0.72	0.66	0.71	0.61	0.77	0.66	0.63
Validity	0.85	0.81	0.84	0.78	0.88	0.81	0.79

Retest was also conducted on a sample of 200 with a gap of 20 days. The test-retest validity and reliability for each factor are given in Table 4.5.

TABLE 4.5: Reliability and Validity of HSPQ Form-A using Test-Retest Technique

Factor	A	B	C	D	E	F	G
0	1	2	3	4	5	6	7
Reliability	0.61	0.73	0.77	0.69	0.82	0.78	0.82
Validity	0.78	0.85	0.88	0.83	0.9	0.88	0.9

Factor	H	I	J	O	Q_2	Q_3	Q_4
0	8	9	10	11	12	13	14
Reliability	0.72	0.67	0.67	0.63	0.77	0.67	0.71
Validity	0.85	0.82	0.82	0.79	0.88	0.82	0.84

Final Study (HSPQ)

The Telugu version of the HSPQ was administered on entire sample of 1200 intermediate students and the scoring was done as per the instructions given in HSPQ manual.

SELF-CONCEPTS SCALE (SCS)

The self-concept is a theoretical construct, which allows the integration of all areas of social and emotional development of an individual into a single system. It has been variously defined as "the self as known to the self" (Murphy, 1947) and "those aspects of the individual, which seem most vital and important to the person" (Jersield, 1960)

Children do not have any self-concepts by the time of their birth. They acquire it by means of incidental learning like their different relations with others in the society. Some children are nourished in such a way that they recognize that they are worthy of love and respect, while some others may have different experiences. In the process of learning through interaction with others around, the child develops self-concepts and ideals of her own. Thus self-concept is a key variable in behaviour and ultimately it influences the reading achievement of the pupils.

In psychological and educational discussions self-concept has been described in many ways.

"The individual's perception of him-self as person, which includes his abilities, appearance, performance in his job and other phases of daily living" (Good, 1973).

"How a person sees himself?" (e.g. Competent, amusing, homely, etc.,). This may differ from other people's views of him though it will have been influenced by them (Derek Rowntree, 1981).

1) An individual's perception of self.
2) A psychological contract that is more complex than implied or assumed by most educators. (Singh, 2002)

Self-concept 'refers to the pictures or images a person has of him'. (Taneja, 1991 & A Team of Experts, 2003)

Adoption of the Self-concepts Scale

The self-concepts scale developed by Dr (Miss) Mukta Rani Rastogi (1974) was adopted for the purpose of the present study. This scale consists of 51 items with 10 areas. It is a five point attitude scale with the alternative answers viz., **Strongly Agree, Agree, Undecided, Disagree** and **Strongly Disagree**. The 10 areas are:

1) Health and Sex Appropriateness
2) Abilities
3) Self-confidence
4) Self-acceptance

5) Worthiness
6) Present, Past and Future
7) Beliefs and Convictions
8) Feeling of Shame and Guilt
9) Sociability
10) Emotional Maturity

The adopted scale was translated into Telugu. It had been refined after obtaining the suggestions of the experts. Then it was used for the present investigation.

The item numbers related to each area of the Self-concepts Scale are shown in Table 4.6. The letters 'P' and 'N' below each item show the Positiveness (P) or Negativeness (N) of the items.

Scoring Procedures for the Self-concepts Scale

Each question in the Self-concepts Scale was followed by 5 alternative answers mentioned above. The students were asked to go through the instructions before they attempt to choose from the choice of answers. They were motivated to choose only one answer for each question.

After collecting the answer sheets, the scoring was done with the help of the answer key. The total raw score of the each student was noted on the top of the answer sheet.

Validity of the Inventory

The validity of a test or scale refers to its accuracy. Dr (Miss) Mukta Rani Rastogi (1974) established (i) Criterion Validity, (ii) Content Validity and (iii) Construct Validity of the Self-concept Scale.

Reliability

Reliability can be defined as the degree of consistency between two measures of the same inventory. There are several

TABLE 4.6: The Item Numbers in each area of the Self-concepts Scale

S. No	Description	Item Numbers								
1	Health and Sex Appropriateness	6 P	20 P	29 N	32 N	34 P	& &	46 P		
2	Abilities	4 P	8 P	12 N	23 N	36 P	38 N	39 N	& &	42 P
3	Self Confidence	7 P	9 P	14 N	16 N	& &	44 P			
4	Self Acceptance	2 P	10 N	17 N	& &	35 N				
5	Worthiness	1 P	3 N	19 N	25 P	27 P	41 N	& &	50 P	
6	Present, Past and Future	18 P	22 P	26 N	31 N	& &	40 P			
7	Beliefs and Convictions	24 N	47 P	& &	48 P					
8	Feeling of Shame and Guilt	5 N	13 N	28 N	30 N	& &	51 N			
9	Sociability	33 N	37 P	43 P	& &	45 N				
10	Emotional Maturity	11 N	15 N	21 N	& &	49 N				

methods to estimate the reliability of a test. The common methods in the text manuals are:

1) Test-retest Reliability
2) Measures of Equivalence
3) Measures of Internal Consistency
4) Split-Half Technique
5) K.R. Formula-20

For the present study internal consistency was measured through Split-Half technique. The procedure suggested by Garrett (1973) was applied. The correlation coefficient for the half test with a sample of 250 was 0.87. The correlation coefficient for the full test is 0.93. It shows that the reliability of the instrument was very high.

STUDY HABITS INVENTORY

The complex of reading behaviour of a person, resulting from varying degrees of interaction, of a number of variable factors, may be defined as a study habit.

The ability to schedule his aims, the habit of note-taking, reviewing, judicious application of whole and part methods etc., form a learner's study habits.

The study habits may be noted as the evaluation of pupil's behaviour in terms of attitudes, appreciation and habits of work in fundamental to well-rounded study of outcomes of teaching.

The word 'study habits' is used to refer to the pupil or student's way of studying whether systematic or unsystematic, efficient or inefficient. (Good, 1973).

Study Habits includes students' habit of concentration, note taking, time budgeting and study methods (Smith, 1961).

The complex of reading behaviour of a person resulting from the varying degrees of interaction of a number of variable factors. Study Habits are regular reading hours and routine characteristics most of general features. In preparing for examinations, greater reliance is placed on textbooks and self prepared text. (Kunchu, 1989).

The study habits of a student means the ability to schedule his time, the plan of his study, the habit of concentration, note-taking, mental review, over learning, massed and distributed learning and so on.

Study habits mainly depend on motivation for reading, interest in subject, attitude, encouragement by others, personality traits etc. Effective learning takes place with good study habits.

Factors Affecting Study Habits

Some of the notes worthy factors are affecting the Study Habits are:

Home

For every child the parents are first teachers and home is the first place of learning. Child's parents and other family members may influence the child's learning methods and study habits. The educational level and the occupations of the parents also show influence on children's study habits.

Intelligence

Brilliant students can quickly develop good study habits than the dull students.

Personality

A student, who can have better adjust to the environment, can develop better study habits.

Community

Community resources like library and meetings with learned people inculcate good study habits among the students.

School

The school administrators and teachers play an important role in developing good or bad study habits.

Curriculum

The curriculum should be suitable for the standard of the child. It should encourage the practical, easy learning that helps to motivate towards good study habits. If the curriculum is above standard, pupils may be frustrated and may develop bad study habits.

Demographic Factors

Locality, sex, caste, father education, mother education, number of members in the family, income of the family, physical environment, social status of the family etc., influence the study habits of the students.

Adoption of the Study Habits Inventory

Looking to the importance of good study habits for good scholastic achievement, it was thought to adopt Study Habits Inventory constructed and standardized by B.V. Patel as a tool to assess the study habits of the sample for the present study.

Five judges who were well versed in psychological testing checked the Telugu version. The statements thus prepared were tried out on a small sample with a view to find out the ambiguity in the wording. A few statements were corrected to remove the ambiguity in the wording.

Scoring Procedure

The statements that are prepared thus, fall into the following seven areas.

1. Home environment and planning of work

2. Reading and note-taking
3. Planning of subject
4. Habits of concentration
5. Preparation for examinations
6. General habits and attitudes
7. School environment

There are 7 items in area one, 9 items in area two, 5 items in area three, 4 items in area four, 6 items in area five, 8 items in area six and 6 items in area seven, a total of 45 items in the inventory. Among them 18 items are negative and 27 items are positive. Five alternative choices of options were given to get more exact responses from the students. The five points are:

1) Always
2) Often
3) Sometimes
4) Seldom and
5) Never

In case of the item depicting good study habits, the student is to give five marks if he puts a tick (✓) in the column of 'always'; four, three, two and one are to be given if he puts the tick mark in the columns of 'often', 'sometimes', 'hardly', and 'never' respectively. In case of the statement depicting bad study habits, the score is to be assigned in the reverse order. Thus the high score on the inventory will indicate good study habits and *vice-versa*.

The areas, item numbers with Positive (P) and Negative (N) nature in Study Habits Inventory are presented in Table 4.7.

Reliability and Validity

For calculating reliability and validity, the procedure suggested by Garrett (1973) was followed.

TABLE 4.7: The Item Numbers in each area of the Study Habits Inventory

S No	Description	Item Numbers								
1.	Home environment and planning of work	1, P	2, P	3, P	4, P	5, N	6, N	7 N		
2.	Reading and note-taking	8, P	9, P	10, P	11, P	12, P	13, P	14, N	15, N	16 P
3.	Planning of subject	17, P	18, P	19, P	20, N	21 N				
4.	Habits of concentration	22, P	23, N	24, N	25 N					
5.	Preparation for examinations	26, P	27, N	28, N	29, N	30, N	31 N			
6.	General habits and attitudes	32, P	33, P	34, N	35, N	36, P	37, P	38, P	39 P	
7.	School environment	40, P	41, P	42, P	43, P	44, P	45 N			

The split-half reliability on a sample of 250 for the half test was 0.88 and for full test was 0.94. Test-retest reliability on a sample of 250 with a gap of 20 days was 0.96. It reveals that the study habits inventory is highly valid and reliable.

FINAL STUDY

Tools Used

The investigator used the following tools for the present investigation.

1) Moral Values Inventory (Telugu Version)
2) Socio-Demographic Scale (English Version)
3) Junior-Senior High School Personality Questionnaire (HSPQ) Form-A (Telugu Version)
4) Self-concepts Scale (Telugu Version)
5) Study Habits Inventory (Telugu Version)

Sample Frame

The sample of the investigation consisted of 1200 Senior Intermediate (XII class) College Students. The stratified random sampling was applied. There are three types of managements namely Aided, Private and Government in intermediate education system both in rural and urban areas. 16 colleges were selected in the above mentioned areas of management and locality by covering all the revenue divisions in the Chittoor District of Andhra Pradesh State. In total 600 girls and 600 boys were included in the above study. The sample frame is 3 × 3 × 2 factorial design with three types of managements situated in three types of locality namely 1) City/municipal town, 2) Small Town and 3) Village with two divisions in gender. The sample design is a stratified random sampling. The sample design is shown in Table 4.8.

TABLE 4.8: Sample design for Final Study

Managements	Locality				Sex		
	City/ Muni	Small Town	Village	Total	Male	Female	Total
Government	11	28	159	198	110	88	198
Aided	169	63	600	832	385	447	832
Private	29	32	109	170	105	65	170
Total	209	123	868	1200	600	600	1200
Grand total		1200		1200		1200	1200

Data Collection

The investigator obtained the list of colleges in the district along with strength particulars of the students from the district authorities concerned. Colleges were selected using stratified random sampling technique. The Principals of the colleges were requested to permit the researcher for collection of data in their institutions. The programme and the time schedule were communicated to all the heads of the colleges well in advance and obtained permission from them.

In each college, the required number of senior intermediate students had been selected using random sampling method. The students were well motivated before attempting the tests.

The booklets and answer sheets were distributed among the selected students. The instructions were read out and the purpose of investigation was explained to motivate them to give answers in a proper manner. Sufficient time was provided for the students to give answers to the questionnaires. The investigator took care to ensure that all the questions were answered by the students following the instructions.

Moral Values Inventory and HSPQ were distributed in the morning one after the other with a break of 10 minutes. After providing sufficient time the investigator had collected the booklets and answer sheets.

In the afternoon the Socio-Demographic Scale, Self-concept Scale and Study Habits Inventory were distributed one after another to the same group of students with a break of 10 minutes between each test. Students were instructed on how to answer each questionnaire. They were assured that the information given by them would be kept confidential. The investigator requested the students to respond to the questions genuinely to help him to find solutions to the research problems. The investigator helped the students wherever they raise doubts in understanding the questions.

After successful completion of the test, the investigator collected the booklets and answer sheets thanking the students for their good cooperation.

Scoring and Analysis

The data collected using the selected tools were scored following the procedures already described to obtain measures of different variables. The analysis was carried out basing on the objectives of the study and the hypotheses formulated employing appropriate statistical techniques. Tables and graphs were used wherever necessary to present the data.

Statistical Techniques Employed

Frequency distribution tables were prepared for Moral Values for all the groups. Mean, median, mode, range, Quartile Deviation, Standard Deviation, Skewness, Kurtosis, Coefficient of Variation and Standard Error of Mean were calculated wherever necessary. The significance tests like 't' test and 'F' test were employed. Multiple 'R' was calculated by carrying out step-wise regression analysis to predict the Moral Values scores of the pupils. The obtained numerical results were adumbrated by graphical representations.

For statistical formulae, the following books were referred:

1. 'Statistical Analysis in Educational Research' Lind Quist (1940)
2. 'Statistical Works for Research Workers' by Fisher (1950)
3. 'Fundamental Statistics in Psychology and Education' by Guilford (1950)
4. 'Statistics in Psychology and Education' by Garrett and Woodworth (1961)
5. 'Statistics in Education and Psychology' by Yate (1965)
6. 'Statistical Principles in Experimental Design' by Edwards (1971)
7. 'Experimental Design in Psychological Research' by Edwards (1971)
8. 'Statistics in Psychology and Education' by Garrett (1973)
9. 'Statistical Methods' by Guptha (1974)
10. 'Applied Regression Analysis' by Draper and Smith (1981)
11. 'Statistics in Psychology and Education' by Mangal (2002)

The significant levels employed with respective symbols are given below.

** Indicates significant at 0.01 level.

* Indicates significant at 0.05 level.

@ Indicates not significant at 0.05 level.

5

ANALYSIS AND INTERPRETATION OF DATA

This chapter deals with analysis and interpretation of data. The data is presented in the form of:

1) Frequency distribution tables.
2) Factorial designs.
3) 't' values and 'F' ratios to know the influence of the independent variables on dependent variable.
4) Regression analysis.

DISTRIBUTION CHARACTERISTICS OF MORAL VALUE SCORES

The Distribution characteristics namely Mean (M), Median (Md), Mode (Mo), Range (R), Quartile Deviation (QD), Standard Deviation (SD), Skewness (Sk), Kurtosis (Ku), Coefficient of Variation (CV) and Standard Error of Mean (SE_M) for various divisions of the sample on Moral Value Scores are studied. The Kurtosis and the Skewness are used wherever necessary. For Normal Distribution the value of skewness is 0.00 and kurtosis (using moments) is 3.00. The distribution characteristics are presented and discussed hereunder.

Frequency Distribution of Moral Value Scores for the Whole Group (Total Sample)

The investigator measured the Moral Value Scores of the Intermediate students by using the constructed and standardized Moral Values Inventory (MVI) developed by the investigator. The Moral Value score means the total score on all the items (79) of the Moral Values Inventory. It is an attitude scale with 5-alternatives: Strongly Agree, Agree, Doubtful, Disagree and Strongly Disagree. The maximum and minimum scores on total Moral Values Inventory are 79 and 395 respectively. The frequency distribution of Moral Values scores for the whole group (N=1200) is presented in Table 5.1.

TABLE 5.1: Frequency Distribution of Moral Value Scores for the Whole Group

Sl. No.	Class Interval	Limits	Mid point	f	Cf	CPf
1	211-230	210.5-230.5	220.5	3	3	0.25
2	231-250	230.5-250.5	240.5	2	5	0.41
3	251-270	250.5-270.5	260.5	6	11	0.91
4	271-290	270.5-290.5	280.5	36	47	3.91
5	291-310	290.5-310.5	300.5	98	145	12.08
6	311-330	310.5-330.5	320.5	257	402	33.5
7	331-350	330.5-350.5	340.5	337	739	61.58
8	351-370	330.5-370.5	360.5	333	1072	89.33
9	371-390	370.5-390.5	380.5	111	1183	98.58
10	391-410	390.5-410.5	400.5	17	1200	100.00

Mean (M)	: 339.68	Coefficient of variation (CV)	: 7.676
Median (Md)	: 341.622		
Mode (Mo)	: 351	Standard Error of Mean (SE_M)	: 0.75
Range (R)	: 180		
Quartile Deviation (QD)	: 17.54	Kurtosis (Ku)	: 0.958
Standard Deviation (SD)	: 26.07		
Skewness (Sk)	: -0.631		

It is observed from Table 5.1 that the mean Moral Value score is 339.68. There are 79 items in the Moral Values Inventory. The neutral value of the Moral Values Inventory is 237 (79 × 3 = 237). The mean Moral Value score is far greater than the neutral value. Hence it is concluded that the Intermediate Students have high Moral Values. The values of Skewness (Sk) and Kurtosis (Ku) are –0.631 and 0.958 respectively. For the normal distribution, the values of Skewness and Kurtosis are 0.00 and 3.00 respectively. Hence, the frequency distribution of Moral Value Scores for the total sample is slightly negatively Skewed and Lepto Kurtic.

The Bar diagram for the distribution of Moral Value Scores for the whole group is given in Fig. 5.1.

The Frequency polygon for the distribution of Moral Value Scores for the whole group is shown in Fig. 5.2.

The Ogive for the distribution of Moral Value Scores for the whole group is presented in Fig 5.3.

Frequency Distribution of Moral Value Scores for Male and Female Students

Frequency distribution of Moral Value Scores for Male Students (N=600) is given in Table 5.2.

It is observed from Table 5.2 that the mean Moral Value score of male students is 334.53. The mean Moral Value score is far greater than the neutral value. Hence it is concluded that the male students have high Moral Values. The values of Skewness (Sk) and Kurtosis (Ku) are -0.401 and -0.022 respectively. For the normal distribution, the values of Skewness and Kurtosis are 0.00 and 3.00 respectively. Hence, the frequency distribution of Moral Value Scores for male students is slightly negatively Skewed and Lepto Kurtic.

TABLE 5.2: Frequency Distribution of Moral Value Scores for Male Students

S.No.	Class Interval	Limits	Mid point	F	CF	CPF
1	231-250	230.5-250.5	240.5	1	1	0.16
2	251-270	250.5-270.5	260.5	3	4	0.66
3	271-290	270.5-290.5	280.5	25	29	4.83
4	291-310	290.5-310.5	300.5	70	79	13.16
5	311-330	310.5-330.5	320.5	144	223	37.16
6	331-350	330.5-350.5	340.5	177	400	66.66
7	351-370	330.5-370.5	360.5	141	541	90.16
8	371-390	370.5-390.5	380.5	36	577	96.16
9	391-410	390.5-410.5	400.5	3	600	100.00

M :	334.53	R :	146	Sk :	-0.401
Md :	335.50	QD :	17	Ku :	-0.022
Mo :	337.44	SD :	24.96	CV :	7.462
SE_M :	1.01				

Frequency distribution of Moral Value Scores for Female Students (N=600) is given in Table 5.3.

It is clear from Table 5.3 that the mean Moral Value score of female students is 344.83. The mean Moral Value score is far greater than the neutral value. Hence it is concluded that the female students have high Moral Values. The values of Skewness (Sk) and Kurtosis (Ku) are –0.957 and 2.404 respectively. For the normal distribution, the values of Skewness and Kurtosis are 0.00 and 3.00 respectively. Hence, the frequency distribution of Moral Value Scores for female students is slightly negatively Skewed and Lepto Kurtic.

The Bar diagram for the distribution of mean Moral Value Scores of male and female students is given in Fig. 5.4.

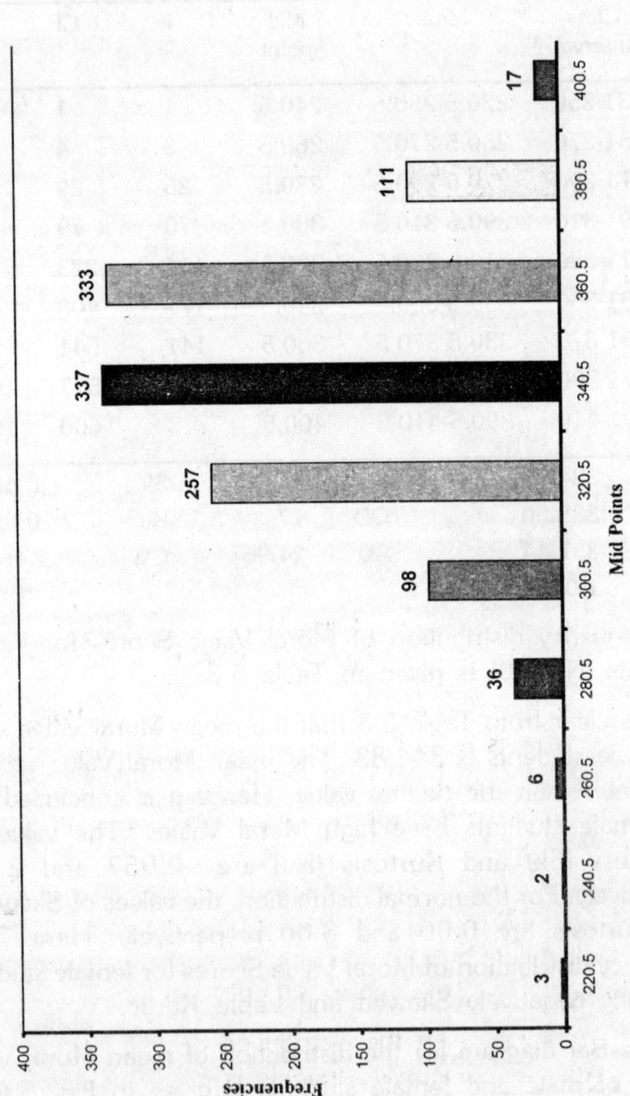

Fig. 5.1: Bar diagram for the distribution of Moral Value Scores for the Whole Group

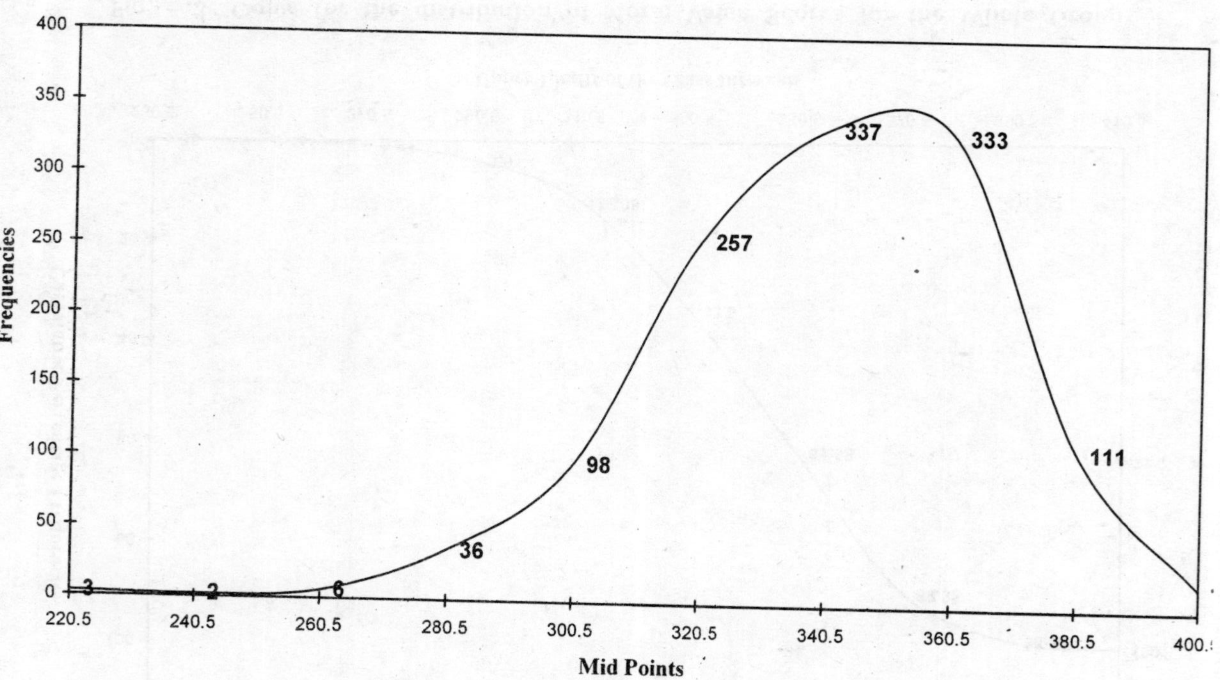

Fig 5.2: Frequency Polygon for the distribution of Moral Value Scores for the

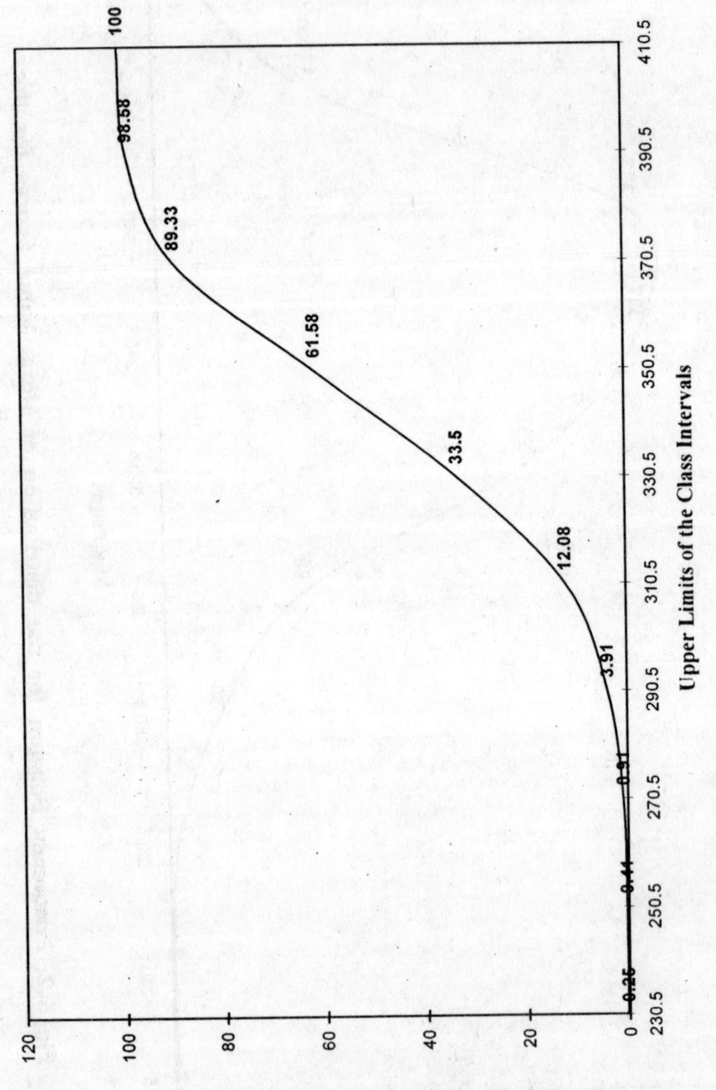

Fig. 5.3: Ogive for the distribution of Moral Value Scores for the Whole Group

TABLE 5.3: Frequency Distribution of Moral Value Scores for Female Students

S.No.	Class Interval	Limits	Mid point	F	CF	CPF
1	211-230	210.5-230.5	220.5	3	3	0.50
2	231-250	230.5-250.5	240.5	1	4	0.66
3	251-270	250.5-270.5	260.5	3	7	1.16
4	271-290	270.5-290.5	280.5	11	18	3.00
5	291-310	290.5-310.5	300.5	28	46	7.66
6	311-330	310.5-330.5	320.5	113	159	26.50
7	331-350	330.5-350.5	340.5	160	319	53.16
8	351-370	330.5-370.5	360.5	192	511	85.16
9	371-390	370.5-390.5	380.5	75	586	97.66
10	391-410	390.5-410.5	400.5	14	600	100.00

M	: 344.83	R	: 180	Sk	: -0.957
Md	: 348	QD	: 17	Ku	: 2.40
Mo	: 354.34	SD	: 26.16	CV	: 7.587
SE_M	: 1.06				

Frequency Distribution of Moral Value Scores for Muslim, Christian and Hindu Students.

Frequency distribution of Moral Value Scores for Muslim students is presented in Table 5.4.

It is seen from Table 5.4 that the mean Moral Value score of Muslim students is 345.78. The mean Moral Value score is far greater than the neutral value. Hence it is concluded that the Muslim students have high Moral Values. The values of Skewness (Sk) and Kurtosis (Ku) are −1.351 and 2.092 respectively. Hence, the frequency distribution of Moral Value Scores for Muslim students is slightly negatively Skewed and Lepto Kurtic.

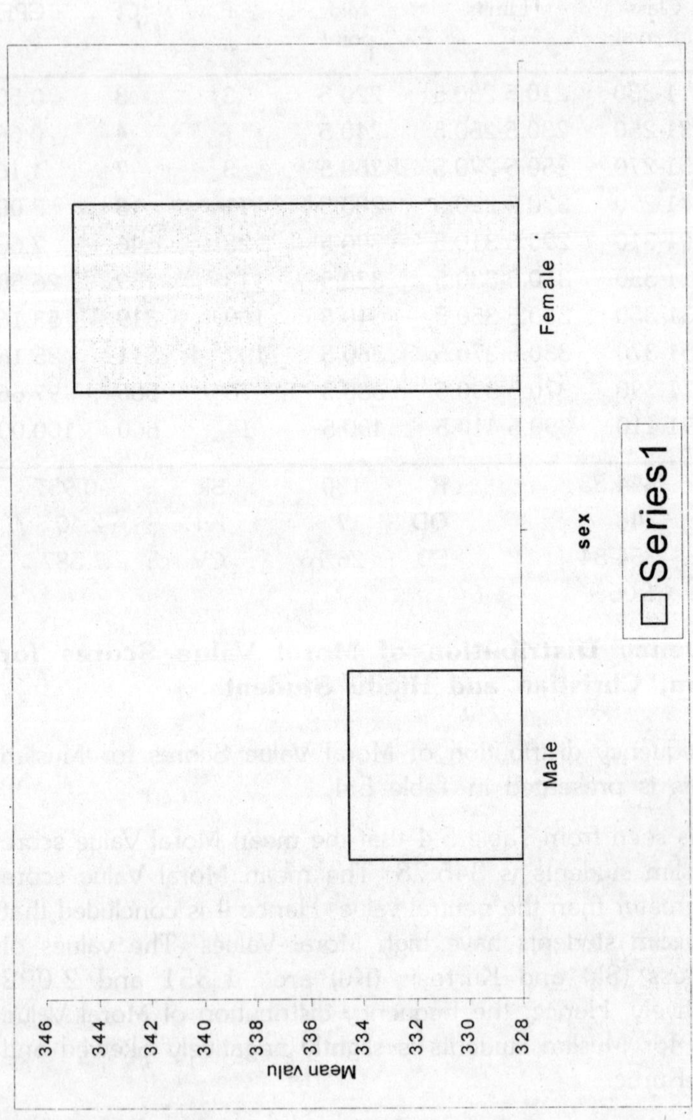

Fig. 5.4: Bar diagram for the mean Moral Value Scores of the Male and Female Students

TABLE 5.4: Frequency Distribution of Moral Value Scores for Muslim Students

S.No.	Class Interval	Limits	Mid point	F.	CF	CPF
1	211-230	210.5-230.5	220.5	0	0	0
2	231-250	230.5-250.5	240.5	0	0	0
3	251-270	250.5-270.5	260.5	0	0	0
4	271-290	270.5-290.5	280.5	1	1	2.63
5	291-310	290.5-310.5	300.5	3	4	10.52
6	311-330	310.5-330.5	320.5	2	6	15.78
7	331-350	330.5-350.5	340.5	12	18	47.36
8	351-370	330.5-370.5	360.5	15	33	86.84
9	371-390	370.5-390.5	380.5	5	38	100.00
10	391-410	390.5-410.5	400.5	0	38	100.00

M	: 345.78	R	: 106	Sk	: -0.1.35
Md	: 351	QD	: 13	Ku	: 2.09
Mo	: 361.44	SD	: 23.50	CV	: 6.797
SE_M	: 3.81				

Frequency distribution of Moral Value Scores for Christian students is given in Table 5.5.

It is clear from Table 5.5 that the mean Moral Value score for Christian students is 331.11. The mean Moral Value score is far greater than the neutral value. Hence it is concluded that the Christian students have high Moral Values. The values of Skewness (Sk) and Kurtosis (Ku) are –0.53 and 1.46 respectively. Hence, the frequency distribution of Moral Value Scores for Christian students is slightly negatively Skewed and Lepto Kurtic.

Frequency distribution of Moral Value Scores for Hindu students is given in Table 5.6.

TABLE 5.5: Frequency Distribution of Moral Value Scores for Christian Students

Sl. No.	Class Interval	Limits	Mid point	F	CF	CPF
1	211-230	210.5-230.5	220.5	1	1	1.85
2	231-250	230.5-250.5	240.5	0	1	1.85
3	251-270	250.5-270.5	260.5	0	1	1.85
4	271-290	270.5-290.5	280.5	4	5	9.25
5	291-310	290.5-310.5	300.5	6	11	20.37
6	311-330	310.5-330.5	320.5	16	27	50.00
7	331-350	330.5-350.5	340.5	13	40	74.07
8	351-370	330.5-370.5	360.5	9	49	90.74
9	371-390	370.5-390.5	380.5	3	52	96.29
10	391-410	390.5-410.5	400.5	2	54	100.00

M : 331.11		R : 170		Sk : -0.53		SE_M : 4.28	
Md : 330		QD : 19.25		Ku : 1.46			
Mo : 327.78		SD : 31.52		CV : 9.519			

It is observed from Table 5.6 that the mean Moral Value score of Hindu students is 339.89. The mean Moral Value score is far greater than the neutral value. Hence it is concluded that the Hindu students have high Moral Values. The values of Skewness (Sk) and Kurtosis (Ku) are -0.60 and 0.86 respectively. Hence, the frequency distribution of Moral Value Scores for Hindu students is slightly negatively Skewed and Lepto Kurtic.

The Bar diagram for the mean Moral Value Scores for Muslim, Christian and Hindu students is shown in Fig. 5.5.

Frequency Distribution of Moral Value Scores for SC/ ST, BC and OC Students.

Frequency distribution of Moral Value Scores for SC/ST students is presented in Table 5.7.

TABLE 5.6: Frequency Distribution of Moral Value Scores for Hindu Students

Sl. No.	Class Interval	Limits	Mid point	F	CF	CPF
1	211-230	210.5-230.5	220.5	2	2	0.18
2	231-250	230.5-250.5	240.5	2	4	0.36
3	251-270	250.5-270.5	260.5	6	10	0.90
4	271-290	270.5-290.5	280.5	31	41	3.70
5	291-310	290.5-310.5	300.5	89	130	11.73
6	311-330	310.5-330.5	320.5	239	369	33.30
7	331-350	330.5-350.5	340.5	312	681	61.46
8	351-370	330.5-370.5	360.5	309	990	89.35
9	371-390	370.5-390.5	380.5	103	1093	98.64
10	391-410	390.5-410.5	400.5	15	1108	100.00

M : 339.89 R : 180 Sk : -0.60 SE_M : 0.77
Md : 342.00 QD : 17.37 Ku : 0.86
Mo : 346.22 SD : 25.79 CV : 7.589

It is clear from Table 5.7 that the mean Moral Value Score of SC/ST students is 337.22. The mean Moral Value Score is far greater than the neutral value. Hence it is concluded that the SC/ST students have high Moral Values. The values of Skewness (Sk) and Kurtosis (Ku) are -0.59 and 1.08 respectively. Hence, the frequency distribution of Moral Value Scores for SC/ST students is slightly negatively Skewed and Lepto Kurtic.

Frequency distribution of Moral Value Scores for BC students is given in Table 5.8. It is observed from Table 5.8 that the mean Moral Value score of BC students is 342.39. The mean Moral Value score is far greater than the neutral value. Hence it is concluded that the BC students have high Moral Values. The values of Skewness (Sk) and Kurtosis (Ku) are -0.658 and 1.11 respectively. Hence, the frequency distribution of Moral Value Scores for BC students is slightly negatively Skewed and Lepto Kurtic.

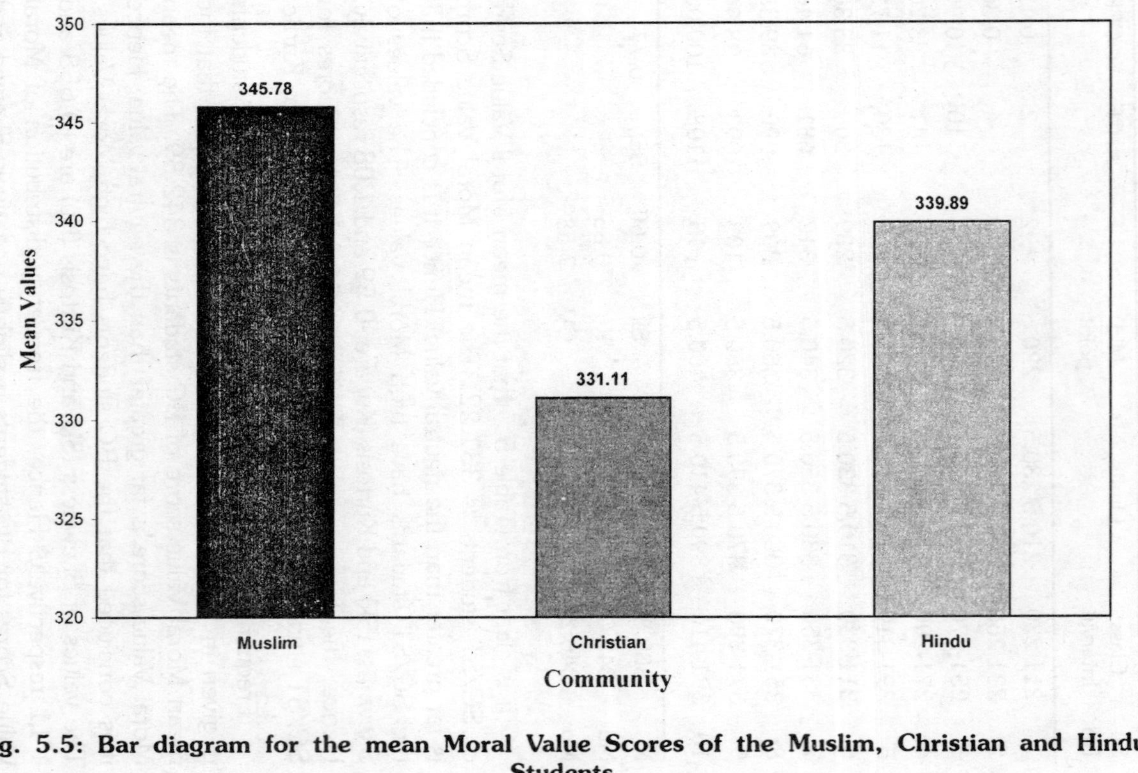

Fig. 5.5: Bar diagram for the mean Moral Value Scores of the Muslim, Christian and Hindu Students

TABLE 5.7: Frequency Distribution of Moral Value Scores for SC/ST Students

Sl. No.	Class Interval	Limits	Mid point	F	CF	CPF
1	211-230	210.5-230.5	220.5	2	2	0.34
2	231-250	230.5-250.5	240.5	1	3	0.51
3	251-270	250.5-270.5	260.5	2	5	0.86
4	271-290	270.5-290.5	280.5	20	25	4.31
5	291-310	290.5-310.5	300.5	52	77	13.29
6	311-330	310.5-330.5	320.5	140	217	37.47
7	331-350	330.5-350.5	340.5	154	371	64.07
8	351-370	330.5-370.5	360.5	161	532	91.88
9	371-390	370.5-390.5	380.5	41	573	98.96
10	391-410	390.5-410.5	400.5	6	579	100.00

M : 337.22 R : 180 Sk : -0.59 SE_M : 1.07
Md : 339 QD : 17 Ku : 1.08
Mo : 342.56 SD : 25.92 CV : 7.688

TABLE 5.8: Frequency Distribution of Moral Values Scores for BC Students

S.No.	Class Interval	Limits	Mid point	F	CF	CPF
1	2	3	4	5	6	7
1	211-230	210.5-230.5	220.5	1	1	0.27
2	231-250	230.5-250.5	240.5	0	1	0.27
3	251-270	250.5-270.5	260.5	1	2	0.55
4	271-290	270.5-290.5	280.5	10	12	3.31
5	291-310	290.5-310.5	300.5	24	36	9.94
6	311-330	310.5-330.5	320.5	67	103	28.45
7	331-350	330.5-350.5	340.5	116	219	60.49
8	351-370	330.5-370.5	360.5	94	313	86.46
9	371-390	370.5-390.5	380.5	42	355	98.06
10	391-410	390.5-410.5	400.5	7	362	100.00

M : 342.39 R : 170 Sk : -0.658 SE_M : 1.35
Md : 343 QD : 16.62 Ku : 1.11
Mo : 344.22 SD : 25.75 CV : 7.521

Frequency distribution of Moral Value Scores for OC students is given in Table 5.9. It is observed from Table 5.9 that the mean Moral Value score of OC students is 341.40. The mean Moral Value score is far greater than the neutral value. Hence it is concluded that the OC students have high Moral Values. The values of Skewness (Sk) and Kurtosis (Ku) are -0.714 and 0.718 respectively. Hence, the frequency distribution of Moral Value Scores for OC students is slightly negatively Skewed and Lepto Kurtic. The Bar diagram for the distribution of mean Moral Value Scores for SC/ST, BC and OC students is given in the Fig. 5.6.

TABLE 5.9: Frequency Distribution of Moral Values Scores for OC Students

Sl. No.	Class Interval	Limits	Mid point	F	CF	CPF
1	211-230	210.5-230.5	220.5	0	0	0
2	231-250	230.5-250.5	240.5	1	1	0.38
3	251-270	250.5-270.5	260.5	3	4	1.54
4	271-290	270.5-290.5	280.5	6	10	3.86
5	291-310	290.5-310.5	300.5	22	32	12.35
6	311-330	310.5-330.5	320.5	50	82	31.66
7	331-350	330.5-350.5	340.5	67	149	57.52
8	351-370	330.5-370.5	360.5	78	227	87.64
9	371-390	370.5-390.5	380.5	28	255	98.45
10	391-410	390.5-410.5	400.5	4	259	100.00

M : 341.40	R : 150	Sk : -0.714	SE_M : 1.64
Md : 347	QD : 17.5	Ku : 0.718	
Mo : 358.2	SD : 26.43	CV : 7.743	

The Values of N, M, Md, Mo, R, QD, SD, Sk, Ku, CV and SE_M for all theSex, Community and Caste on Moral Value Scores

The values of N, M, Md, Mo, R, QD, SD, Sk, Ku, CV and SE_M for all the Sex, Community and Caste on Moral Value Scores are presented in Table 5.10.

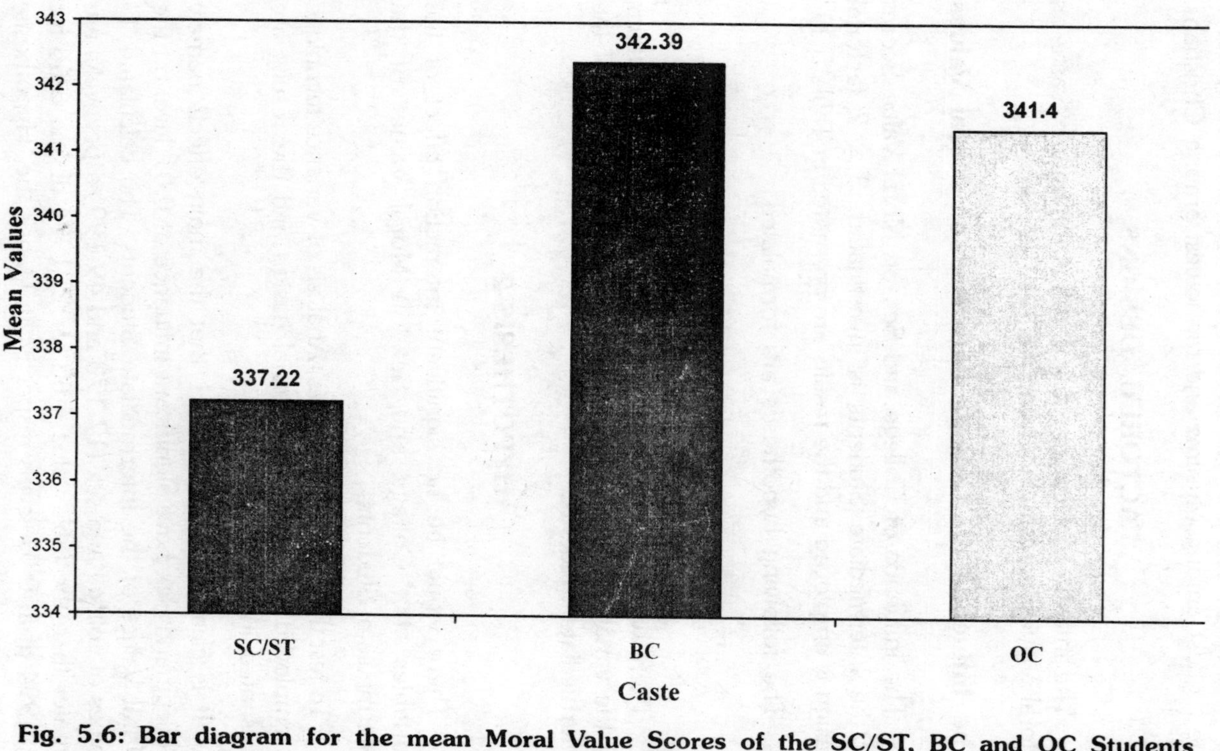

Fig. 5.6: Bar diagram for the mean Moral Value Scores of the SC/ST, BC and OC Students

It is clear from Table 5.10 that the mean Moral Values is the highest among Muslims and the lowest among Christians.

FACTORIAL DESIGNS

The influence of college x sex and community x caste on Moral Values are studied using factorial designs.

The Influence of 'College and Sex' on Moral Values

The influence of College and Sex on Moral Value Scores of the Intermediate Students is investigated. 3 × 2 factorial design is employed and the results are presented in Table 5.11.

The following hypotheses are formulated:

HYPOTHESIS-1

There would be no significant influence of the main effects of the variables viz., College and Sex on Moral Values of the Intermediate Students.

HYPOTHESIS-2

There would be no significant interaction effect of the variables viz., College and Sex on Moral Values of the Intermediate Students.

To test the above hypotheses, Analysis of Variance technique is employed using 3 × 2 factorial design and the results are presented in the Table 19.

It is clear from Table 5.11 that the main effects namely College and Sex have significant influence at 0.01 level on the Moral Values of the Intermediate Students. The calculated 'F' values of college and sex (17.173 and 49.199 respectively) are greater than the table value 4.63 for 2, 1994 df and 6.66 for 1, 1994 df at 0.01 levels respectively. Hence the 'Hypothesis-

TABLE 5.10: The values of N, M, Md, Mo, R, QD, SD, Sk, Ku, CV and SE_M for all the Sex, Community and Caste on Moral Value Scores

S.No.	Group	N	M	Md	Mo	R	QD	SD	Sk	Ku	CV	SE_M
1	**Whole**	1200	339.68	341.622	351.00	180	17.54	26.07	-0.631	0.958	7.676	0.75
2	**Male**	600	334.53	335.500	337.44	146	17.00	24.96	-0.401	-0.022	7.462	1.01
3	**Female**	600	344.83	348.000	354.34	180	17.00	26.16	-0.957	2.400	7.587	1.06
4	**Muslim**	38	345.78	351.000	361.44	106	13.00	23.50	-1.350	2.090	6.797	3.81
5	**Christian**	54	331.11	330.000	327.78	170	19.25	31.52	-0.530	1.460	9.519	4.28
6	**Hindu**	1108	339.89	342.000	346.22	180	17.37	25.79	-0.600	0.860	7.589	0.77
7	**SC/ST**	579	337.22	339.000	342.56	180	17.00	25.92	-0.590	1.080	7.688	1.07
8	**BC**	362	342.39	343.00	344.22	170	16.62	25.75	-0.658	1.110	7.521	1.35
9	**OC**	259	341.40	347.00	358.20	150	17.50	26.43	-0.714	0.718	7.743	1.64

TABLE 5.11: Results of Analysis of Variance (ANOVA) for the attitudinal scores of Intermediate Students towards Moral Values under 3X2 (College X Sex) Factorial Design

S.No.	Source of variance	Sum of squares	df	Mean Square	F	Level of significance
1	COL	21902.693	2	10951.347	17.173	**
2	SEX	31374.892	1	31374.892	49.199	**
3	COL * SEX	517.135	2	258.568	0.405	@
4	Error	761429.839	1194	637.713	—	
5	Total	815224.559	1199	—	—	

College (COL) -3 levels SEX-2 levels

1' is rejected. It is concluded that college and sex have significant influence on Moral Values of Intermediate Students.

Students studying in the Government colleges have significantly better Moral Values than the students studying in Aided colleges and Private colleges. The students studying in Private colleges have significantly least Moral Values than the students studying in Government colleges and Aided colleges. Female students have significantly better Moral Values than the male students.

The two factor interaction effect namely College × Sex doesn't have significant influence on Moral Values of the Intermediate Students. It is also evident from the Table-19 that the calculated value of 'F' for College × Sex is 0.405 which is less than the table value 3.00 for 2, 1994 df at 0.05 level. Hence the 'Hypothesis-2' is accepted. It is concluded that there is no interaction effect of College × Sex on Moral Values of the Intermediate Students.

The influence of Community × Caste on Moral Values

The influence of Community and Caste on Moral Value Scores of the Intermediate Students is investigated. 3x3 factorial design is employed and the results are presented in the Table 5.12.

The following hypotheses are formulated:

HYPOTHESIS-3

There would be no significant influence of the main effects of the variables viz., Community and Caste on Moral Values of the Intermediate Students.

HYPOTHESIS-4

There would be no significant interaction effect of the variables viz., Community and Caste on Moral Values of the Intermediate Students.

TABLE 5.12: Results of Analysis of Variance (ANOVA) for the attitudinal scores of Intermediate Students towards Moral Values under 3X3 (Community X Caste) Factorial Design

S.No.	Source of variance	Sum of squares	df	Mean Square	F	Level of significance
1	COMMUNITY	5434.265	2	2717.132	4.037	*
2	CASTE	5862.465	2	2931.232	4.355	*
3	COM * CASTE	2263.050	4	565.762	0.841	@
4	Error	801664.780	1191	673.102	—	
5	Total	815224.559	1199	—	—	

Community- 3 levels Caste- 3 levels

To test the above hypotheses, Analysis of Variance technique is employed using 3 × 3 factorial design and the results are presented in Table 5.12.

It is observed from Table 5.12 that the main effects of Community and Caste have significant influence at 0.05 level on the Moral Values of the Intermediate Students. The calculated values of 'F' for Community and Caste (4.037 and 4.355 respectively) are greater than the table value 3.00 for 2, 1991 df at 0.05 level. Hence the 'Hypothesis-3' is rejected. It is concluded that community and caste have significant influence on Moral Values of Intermediate Students.

The two factor interaction effect namely Community × College doesn't have significant influence on Moral Values of the Intermediate Students. It is also seen from Table 5.12 that the calculated value of 'F' for Community × Caste is 0.841 less than the table value 2.38 for 4, 1991 df at 0.05 level. Hence the 'Hypothesis-4' is accepted. It is concluded that there is no interaction effect of Community × Caste on Moral Values of the Intermediate Students.

It is observed that the Muslim students have significantly better Moral Values than Christian and Hindu students. The Christian students have significantly least Moral Values than Hindu and Muslim students. B.C. students have significantly better Moral Values than OC and SC/ST students. SC/ST students have significantly least Moral Values than OC and BC students.

INFLUENCE OF SOCIO-DEMOGRAPHIC VARIABLES ON MORAL VALUES

The influence of some of the socio-demographic variables viz., Residence, Medium of Study, Religious Festivals, Religious Discourses, Type of Family, Age, Family Annual Income, Educational Qualification of Mother, Educational Qualification of Father, Fathers' Occupation, Mothers' Occupation, Type of

Family, Native Place, Family Economic Position, Visiting Temple, When You go Wrong Who corrects You and Group Subjects on Moral Values of the Intermediate Students are investigated.

1. *Influence of 'Residence' on Moral Values*

The influence of Residence of the students on Moral Values is investigated. The students are divided into 2 groups on the basis of their residence, namely:

1) Day Scholar, and

2) Hostler.

The following hypothesis is formulated:

HYPOTHESIS-5

There would be no significant influence of residence of the students on Moral Values.

The above hypothesis is tested using 't' technique and the results are presented in Table 5.13.

TABLE 5.13: Influence of 'Residence' on Moral Values

S. No.	Residence	No. of observations	Mean value	Standard deviation	't' value	Level of significance
1.	Days Scholar	623	341.66	25.86	2.737	**
2.	Hostler	577	337.55	26.15		

df: 1198 Grand Mean: 339.605

It is observed from Table 5.13 that the computed 't' value is 2.737, which is greater than the table value of 't' (2.58) for 1198 df at 0.01 level. Hence 'Hypothesis-5' is rejected at 0.01 level. It is concluded that residence has significant influence on Moral Values of Intermediate Students. It is clear from the mean values that the day scholars have significantly better Moral Values than the hostellers.

2. Influence of 'Medium of Study' on Moral Values

The influence of Medium of Study of the students on Moral Values is investigated. The students are divided into 2 groups on the basis of their medium of study, namely:

1) Telugu, and
2) English.

The following hypothesis is formulated:

HYPOTHESIS-6

There would be no significant influence of medium of study on the Moral Values of students.

The above hypothesis is tested using 't' technique and the results are presented in Table 5.14.

TABLE 5.14: Influence of 'Medium of Study' on Moral Values

S. No.	Residence	No. of observations	Mean value	Standard deviation	't' value	Level of significance
1.	Telugu	992	339.84	25.38	0.467	@
2.	English	208	338.91	29.18		

df: 1998 Grand Mean: 339.375

It is clear from Table 5.14 that the computed 't' value is 0.467, which is less than the table value of 't' (1.96) for 1198 df at 0.05 level. Hence 'Hypothesis-6' is accepted at 0.05 level. It is concluded that medium of study has no significant influence Moral Values of Intermediate Students.

3 Influence of 'Religious Festivals' on Moral Values

The influence of religious festivals of the students on Moral Values is investigated. The students are divided into 2 groups on the basis of their celebration of religious festivals, namely: 1) No, 2) Yes.

The following hypothesis is formulated:

HYPOTHESIS-7

There would be no significant influence of religious festivals on the Moral Values of students.

The above hypothesis is tested using 't' technique and the results are presented in Table 5.15

TABLE 5.15: Influence of 'Religious Festivals' on Moral Values

Sl. No.	Religious Festivals	No. of observations	Mean value	Standard deviation	't' value	Level of significance
1.	No	62	339.74	28.49	0.017	@
2.	Yes	1138	339.68	25.95		

df: 1998 Grand Mean: 339.71

It is observed from Table 5.15 that the computed 't' value is 0.017, which is less than the table value of 't' (1.96) for 1198 df at 0.05 level. Hence 'Hypothesis-7' is accepted at 0.05 level. It is concluded that religious festivals have no significant influence on Moral Values of Intermediate Students.

4. Influence of 'Religious Discourses' on Moral Values

The influence of religious discourses of the students on Moral Values is investigated. The students are divided into 2 groups on the basis of their religious discourses , namely: 1) No, 2) Yes.

The following hypothesis is formulated:

HYPOTHESIS-8

There would be no significant influence of religious discourses on the Moral Values of students.

The above hypothesis is tested using 't' technique and the results are presented in Table 5.16.

TABLE 5.16: Influence of 'Religious Discourses' on Moral Values

Sl. No.	Religious Discourses	No. of observations	Mean value	Standard deviation	't' value	Level of significance
1.	No	403	339.60	26.55	0.078	@
2.	Yes	797	339.72	25.84		
df: 1998			Grand Mean: 339.66			

It is clear from Table 5.16 that the computed 't' value is 0.078, which is less than the table value of 't' (1.96) for 1198 df at 0.05 level. Hence 'Hypothesis-8' is accepted at 0.05 level. It is concluded that religious discourses have no significant influence on Moral Values of Intermediate Students.

5. Influence of 'Type of Family' on Moral Values

The influence of type of family of the students on Moral Values is investigated. The students are divided into 2 groups on the basis of their type of family, namely: 1) Nuclear, 2) Joint.

The following hypothesis is formulated.

HYPOTHESIS-9

There would be no significant influence of type of family of the students on Moral Values.

The above hypothesis is tested using 't' technique and the results are presented in Table 5.17

TABLE 5.17: Influence of 'Type of Family' on Moral Values

S. No.	Type of Family	No. of observations	Mean value	Standard deviation	't' value	Level of significance
1.	Nuclear	758	340.13	24.86	0.774	@
2.	Joint	442	338.92	28.04		
df: 1998			Grand Mean: 339.525			

It is seen from the Table-25 that the computed 't' value is 0.774, which is less than the table value of 't' (1.96) for 1198 df at 0.05 level. Hence 'Hypothesis-6' is accepted at 0.05 level. It is concluded that type of family has no significant influence on Moral Values of Intermediate Students.

6. Influence of 'Age' on Moral Values

The influence of age of the students on Moral Values is investigated. The students are divided into 3 groups on the basis of their age, namely: 1) 16 years, 2) 17 years, 3) 18 years and above.

The following hypothesis is formulated.

HYPOTHESIS-10

There would be no significant influence of age of the students on Moral Values. The above hypothesis is tested using 'F' technique and the results are presented in Table 5.18.

TABLE 5.18: Analysis of variance (ANOVA) for the attitudinal scores of Intermediate Students towards Moral Values under the variable 'Age'

S. No.	Source of Variation	Sum of SquaresSS	df	Mean Square (MS)	'F' value	Level of significance
1.	Between Groups	6454.611	2	3227.306	4.776	**
2.	Within Groups	808769.95	1197	675.664		
3.	Total	815224.56	1999	—		

It is seen from Table 5.18 that the calculated 'F' value 4.776 is greater than the table value 4.63 for 2 and 1197 df at 0.01 level. Hence 'Hypothesis-10' is rejected. It is concluded that age has significant influence on Intermediate Students towards Moral Values. It is observed from the mean values that the lower age is associated with significantly better Moral Values.

This result is intune with the findings of Sibia, Sukhvinder (1990) and Shama and Kaur (1992). This result is not intune with the findings of Wright and Cox (1967) and Ravan Hushim Rowahan (1974).

7. *Influence of 'Family Annual Income' on Moral Values*

The influence of family annual income of the students on Moral Values is investigated. The students are divided into 4 groups on the basis of their family annual income, namely: 1) up to Rs. 25,000, 2) Rs. 25,001 - 50,000, 3) Rs. 50,001- 1 lakh, 4) Rs. above 1 lakh

The following hypothesis is formulated.

HYPOTHESIS-11

There would be no significant influence of family annual income of the students on Moral Values.

The above hypothesis is tested using 'F' technique and the results are presented in Table 5.19.

TABLE 5.19: Analysis of variance (ANOVA) for the attitudinal scores of Intermediate Students towards Moral Values under the variable 'Family Annual Income'

Sl. No.	Source of Variation	Sum of SquaresSS	df	Mean Square (MS)	'F' value	Level of significance
1.	Between Groups	10456.573	3	3485.524	5.180	**
2.	Within Groups	804767.99	1196	672.883		
3.	Total	815224.56	1999	—		

It is clear from Table 5.19 that the calculated 'F' value 5.180 is greater than the table value 3.80 for 3 and 1196 df at 0.01 level. Hence 'Hypothesis-11' is rejected. It is concluded that family annual income has significant influence on Moral Values of Intermediate Students. It is seen from the mean values that the students with Annual Income group of Rs. 25001 to Rs. 50000 have significantly better Moral Values than the other three groups. The students with Annual Income group of Rs. 50001 to Rs. 1 lakh have the lowest Moral Values among the four groups of students.

This result is intune with the findings of Arokiaswamy (1993) and Shaik Shamshuddin (2005).

8. Influence of 'Educational qualifications of Mother' on Moral Values

The influence of educational qualifications of mother of the students on Moral Values is investigated. The students are divided into 3 groups on the basis of their educational qualification of mother, namely: 1) up to X class, 2) Degree, 3) P.G. and Professional.

The following hypothesis is formulated.

HYPOTHESIS-12

There would be no significant influence of educational qualifications of mother of the students on Moral Values.

The above hypothesis is tested using 'F' technique and the results are presented in Table 5.20.

It is seen from Table 5.20 that the calculated 'F' value 0.119 is less than the table value 3.00 for 2 and 1197 df at 0.05 level. Hence 'Hypothesis-12' is accepted. It is concluded that family annual income has no significant influence on Intermediate Moral Values of Intermediate Students.

TABLE 5.20: Analysis of variance (ANOVA) for the attitudinal scores of Intermediate Students towards Moral Values under the variable 'Educational Qualifications of the Mother'

Sl. No.	Source of Variation	Sum of SquaresSS	df	Mean Square (MS)	'F' value	Level of significance
1.	Between Groups	162.208	2	81.104	0.119	@
2.	Within Groups	815062.35	1197	680.921		
3.	Total	815224.56	1999	—		

This result is intune with the findings of Dhul and Khatri (2002) and is not intune with the findings of Sinha (1981) and Shaik Shamshuddin (2005).

9. Influence of 'Educational qualifications of Father' on Moral Values

The influence of educational qualifications of father of the students on Moral Values is investigated. The students are divided into 3 groups on the basis of their educational qualifications of father, namely: 1) up to X class, 2) Degree, 3) P.G. and Professional.

The following hypothesis is formulated.

HYPOTHESIS-13

There would be no significant influence of educational qualification of father of the students on Moral Values.

The above hypothesis is tested using 'F' technique and the results are presented in Table 5.21.

TABLE 5.21: Analysis of variance (ANOVA) for the attitudinal scores of Intermediate Students towards Moral Values under the variable 'Educational Qualifications of the Father'

Sl. No.	Source of Variation	Sum of SquaresSS	df	Mean Square (MS)	'F' value	Level of significance
1.	Between Groups	2010.876	2	1005.438	1.480	@
2.	Within Groups	813213.68	1197	679.377		
3.	Total	815224.56	1999	—		

It is observed from Table 5.21 that the calculated 'F' value 1.480 is less than the table value 3.00 for 2 and 1197 df at 0.05 level. Hence 'Hypothesis-13' is accepted. It is concluded that family annual income has no significant influence on Moral Values of Intermediate Students.

This result is intune with the findings of Dhul and Khatri (2002) and not intune with the findings of Sinha (1981) and Shaik Shamshuddin (2005).

10. Influence of 'Father Occupation' on Moral Values

The influence of Occupation of Father of the students on Moral Values is investigated. The students are divided into three groups on the basis of their fathers' occupation, namely: 1) Labour, 2) Agriculture/Caste based occupation, 3) Government Employee

The following hypothesis is formulated.

HYPOTHESIS-14

There would be no significant influence of fathers' occupation of the students on Moral Values.

The above hypothesis is tested using 'F' technique and the results are presented in Table 5.22.

TABLE 5.22: Analysis of variance (ANOVA) for the attitudinal scores of Intermediate Students towards Moral Values under the variable 'Father's Occupation'

Sl. No.	Source of Variation	Sum of SquaresSS	df	Mean Square (MS)	'F' value	Level of significance
1.	Between Groups	544.327	2	272.163	0.400	@
2.	Within Groups	814680.23	1197	680.602		
3.	Total	815224.56	1999	—		

It is clear from the Table-30 that the calculated 'F' value 0.400 is less than the table value 3.00 for 2 and 1197 df at 0.05 level. Hence 'Hypothesis-14' is accepted. It is concluded that fathers' occupation has no significant influence on Moral Values of Intermediate Students.

This result is intune with the findings of Shaik Shamshuddin (2005).

11. Influence of 'Mother Occupation' on Moral Values

The influence of Occupation of Mother of the students on Moral Values is investigated. The students are divided into 3 groups on the basis of their mothers' occupation, namely: 1) Labour, 2) House Wife, 3) Government Employee

The following hypothesis is formulated.

HYPOTHESIS-15

There would be no significant influence of mothers' occupation of the students on Moral Values.

The above hypothesis is tested using 'F' technique and the results are presented in Table 5.23.

TABLE 5.23: Analysis of variance (ANOVA) for the attitudinal scores of Intermediate Students towards Moral Values under the variable 'Mother's Occupation'

S. No.	Source of Variation	Sum of SquaresSS	df	Mean Square (MS)	'F' value	Level of significance
1.	Between Groups	3593.142	2	1796.571	2.650	@
2.	Within Groups	811631.42	1197	678.055		
3.	Total	815224.56	1999	—		

It is clear from Table 5.23 that the calculated 'F' value 2.650 is less than the table value 3.00 for 2 and 1197 df at 0.05 level. Hence 'Hypothesis-15' is accepted. It is concluded that mothers' occupation has no significant influence on Moral Values of Intermediate Students.

This result is intune with the findings of Shamshuddin (2005).

12. Influence of 'Birth Order' on Moral Values

The influence of birth order of the students on Moral Values is investigated. The students are divided into 3 groups on the basis of their birth order, namely: 1) 3 and above, 2) 2, 3) 1.

The following hypothesis is formulated.

HYPOTHESIS-16

There would be no significant influence of birth order of the students on Moral Values.

The above hypothesis is tested using 'F' technique and the results are presented in Table 5.24.

TABLE 5.24: Analysis of variance (ANOVA) for the attitudinal scores of Intermediate Students towards Moral Values under the variable 'Birth Order'

S. No.	Source of Variation	Sum of SquaresSS	df	Mean Square (MS)	'F' value	Level of significance
1.	Between Groups	2681.376	2	1340.688	1.975	@
2.	Within Groups	812543.18	1197	678.813		
3.	Total	815224.56	1199	—		

It is observed from Table 5.24 that the calculated 'F' value 1.975 is less than the table value 3.00 for 2 and 1197 df at 0.05 level. Hence 'Hypothesis-16' is accepted. It is concluded that birth order has no significant influence on Moral Values of Intermediate Students.

This result is not intune with the findings of Shama and Kaur (1992).

13. Influence of 'Total Members in the Family' on Moral Values

The influence of total members in the family of the students on Moral Values is investigated. The students are divided into 3 groups on the basis of total members in the family, namely: 1) 5 and above, 2) 4, 3) 3 and below.

The following hypothesis is formulated.

HYPOTHESIS-17

There would be no significant influence of total members in the family of the students on Moral Values.

The above hypothesis is tested using 'F' technique and the results are shown in Table 5.25.

TABLE 5.25: Analysis of variance (ANOVA) for the attitudinal scores of Intermediate Students towards Moral Values under the variable 'Total Members in the Family'

Sl. No.	Source of Variation	Sum of SquaresSS	df	Mean Square (MS)	'F' value	Level of significance
1.	Between Groups	402.651	2	202.826	0.298	@
2.	Within Groups	814818.91	1197	680.718		
3.	Total	815224.56	1999	—		

It is clear from Table 5.25 that the calculated 'F' value 0.298 is less than the table value 3.00 for 2 and 1197 df at 0.05 level. Hence 'Hypothesis-17' is accepted. It is concluded that total members in the family has no significant influence on Moral Values of Intermediate Students.

This result is intune with the findings of Rangaswamy (2006) and not intune with the findings of Annamma (1984).

14. Influence of 'Native Place' on Moral Values

The influence of native place of the students on Moral Values is investigated. The students are divided into 3 groups on the basis of their native place, namely: 1) City/Municipal Town, 2) Small Town, 3) Village.

The following hypothesis is formulated.

HYPOTHESIS-18

There would be no significant influence of native place of the students on Moral Values.

The above hypothesis is tested using 'F' technique and the results are given in Table 5.26.

TABLE 5.26: Analysis of variance (ANOVA) for the attitudinal scores of Intermediate Students towards Moral Values under the variable 'Native Place'

Sl. No.	Source of Variation	Sum of SquaresSS	df	Mean Square (MS)	'F' value	Level of significance
1.	Between Groups	874.766	2	437.383	0.643	@
2.	Within Groups	814349.79	1197	680.326		
3.	Total	815224.56	1999	—		

It is clear from Table 5.26 that the calculated 'F' value 0.643 is less than the table value 3.00 for 2 and 1197 df at 0.05 level. Hence 'Hypothesis-18' is accepted. It is concluded that native place has no significant influence on Moral Values of Intermediate Students.

This result is intune with the findings of Dwivedi, Om Prakash (1983), Reddy (2005), Shaik Shamshuddin (2005) and Rangaswamy (2006).

This result is not intune with Gaur (1975), Begum Shahina (1983) and Yella Reddy (2004).

15. Influence of 'Family Economic Position' on Moral Values

The influence of family economic position of the students on Moral Values is investigated. The students are divided into 3 groups on the basis of their family economic position, namely: 1) Rich, 2) Medium, 3) Poor.

The following hypothesis is formulated.

HYPOTHESIS-19

There would be no significant influence of family economic position of the students on Moral Values.

The above hypothesis is tested using 'F' technique and the results are shown in Table 5.27.

TABLE 5.27: Analysis of variance (ANOVA) for the attitudinal scores of Intermediate Students towards Moral Values under the variable 'Family Economic Position'

Sl. No.	Source of Variation	Sum of SquaresSS	df	Mean Square (MS)	'F' value	Level of significance
1.	Between Groups	6157.885	2	3078.943	4.555	*
2.	Within Groups	809066.67	1197	675.912		
3.	Total	815224.56	1999	—		

It is clear from Table 5.27 that the calculated 'F' value 4.555 is greater than the table value 3.00 for 2 and 1197 df at 0.05 level. Hence 'Hypothesis-19' is rejected. It is concluded that family economic position has significant influence on Moral Values of Intermediate Students. It is observed from the mean values that the students belonging to medium 'Family Economic Position' have significantly better Moral Values than the other two groups. The students belonging to rich 'Family Economic Position' have the lowest Moral Values as compared with other two groups.

This result is intune with Dhull and Mahashweta (2005) and Shaik Shamshuddin (2005).

16. Influence of 'Visiting Temple' on Moral Values

The influence of visiting temple of the students on Moral Values is investigated. The students are divided into 3 groups on the basis of their visiting temple, namely: 1) Never, 2) Occasionally, 3) Regularly.

The following hypothesis is formulated.

HYPOTHESIS-20

There would be no significant influence of visiting temple of the students on Moral Values.

The above hypothesis is tested using 'F' technique and the results are given in Table 5.28.

TABLE 5.28: Analysis of variance (ANOVA) for the attitudinal scores of Intermediate Students towards Moral Values under the variable 'Visiting Temple'

Sl. No.	Source of Variation	Sum of SquaresSS	df	Mean Square (MS)	'F' value	Level of significance
1.	Between Groups	4426.662	2	2213.331	3.268	*
2.	Within Groups	810797.90	1197	677.358		
3.	Total	815224.56	1999	—		

It is clear from Table 5.28 that the calculated 'F' value 3.268 is greater than the table value 3.00 for 2 and 1197 df at 0.05 level. Hence 'Hypothesis-20' is rejected. It is concluded that visiting temple has significant influence on Moral Values of Intermediate Students. The students who are visiting temple occasionally have significantly better Moral Values than the other students. The students who never visit the temple have significantly least Moral Values than the other students.

17. *Influence of 'When you go Wrong who corrects you' on Moral Values*

The influence of 'When you go Wrong who corrects you' on Moral Values is investigated. The students are divided into 4 groups on the basis of their 'when you wrong who corrects you', namely: 1) Others/Friends, 2) Teacher, 3) Father, 4) Mother

The following hypothesis is formulated.

HYPOTHESIS-21

There would be no significant influence of total members in the family of the students on Moral Values.

The above hypothesis is tested using 'F' technique and the results are presented in Table 5.29.

TABLE 5.29: Analysis of variance (ANOVA) for the attitudinal scores of Intermediate Students towards Moral Values under the variable 'When you go wrong who corrects you'

Sl. No.	Source of Variation	Sum of SquaresSS	df	Mean Square (MS)	'F' value	Level of significance
1.	Between Groups	4688.253	3	1562.751	2.306	@
2.	Within Groups	810536.31	1196	677.706		
3.	Total	815224.56	1999	—		

It is clear from Table 5.29 that the calculated 'F' value 2.306 is less than the table value 2.61 for 3 and 1196 df at 0.05 level. Hence 'Hypothesis-21' is accepted. It is concluded that the variable 'when you go wrong who corrects you' has no significant influence on Moral Values of Intermediate Students.

18. Influence of 'Group Subjects' on Moral Values

The influence of group subjects of the students on Moral Values is investigated. The students are divided into 4 groups on the basis of their group subjects viz., 1) H.E.C., 2) C.E.C., 3) Bi.P.C., 4) M.P.C.

The following hypothesis is formulated.

HYPOTHESIS-22

There would be no significant influence of group subjects of the students on Moral Values.

The above hypothesis is tested using 'F' technique and the results are shown in Table 5.30.

TABLE 5.30: Analysis of variance (ANOVA) for the attitudinal scores of Intermediate Students towards Moral Values under the variable 'Group Subjects'

Sl. No.	Source of Variation	Sum of SquaresSS	df	Mean Square (MS)	'F' value	Level of significance
1.	Between Groups	44574.680	3	14858.227	23.059	**
2.	Within Groups	770649.88	1196	644.356		
3.	Total	815224.56	1999	—		

It is clear from Table 5.30 that the calculated 'F' value 23.059 is greater than the table value 3.80 for 3 and 1196 df at 0.01 level. Hence 'Hypothesis-22' is rejected. It is concluded that group subjects has significant influence on Moral Values of Intermediate Students. The students with 'Group Subjects' namely Mathematics, Physics and Chemistry (MPC) have significantly better Moral Values than the others. The students with 'Group Subjects' namely History, Economics and Civics (HEC) have significantly least Moral Values than the others.

This result is intune with the findings of Arokiaswamy (1993), Shaik shamshuddin (2005) and Rangaswamy (2006).

INFLUENCE OF 14 PERSONALITY FACTORS OF HSPQ ON MORAL VALUE SCORES

The effect of 14 personality factors of HSPQ on Moral Values of the Intermediate Students is investigated. The raw scores on each personality factor for the total sample are converted into stens. On the basis of the sten values; the students are divided into three groups, namely: (1) students with sten values 1-4 (2) students with sten values 5-6 (3) students with sten values 7-10. The influence of each personality factor on the Moral Values of the Intermediate Students is investigated.

The following hypothesis is formulated.

HYPOTHESIS-23

There would be no significant influence of 14 personality factors of HSPQ on Moral Values of the Intermediate Students.

Hypothesis-23 is tested by employing 'F' technique and the results are presented in Table 5.31.

The table value of 'F' for 2 and 1197 df at 0.05 level is 3.00 and at 0.01 level is 4.63. It is evident from the Table 5.31 that the Personality Factors-C (Emotionally less stable Vs Emotionally stable), Factor I (Though minded Vs Tense minded), Factor O (Placid Vs Apprehensive), Factor Q_2 (Group Dependent Vs Controlled), Factor Q_3 (Undisciplined Vs Controlled) and Factor Q_4 (Relaxed Vs Tense) are significant at 0.01 level. Hence the Hypothesis-23 is rejected for the personality factors C, I, O, Q_2, Q_3 and Q_4. It is concluded that the personality factors C, I, O, Q_2, Q_3 and Q_4 have significant influence on Moral Values of the Intermediate Students.

The Factor-B (Less Intelligent Vs More Intelligent) and Factor E (Obedient Vs Assertive) are significant at 0.05 level. Hence the Hypothesis-23 is rejected at 0.05 level. It is concluded that the personality Factors-B and E have significant influence on Moral Values of the Intermediate Students. It is observed from the mean values that the students with personality characteristics (1) High Intelligence; (2) Emotionally Stable, Mature, Faces Reality, Calm; (3) Obedient, Mild, Easily Led, Docile, Accommodating; (4) Tough-minded, Rejects Illusions; (5) Self-assured, Placid, Secure, Complacent, Serene; (6) Sociably Group Dependent, A Joiner and Sound Follower; (7) Uncontrolled, Lax, Follows Own Urges, Careless of Social Rules; (8) Relaxed, Tranquil, Torpid, Unfrustrated, Composed have significantly better

TABLE 5.31: Influence of 14 Personality Factors of HSPQ on Moral Values

Sl. No.	Factors	No. of observations			Means			SDs			'F' Value	Level of Signi
		I	II	III	I	II	III	I	II	III		
1	**A**	81	523	596	343.877	339.306	339.45	25.6054	26.816	25.4662	1.126	@
2	**B**	115	408	677	334.452	339.355	340.774	24.8163	26.982	25.6488	2.948	*
3	**C**	132	476	592	333.864	338.609	341.85	24.1973	26.2588	26.1196	5.78	**
4	**D**	392	590	218	340.829	339.276	338.739	26.6521	25.7396	25.9784	0.553	@
5	**E**	198	475	527	342.869	340.282	337.953	23.0566	26.0951	27.0181	2.772	*
6	**F**	262	552	386	341.118	338.431	340.508	24.2449	26.9237	26.0233	1.227	@
7	**G**	373	521	306	337.869	340.697	340.18	26.6796	26.3761	24.75	1.353	@
8	**H**	107	543	550	340.598	340.954	338.256	23.2561	26.8337	25.8038	1.535	@
9	**I**	540	270	390	343.339	337.922	335.849	26.1173	26.5558	25.0489	10.297	**
10	**J**	83	386	731	335.843	340.023	339.944	25.7438	25.0769	26.6241	0.969	@
11	**O**	542	496	162	342.757	337.883	334.932	26.2263	26.0325	24.5802	7.721	**
12	**Q_2**	307	498	395	344.713	338.207	337.643	25.3821	26.1201	26.1051	7.807	**
13	**Q_3**	229	590	381	344.48	340.778	335.113	26.2893	26.0163	25.3942	10.409	**
14	**Q_4**	229	598	373	345.799	340.306	334.938	23.9263	26.3371	26.0996	12.896	**

** Significant at 0.01 level * Significant at 0.05 level @ Not Significant at 0.05 level

Moral Values than the students with personality characteristics (1) Low Intelligence; (2) Affected by feelings, Emotionally Less Stable, Easily upset, Changeable; (3) Assertive, Aggressive, Competitive, Stubborn; (4) Tender-minded, Sensitive, Dependent, Overprotected; (5) Apprehensive, Self-reproaching, Insecure, Worrying, Troubled; (6) Self-sufficient, Resourceful, Prefers Own Decisions; (7) Controlled, Exacting Will Power, Socially Precise, Compulsive, Following Self-image; and (8) Tense, Frustrated, Driven, Overwrought, Fretful.

The 'F' values for the remaining personality factors viz., A (Reserved Vs Outgoing), D (Phlegmatic Vs Excitable), F (Sober Vs Happy go lucky), G (Moral Standards Vs Super ego strength) and H (Shy Vs Venturesome) are not significant at 0.05 level. Hence the Hypothesis-23 is accepted. It is concluded that the personality factors A, D, F, G and H don't have significant influence on Moral Values of the Intermediate Students.

The results of the Factors A, D, E, F, H and J are intune with the findings of Rangaswamy (2006) and the results of the Factor-G are not intune with the findings of Rangasway (2006).

INFLUENCE OF SELF-CONCEPTS ON MORAL VALUES

The influence of 10 areas of Self-concepts and Total score of Self-concepts on Moral Values of the Intermediate Students is investigated.

The raw score on each area of the Self-concepts and also the total score are converted into Quratiles. On the basis of Quartile values, the students are divided into 3 groups, on each area of Self-concepts and also on Total Score of Self-concepts. Group I is formed with students upto Q_1, Group II is formed with students above Q_1 and upto Q_3 and Group III is formed with students above Q_3.

The following hypothesis is formulated.

HYPOTHESIS-24

There would be no significant influence of the different areas of Self-concepts and the total score of the Self-concepts on Moral Values of the Intermediate Students.

Hypothesis-24 is tested with the help of 'F' technique and the results are presented in Table 5.32.

The table value of 'F' for 2 and 1197 df at 0.01 level is 4.63 and 3.00 at 0.05 level. It is observed from the Table 5.32 that the computed values of 'F', for the areas B (Abilities), F (Self Acceptance), H (Worthiness), S_3 (Sociability) and T (Total of Self-concepts) are greater than the table values. Hence the Hypothesis-24 is rejected. It is concluded that the areas B, F, H, S_3 and T (Total of Self-concepts) have significant influence on Moral Values of the Intermediate Students. The computed 'F' value of the area P of Self-Concepts is greater than the table values 3.00 at 0.05 level. Hence the Hypothesis-24 was rejected at 0.05 level and it is concluded that the area P factor of Self-Concepts has significant influence on Moral Values of Intermediate Students. It is observed from Table-40 that the students who scored Q_3 and above in the self-concepts areas (1) Abilities, (2) Self-acceptance, (3) Worthiness, (4) Present, Past and Future, and (5) Self-concepts total score have significantly better than the students who scored up to Q_1. It indicates that better self-concepts leads to better Moral Values.

The computed 'F' values for the area A (Health & Sex Appropriateness), E (Self Confidence), S_1 (Beliefs and Convictions), S_2 (Feelings of Shame and Guilt) and W (Emotional Maturity) are less than the table value 3.00 at 0.05 level. Hence the Hypothesis-24 is accepted. It concluded that the area A, E, S_1, S_2 and W of Self-concepts have no significant influence on Moral Values of Intermediate Students.

TABLE 5.32: Influence of Self-concepts on Moral Values

Sl. No.	Variables	No. of observations			Means			SDs			'F' Value	Level of Signi.
		I	II	III	I	II	III	I	II	III		
1	**A**	346	634	220	339.575	338.816	342.368	27.8501	25.8395	23.6916	1.522	@
2	**B**	339	611	250	332.926	339.974	348.148	27.5824	25.5691	22.4799	25.602	**
3	**E**	422	483	295	338.18	339.286	342.495	26.2588	26.5054	24.9455	2.478	@
4	**F**	346	608	246	336.812	338.413	346.874	25.3237	27.5009	21.9789	12.405	**
5	**H**	363	646	191	335.276	340.322	345.916	25.7067	26.3876	24.2952	11.018	**
6	**P**	324	586	290	337.833	339.16	342.817	27.1105	26.2254	24.3506	3.038	*
7	S_1	352	692	156	338.986	339.08	343.955	25.8371	25.6743	28.073	2.411	@
8	S_2	383	527	290	338.475	339.624	341.397	25.1093	26.1587	27.1508	1.038	@
9	S_3	453	489	258	342.185	339.264	336.097	25.9074	25.9468	26.2482	4.617	**
10	**W**	403	530	267	338.598	340.896	338.925	26.0581	26.1551	25.9385	1.035	@
11	**T**	327	590	283	334.749	339.127	346.555	27.3646	25.7995	23.637	16.216	**

** Significant at 0.01 level   * Significant at 0.05 level   @ Not Significant at 0.05 level

INFLUENCE OF STUDY HABITS ON MORAL VALUES

The influence of seven areas of Study Habits and Total score of Study Habits on Moral Values of the Intermediate Students is investigated.

The raw score on each area of the Study Habits and also the total score are converted into quartiles. The students are divided into 3 groups, on each area of Study Habits and also on Total Score of Study Habits. Three Groups are formed based on quartiles; 1) Group I (Up to Q_1), 2) Group II (Above Q_1 and up to Q_3), and 3) Group III (AboveQ_3).

The following hypothesis is formulated.

HYPOTHESIS-25

There would be no significant influence of the different areas of Study Habits and the total score of the Study Habits on Moral Values of the Intermediate Students.

Hypothesis-25 is tested with the help of 'F' technique and the results are presented in Table 5.33.

The computed 'F' values for all the areas of Study Habits and for Total score of Study Habits are grater than the table value 4.63 for 2 and 1197 df at 0.01 level. Hence the Hypothesis-25 is rejected. It concluded that all the areas of Study Habits SH_1 (Home environment and Planning of work), SH_2 (Reading and note taking), SH_3 (Planning of Subject), SH_4 (Habits of concentration), SH_5 (Preparation for examination), SH_6 (General Habits & Attitudes), SH_7 (School Environment) and SHT (Study Habits Total Score) have no significant influence on Moral Values of Intermediate Students.

It is clear from Table 5.33 that the students who scored Q_3 and above in all the seven areas of Study Habits namely (1) Home Environment and Planning, (2) Reading and note-taking, (3) Planning of subject, (4) Habits of concentration,

TABLE 5.33: Influence of Study Habits on Moral Values

Sl. No.	Variables	No. of observations			Means			SDs			'F' Value	Level of Signi.
		I	II	III	I	II	III	I	II	III		
1	**SH_1**	364	603	233	335.396	340.683	343.807	26.7216	24.9768	27.0074	8.38	**
2	**SH_2**	322	626	252	335.379	338.757	347.496	26.8816	25.5895	24.6176	16.51	**
3	**SH_3**	481	533	186	337.056	339.737	346.339	26.1592	26.5056	23.4167	8.609	**
4	**SH_4**	308	617	275	335.026	339.011	346.418	27.3706	25.9747	23.4129	14.615	**
5	**SH_5**	362	604	234	335.53	339.336	347.017	25.569	26.8118	23.331	14.206	**
6	**SH_6**	353	600	247	336.853	338.383	346.899	27.1127	25.8846	23.7218	12.518	**
7	**SH_7**	330	637	233	335.191	339.929	345.386	26.9584	26.2762	22.9999	10.668	**
8	**SHT**	304	598	298	334.872	337.467	349.05	27.852	25.4801	22.952	27.75	**

** Significant at 0.01 level

(5) Preparation for examinations, (6) General habits and attitudes and (7) School Environment and also in Study Habits Total Score have Significantly better Moral Values than other two groups. It is concluded that better Study Habits leads to better Moral Values.

MULTIPLE REGRESSION ANALYSIS

This section deals with the analysis of the relative contribution or magnitude of the effect of each of the different independent variables to the dependent variable.

The analysis is presented in 5 parts. Moral Value Scores (MVS) is the dependent variable for all the parts. There are 56 variables for the purpose of regression analysis in this study. 55 variables are independent variables and 1 variable is dependent. The Variable Number (VN) description of the variable and symbol used are presented in Table 42.

Variable Number (VN) 56 that is Moral Value Scores in the Table 5.34 is dependent variable and all the other 55 variables are independent variables in this study. The Moral Values are very important for all types of students in the society. Moral Values have relation with Personality Factors, Study Habits and Self-Concepts and Socio-Demographic variables.

TABLE 5.34: Variables used for Regression Analysis

Variable No.	Variable	Symbol
1	College	C
2	Age	A
3	Family Annual Income	FAI
4	Educational Qualification Mother	EQM
5	Educational Qualification of Father	EQF
6	Father Occupation	FO
7	Mother Occupation	MO
8	Birth Order	BO

(*contd.*)

Variable No.	Variable	Symbol
9	Total Members in the Family	TMF
10	Residence	R
11	Sex	S
12	Community	Co
13	Caste	Ca
14	Native Place	NP
15	Family Economic Position	FEP
16	Medium of Study	MS
17	Religious Festivals	RF
18	Religious Discourses	RD
19	Visiting Temple	VT
20	When you go wrong who corrects you	WW
21	Type of Family	TF
22	Group Subjects	GS
23	Reserved Vs Outgoing (HSPQ-A)	HA
24	Less Intelligent Vs More Intelligent (HSPQ-B)	HB
25	Emotionally less stable Vs Emotionally stable (HSPQ-C)	HC
26	Phlegmatic Vs Excitable (HSPQ-D)	HD
27	Obedient Vs Assertive (HSPQ-E)	HE
28	Sober Vs Happy go lucky (HSPQ-F)	HF
29	Moral standards Vs Super ego strength (HSPQ-G)	HG
30	Shy Vs Venturesome (HSPQ-H)	HH
31	Though minded Vs Tense minded (HSPQ-I)	HI
32	Vigorous Vs Doubting (HSPQ-J)	HJ
33	Placid Vs Apprehensive (HSPQ-O)	HO
34	Group dependent Vs Self-sufficient (HSPQ-Q_2)	HQ_2
35	Undisciplined Vs Controlled (HSPQ-Q_3)	HQ_3
36	Relaxed Vs Tense (HSPQ-Q_4)	HQ_4
37	(Self-concept-A)	SC_1
38	(Self-concept-B)	SC_2

Variable No.	Variable	Symbol
39	(Self-concept-E)	SC_3
40	(Self-concept-F)	SC_4
41	(Self-concept-H)	SC_5
42	(Self-concept-P)	SC_6
43	(Self-concept-S_1)	SC_7
44	(Self-concept-S_2)	SC_8
45	(Self-concept-S_3)	SC_9
46	(Self-concept-W)	SC_{10}
47	(Self-concept-T)	SCT
48	Home environment and Planning of Work	SH_1
49	Reading and note taking	SH_2
50	Planning of subject	SH_3
51	Habits of concentration	SH_4
52	Preparation for examination	SH_5
53	General Habits and attitudes	SH_6
54	School Environment	SH_7
55	Total Study Habits Score	SHT
56	Moral Value Score	MVS

Prediction of Moral Value Scores (MVS) with the help of Socio-Demographic variables

The relative contribution of 22 Socio-Demographic variables (variables 1 to 22 in Table 5.34) to the dependent variable MVS (variable 56 in Table 5.34) is studied with the help of Multiple Regression Analysis. The results of regression analysis are presented in Table 5.35.

It could be seen from Table 5.35 that the first variable entered into the step-wise regression analysis is sex (S). The multiple correlation (R) obtained is 0.198, indicating that the strength of the relationship between the two variables (MVS and S) is about 20 per cent. It could seen that the R is significant

TABLE 5.35: Prediction of Moral Values with the help of Socio-Demographic Variables

Sl No	IV (VN)	R	R^2	SER	F-Value for R	b(VN)	t-Value for b	Constant A	β	r	% of Variance
1	2	3	4	5	6	7	8	9	10	11	12
1	**S (11)**	0.198	0.039	25.5721	48.655**	10.298 (11)	6.975**	324.238	0.198	0.0198	3.92
					(1, 1198)		-1198				
2	**C (01)**	0.253	0.064	25.2485	40.904**	10.075 (11)	6.909**	339.285	0.193	-0.163	3.821
					(2, 1197)	-7.443 (01)	5.648**		-0.158		2.575
							-1197				
3	**R (10)**	0.286	0.082	25.0159	35.568**	10.619 (11)	7.328**	351.978	0.204	-0.079	4.039
					(3, 1196)	-8.889 (01)	6.636**		-0.189		3.08
						-7.192 (10)	4.834**		-0.138		1.09
							-1196				
4	**A (02)**	0.299	0.089	24.9248	29.309**	10.061(11)	6.915**	362.305	0.193	-0.083	3.821
					(4, 1195)	-9.223 (01)	6.889**		-0.196		3.319
						-7.900 (10)	5.268**		-0.151		1.192
						-4.041(02)	3.123**		-0.088		0.73
							-1195				

5	**Ca (13)**	0.305	0.093	24.8829	24.533**	9.638 (11)	6.580**	358.355	0.185	0.076	3.663
					(5, 1194)	-9.825 (01)	7.207**		-0.209		3.406
						-6.617 (10)	4.129**		-0.127		1.003
						-4.074 (02)	3.153**		-0.089		0.738
						2.271 (13)	2.243*		0.069		0.524
							-1194				

** Significant at 0.01 level * Significant at 0.05 level VN Variable Number IV Independent Variable

(F = 48.655) beyond 0.01 level of significance for 1 and 1198 df. The coefficient of multiple R^2 is 0.039. This shows that 3.9 per cent of the variance is MVS is accounted by S.

The standard error of R (SER) is 25.5721. From this it may be inferred that nearly 68% of the actual MVS value would lie with in M $\pm$ 25.5721 of MVS value predicted with the help of this variable (S).

The partial regression co-efficient (b) presented in column-7 is 10.298. This value indicates that the MVS value would change by 10.298 units for every unit of change in S. The 't' value for 'b' is 6.975, which is highly significant at 0.01 level (column-8). The value of constant that could be written to predict MVS at this stage is 324.238.

The general form of the multiple regression equation may be written as:

$$Y = A + b_1(X1) + b_2\ (X_2) + b_3(X_3) + \ldots + b_n(X_n)$$

where Y is the predicted score on the dependent variable; A is a constant;

b_1, b_2, b_3, . . . bn are partial regression coefficients; and

X_1, X_2, X_3, . . . X_n are the scores on different independent variables.

Thus, the multiple regression equation at the end of this step could be written as: MVS = 324.238 +10.298 (S)

College (C) entered into the step-wise regression analysis as the second most significant variable. The multiple correlation (R) between MVS on one side, and S and C on the other side is 0.253. Thus, the strength of the relationship between MVS and the two independent variables put together is 25.30% . R is significant at 0.01 level (F = 40.904 at 2, 1197df).

The value of R^2 is 0.064. This shows that the two variables put together could explain 6.4% of variance in the dependent variable MVS. Out of this 3.821% of variance is explained by

S and the remaining 2.575% of variance is accounted by C (Table 5.35, Column-12).

The regression equation to predict MVS with these two variables (S and C) as predictor variables is:

$$MVS = 339.285 + 10.075\ (S) - 7.443\ (C)$$

Where 339.285 is the constant to be considered at this step and 10.075 and -7.443 are partial regression coefficients, and S and C are scores on Sex and College respectively. The 'b' values for these variables are significant at 0.01 level.

There are 5 variables out of 22 socio-demographic variables contributed to predict MVS. These 5 variables are 1.Sex (S), 2. College (C), 3. Residence (R), 4. Age (A) and 5. Caste (Ca). All these 5 socio-demographic variables could explain 9.3% of variance in MVS. The regression equation at the end of 5th step is;

$$MVS = 358.355 + 9.638\ (S) - 9.825\ (C) - 6.617\ (R) - 4.074\ (A) + 2.271\ (Ca)$$

It is observed from Table 5.35 that it could be possible to explain 9.3% of variance with the help of the above five variables in the dependent variable MVS.

It is concluded that the Moral Value Scores could be best predicted with the help of five socio-demographic variables namely 1. Sex (S), 2. College (C), 3. Residence (R), 4. Age (A) and 5. Caste (Ca) out of 22 socio-demographic variables.

Prediction of Moral Value Scores with the help of Personality Factors

In this analysis 14 personality factors of HSPQ (variables 23-36, Table 5.34) are treated as independent variables and MVS (variable 56, Table 5.34) as dependent variable. The effect of 14 personality factors on MVS is pridicted. The results are shown in Table 5.36.

TABLE 5.36: Prediction of Moral Values with the help of HSPQ

Sl. No	IV (VN)	R	R^2	SER	F-Value for R	b(VN)	t-Value for b	Constant A	β	r	% of Variance
1	2	3	4	5	6	7	8	9	10	11	12
1	**HQ_4 (36)**	0.145	0.021	25.8096	25.812**	-5.423 (36)	5.081**	351.182	-0.145	-0.145	2.102
					(1, 1198)		-1198				
2	**HQ_3 (35)**	0.174	0.03	25.7007	18.603**	-4.473 (36)	4.066**	356.95	-0.12	-0.129	1.74
					(2, 1197)	-3.659 (35)	3.343**		-0.098		1.264
							-1197				
3	**HE (27)**	0.196	0.038	25.6042	15.843**	-4.704 (36)	4.283**	365.451	-0.126	-0.068	1.827
					(3, 1196)	-3.955 (35)	3.614**		-0.106		1.367
						-3.246 (27)	3.169**		-0.091		0.618
							-1196				
4	**HO (33)**	0.21	0.044	25.5338	13.848**	-4.198 (36)	3.779**	368.846	-0.112	-0.112	1.624
					(4, 1195)	-3.729 (35)	3.407**		-0.1		1.29
						-3.220 (27)	3.152**		-0.09		0.612
						-2.976 (33)	2.757**		-0.08		0.896
							-1195				

5	**HG (29)**	0.22	0.048	25.4921	12.098**	-4.303 (36)	3.876**	365.566	-0.115	0.035	1.667
					(5, 1194)	-4.045 (35)	3.671**		-0.109		1.406
						-3.228 (27)	3.166**		-0.09		0.612
						-3.027 (33)	2.808**		-0.081		0.907
						2.202 (29)	2.217*		0.063		0.22
							-1194				
6	**HC (25)**	0.228	0.052	25.4542	10.871**	-3.965 (36)	3.541**	358.476	-0.106	0.097	1.537
					(6, 1193)	-3.887 (35)	3.525**		-0.105		1.354
						-3.291 (27)	3.231**		-0.092		0.625
						-2.798 (33)	2.586**		-0.075		0.84
						2.258 (29)	2.276*		0.065		0.227
						3.385 (25)	2.135*		0.062		0.601
							-1193				

** Significant at 0.01 level   * Significant at 0.05 level   VN Variable Number   IV Independent Variable

In this step-wise multiple regression analysis, the first independent variable that entered is Factor-Q_4 (HQ_4) that is variable 36 in the Table 5.34. The values of R and R^2 at this stage are 0.145 and 0.021 respectively. Thus, the amount of variance in MVS explained by this variable is 2.1%. The 't' value for 'b' is 5.081. It is significant at 0.01level (for 1198 df). The value of constant is 351.132. The standard error of R (SER) is 25.8096. From this it may be inferred that nearly 68% of the actual MVS value would lie with in $M \pm 25.8096$ of MVS value predicted with the help of this variable (HQ_4).

The multiple regression equation could be written as:

$$MVS = 351.182\text{-}5.423\ (HQ_4)$$

Six personality factors viz., 1. Factor-Q_4 (Relaxed Vs Tense), 2. Factor-Q_3 (Undisciplined Vs Controlled), 3. Factor E (Obedient Vs Assertive), 4. Factor O (Placid Vs Apprehensive), 5. Factor G (Moral Standards Vs Super ego strength) and 6. Factor C (Emotionally less stable Vs Emotionally Stable) contributed 5.2% of variance in MVS. The 't' values of 'b' for the variables HQ_4 (36), HQ_3 (35), HE (27) and HO (33) are significant at 0.01 level for 1193df and for variables HG (29) and HC(25) are significant at 0.05 level for 1193 df. The value of constant is 358.476.

The regression equation at the end of 6th step could be written as:

$$MVS = 358.476 - 3.965(HQ_4) - 3.887(HQ_3) - 3.291(HE) - 2.798\ (HO) + 2.258\ (HG) + 3.385\ (FC)$$

It is observed from Table 5.36 that it could be possible to explain 5.2% of variance with the help of the above six variables in the variable MVS.

It is concluded that the Moral Value Scores could be best predicted with the help of six Personality Factors namely 1) Factor-Q_4 (HQ_4), 2) Factor-Q_3 (HQ_3), 3) Factor-E (HE), 4) Factor-O (HO), 5) Factor-G (HG) and 6) Factor-C (HC) out of 14 Personality Factors of HSPQ.

Prediction of MVS with the help of Self-Concepts

With the help of 10 areas of Self-concepts and Self-concepts total score (variables 37-47, Table 5.34); MVS is predicted and the results are presented in Table 5.37.

The first predictor variable entered into the multiple regression analysis is self-concepts area SC_2 (Abilities). The R obtained is 0.202 (Column-3, Table 5.37). The 'F' value of R is 51.097 (Column-6, Table 5.37). Hence it is significant at 0.01 level for 1 and 1998 df. The R^2 value is 0.041 (Column-4, Table-45). Therefore it could be inferred that 4.1% of variance in MVS is contributed by this variable. The partial regression coefficient 'b' is 7.567 (Column-7, Table 5.37). It is significant at 0.01 level. This shows that the change in MVS is by 7.567 units for every unit of change in SC_2. The Constant value is 325.113 (Column-9, Table 5.37). The standard error of multiple R (SER) is 25.5470. From this it may be inferred that nearly 68% of the actual MVS value would lie with in M $\pm$ 25.5470 of MVS value predicted with the help of this variable SC_2 (Abilities).

The regression equation could be written as:

$$MVS = 325.113+7.567\ (SC_2)$$

There are four steps in this regression analysis. The 4 variables of self-concepts that have contributed for Moral Values are 1) SC_2 (Abilities), 2) SC_5 (Worthiness), 3) SC_9 (Sociability) and 4) SC_4 (Self-acceptance).

All these four variables could be able to explain 6.1% of variance in the dependent variable MVS.

The multiple regression equation at the end of forth step could be written as:

$$MVS = 321.351 + 6.093(SC_2) + 3.304(SC_5) - 2.725\ (SC_9) + 2.634\ (SC_4)$$

TABLE 5.37: Prediction of Moral Values with the help of Self Concepts

Sl. No	IV (VN)	R	R^2	SER	F-Value for R	b(VN)	t-Value for b	Constant A	2	r	% of Variance
1	2	3	4	5	6	7	8	9	10	11	12
1	**SC_2(38)**	0.202	0.041	25.547	51.097**	7.567 (38)	7.148**	325.113	0.202	0.202	4.08
					(1, 1198)		-1198				
2	**SC_5(41)**	0.222	0.049	25.4445	31.093**	6.789 (38)	6.282**	319.732	0.181	0.134	3.656
					(2, 1197)	3.705 (41)	3.268**		0.094		1.259
							-1197				
3	**SC_9(45)**	0.235	0.055	25.3751	23.359**	6.736 (38)	6.248**	325.037	0.18	-0.087	2.636
					(3, 1196)	3.555 (41)	3.141**		0.091		1.219
						-2.680 (45)	2.748**		-0.077		0.669
							-1196				
4	**SC_4(40)**	0.247	0.061	25.3124	19.341**	6.093 (38)	5.525**	321.351	0.163	0.127	3.292
					(4, 1195)	3.304 (41)	2.915**		0.084		1.125
						-2.725 (45)	2.801**		-0.079		0.687
						2.856 (40)	2.634**		0.076		0.965
							-1195				

** Significant at 0.01 level * Significant at 0.05 level VN Variable Number IV Independent Variable

It is observed from Table 5.37 that it could be possible to explain 6.1% of variance with the help of the above four variables in the dependent variable MVS.

It is concluded that the Moral Value Scores could be best predicted with the help of 1. Abilities (SC_2), 2. Worthiness (SC_5), 3. Sociability (SC_9) and 4. Self Acceptance (SC_4) of self-concepts among the areas of self-concepts.

Prediction of MVS with the help of Study Habits

With the help of seven areas of study habits and study habits total score (variables 48-55, Table 5.34); MVS is predicted and the results are presented in Table 5.38.

The standard error of R (SER) is 25.60006 (column-5, Table 5.38). From this it may be inferred that nearly 68% of the actual MVS value would lie with in M $\pm$ 25.60006 of MVS value predicted with the help of this variable SHT (Study Habits Total score). The R and R^2 values are 0.0192 and 0.037 respectively (columns 3, 4; Table 5.38)

The partial regression coefficient 'b' presented in the column-7 is 7.067. This value indicates that the MVS value would be change by 7.067 units for every unit of change in SHT. The 't' value for 'b' is 6.773, which is highly significant at 0.01 level for 1998 df (column-8, Table 5.38). The value of constant that could be written to predict MVS at this stage is 325.587.

The multiple regression equation at the end of this step could be written as:

MVS = 325.587+7.067 (SHT)

There are only two steps in this step-wise multiple regression analysis. The second and last variable SH_5 (Preparation for Examination) is entered into the multiple regression analysis. The multiple correlation (R) between MVS on one side, and SHT and SH_5 on the other side is 0.0206. Thus, the strength of the relationship between MVS and the two independent

TABLE 5.38: Prediction of Moral Values with the help of Study Habits

S No	IV (VN)	R	R^2	SER	F-Value for R	b(VN)	t-Value for b	Constant A	2	r	% of Variance
1	2	3	4	5	6	7	8	9	10	11	12
1	**SHT (55)**	0.0192	0.037	25.6001	45.871** (1, 1198)	7.067 (56)	6.773** -1198	325.587	0.192	0.192	3.68
2	**SH_5 (52)**	0.0206	0.043	25.536	26.589** (2, 1197)	5.813 (56)	5.087**	322.239	0.158	0.148	3.033
						3.090 (53)	2.660** -1197		0.083		1.228

** Significant at 0.01 level * Significant at 0.05 level VN Variable Number IV Independent Variable

variables put together is 20.6%. The 'F' value of R is 26.589 and it is significant at 0.01 level for 2, 1997df.

The value of R^2 is 0.043. This shows that the two variables put together could explain 4.3% of variance in the dependent variable Moral Value Scores. Out of this 3.033% of variance is explained by SHT and the remaining 1.228% of variance is accounted by SH_5 (column-12, Table-46).

The regression equation to predict MVS with these two variables (SHT and SH_5) is written as:

$$MVS = 322.239+5.813\ (SHT)\ +3.090(SH_5)$$

It is observed from the Table-46 that it could be possible to explain 4.3% of variance with the help of the above two variables in the variable MVS.

It is concluded that Moral Value Scores could be best predicted with the help of 1) Study Habits Total score (SHT) and 2) Preparation for Examination (SH_5) out of 8 variables of study habits.

5.7.5 Prediction of Moral Values with the help of all the 55 Independent variables

With the help of all 55 independent variables (variables 1-55, Table 5.34), the Moral Value Scores of Intermediate Students is predicted, and the results are presented in Table 5.39.

The first most significant variable in the step-wise regression analysis is SC_2.The standard error of R (SER) in the Table 5.39 (column-5) is 25.5470. From this it may be interred that nearly 68% of the actual MVS value would lie with in M $\pm$ 25.5470 of MVS value predicted with the help of the variable SC_2 (column-2, Table 5.39).

The partial regression coefficient 'b' presented in column-7 is 7.567. This value indicates that the MVS value would change by 7.567 units for every unit of change in SC_2. The

TABLE 5.39: Prediction of Moral Values with the help of 55 Independent Variables

S No	IV (VN)	R	R^2	SER	F-Value for R	b(VN)	t-Value for b	Constant A	2	r	% of Variance
1	2	3	4	5	6	7	8	9	10	11	12
1	**SC_2(38)**	0.202	0.041	25.547	51.097**	7.567 (38)	7.148**	325.113	0.202	0.202	4.08
					(1, 1198)		-1198				
2	**S (11)**	0.259	0.067	25.2054	43.093**	6.393 (38)	6.009**	314.468	0.171	0.198	3.454
					(2, 1197)	8.604 (11)	5.805**		0.165.		3.267
							(1197)				
3	**C (01)**	0.295	0.087	24.948	37.933**	5.803 (38)	5.478**	328.828	0.155	-0.163	3.131
					(3, 1196)	8.561 (11)	5.835**		0.164		3.247
						-6.657(01)	5.082**		-0.141		2.298
							(1196)				
4	**R (10)**	0.327	0.107	24.6786	35.887**	6.112 (38)	5.823**	341.815	0.163	-0.079	3.292
					(4, 1195)	9.061 (11)	6.229**		0.174		3.445
						-8.158 (01)	6.146**		-0.173		2.819
						-7.674 (10)	5.220**		-0.147		1.161
							(1195)				

5	**SHT (55)**	0.341	0.116	24.5642	31.411**	4.613 (38)	4.083**	336.86	0.123	0.192	2.484
					(5, 1194)	8.640 (11)	5.947**		0.166		3.286
						-7.720 (01)	5.817**		-0.164		2.673
						-7.734(10)	5.285**		-0.148		1.169
						3.857 (55)	3.487**		0.105		2.016
							(1194)				
6	**A (02)**	0.35	0.123	24.4832	27.835**	4.554 (38)	4.044**	346.751	0.122	-0.083	2.464
					(6, 1193)	8.140 (11)	5.585**		0.156		3.088
						-8.049 (01)	6.064**		-0.171		2.787
						-8.393 (10)	5.690**		-0.161		1.271
						3.811 (55)	3.457**		0.104		1.996
						-3.797 (02)	2.986**		-0.083		0.688
							(1193)				
7	**HE (27)**	0.359	0.129	24.413	25.120**	4.311 (38)	3.828**	351.673	0.115	-0.068	2.323
					(7, 1192)	8.981 (11)	6.052**		0.0172		3.405
						-7.783 (01)	5.865**		-0.165		2.689
						-8.357 (10)	5.681**		-0.16		1.264
						3.757 (55)	3.417**		1.102		1.958
						-3.719 (02)	2.932**		-0.081		0.672
						-2.787 (27)	2.805**		-0.078		
							(1192)				

1	2	3	4	5	6	7	8	9	10	11	12
8	**SC_4 (40)**	0.364	0.132	24.3724	22.675**	3.800 (38)	3.311**	347.92	0.102	0.127	2.06
					(8, 1191)	8.942 (11)	6.035**		0.172		3.405
						-7.801 (01)	5.888**		-0.166		2.705
						-8.090 (10)	5.491**		-0.155		1.224
						3.604 (55)	3.277**		0.098		1.881
						-3.672 (02)	2.900**		-0.08		0.664
						-2.710 (27)	2.730**		-0.076		0.516
						2.334 (40)	2.231**		0.062		0.787
							(1191)				
9	**SC_9 (45)**	0.368	0.136	24.3357	20.726**	3.797 (38)	3.314**	351.5	0.101	-0.087	2.04
					(9, 1190)	8.736(11)	5.892**		0.168		3.326
						-7.649 (01)	5.775**		-0.162		2.64
						-8.037 (10)	5.462**		-0.154		1.216
						3.533 (55)	3.216**		0.096		1.843
						-3.658 (02)	2.893**		-0.08		0.664
						-2.669 (27)	2.692**		-0.074		0.503
						2.372 (40)	2.270*		0.063		0.8
						-2.010 (45)	2.142*		-0.058		0.504
							(1190)				

** Significant at 0.01 level* Significant at 0.05 level**VN** - Variable Number**IV** - Independent Variable

't' value for 'b' is 7.148, which is highly significant at 0.01 level (column-8, Table 5.39). The value of constant that could be written to predict MVS at this stage is 325.113.

The multiple regression equation at the end of the first step could be written as:

$$MVS = 325.113+7.567\ (SC_2)$$

Sex (S) is entered into the step-wise regression analysis as the second most significant variable. The multiple correlation (R) between MVS on one side and SC_2 and S on the other side is 0.259. Thus, the strength of the relationship between MVS and the two independent variables put together 25.90%. The 'F' value of R is 43.093 (column-6, Table 5.39), which is significant at 0.01 level for 2, 1197df.

The value of R^2 is 0.067. This shows that the two variables put together could explain 6.7% of variance in the dependent variable Moral Value Scores. Out of this 3.454% of variance is explained by SC_2 and the remaining 3.267% of variance is accounted by sex 'S' (column-12, Table 5.39).

The regression equation to predict MVS with these two variables (SC_2 and S) as predictor variables is:

$$MVS= 314.468+6.393(SC_2)\ +8.604\ (S)$$

Where 314.468 is the constant to be considered at this step, 6.393 and 8.604 are partial regression coefficients; SC_2 and S are scores on Abilities (self-concepts) and Sex respectively. The 'b' values for the variables are significant at 0.01 level.

There would not be much increase in R^2 after the 9th step. The regression equation at the end of 9th step would be written as:

$$MVS = 351.500+3.797\ (SC_2)\ +8.736\ (S)-7.649\ (C)-8.037\ (R)\ +3.533\ (SHT)-3.658\ (A)-2.669\ (HE)\ +2.372\ (SC_4)-2.010\ (SC_9)$$

It is observed from Table 5.39 that it could be possible to explain 13.6% of va riance with the help of the above nine variables in the variable MVS.

It is concluded that the Moral Value Scores could be best predicted with the help of

1. Sex (S),
2. College (C),
3. Residence (R),
4. Age (A) of socio-demographic variables,
5. Study Habits Total score (SHT), of study habits variable,
6. Factor-E (HE), of HSPQ,
7. Abilities (SC_2),
8. Self-acceptance (SC_4) and
9. Sociability (SC_9)

of self-concepts variables among the 55 independent variables.

6

Summary, Findings, Conclusions, Recommendations and Suggestions

This chapter deals with the Summary, Major findings, Conclusions, Recommendations and Suggestions for further research.

6.1 SUMMARY

Value is "something which pervades everything. It determines the meaning of the world as a whole, as well as the meaning of every person, every event, and every action. It can be said of every thing that is either good or bad; it can be said whether it must not be, or that it ought not to exist, that its existence is right or wrong" (Lossky and Marshall, 1935).

Values are the desirable ends, goals or modes of action which makes human behaviour selective. Value not only orients but also determines human behaviour.

The epics, the *Ramayana* and the *Mahabharata* contain many morals, from which we can learn how to live and conduct ourselves in various situations. The epics are meant for the laymen, people who are serious about their religious duties and salvation, but not enough to make it the single most important thing in their lives and pursue it steadfastly. Since they are in narrative form, their messages, morals and lessons are easy to understand and remember. For the last several centuries, both the epics served people well by inculcating in them a deep sense of reverence, devotion, commitment to the path of righteousness and belief and interest in the life beyond.

Moral education is becoming an increasingly popular topic in the fields of psychology and education. Media reports of increased violent juvenile crime, teenage pregnancy, and suicide have caused many to declare a moral crisis in our nation. While not all of these social concerns are moral in nature, and most have complex origins, there is a growing trend towards linking the solutions to these and related social problems to the teaching of moral and social values in our schools and colleges.

6.1.1 Introduction

Moral values are the standards of good and evil, which govern an individual's behaviour and choices. Individual's morals may derive from society and government, religion, or self. When moral values derive from society and government they, of necessity, may change as the laws and morals of the society change. An example of the impact of changing laws on moral values may be seen in the case of marriage vs. living together.

Moral values also derive from within one's own self. This is clearly demonstrated in the behaviour of older infants and young toddlers. If a child has been forbidden to touch or take a certain object early on, they know enough to slowly look over their shoulder to see if they are being observed before touching said object. There is no need for this behaviour to be taught; it is instinctive. Once, however, any form of discipline is applied to modify the child's behaviour, the child now gains the capacity within himself to distinguish his right behaviour from his wrong behaviour. Now, the child can make correct choices based on his own knowledge. The choices that are made by an individual from childhood to adulthood are between forbidden and acceptable, kind or cruel, generous or selfish. A person may, under any given set of circumstances, decide to do what is forbidden. If this individual possesses moral values, going against them usually produces guilt.

6.1.2 Statement of the Problem

The present study is concerned with the Attitude of Intermediate Students towards Moral Values in relation with certain variables. It examines the differences in the attitudes of intermediate students towards moral values residing in the rural and urban areas, private, aided and government colleges. The study is designed to make an in depth study of Moral Values in relation with certain Socio-Demographic variables, Study Habits, Self –concepts and Personality factors of Intermediate Students.

6.1.3 Title of the Problem

The title of the present study is stated as "Moral Values of Intermediate Students".

6.1.4 Need for the Study

Modern mass society presents a sharp contrast, as the young grow up. They are faced with confusions, delays and discontinuities. Adolescents in particular are uncertain about themselves. Some are in conflict with themselves, bewildered an insecure. In one-way or another, many children are not of step with the life. In short, society is less well coordinated today than at earlier time to advance children into adult.

It follows from what has been said that schools in many complexes industrially developing nations are faced with difficult tasks. They are asked to educate the young, not only in such skills as the three R's but also in many social aspects of culture; they are asked to acculturate young people.

Schools are expected to teach the moral values of society when the values themselves are in conflict. Moreover in the modern world, it is not enough to shape learners in the image of their elders. The aim is to transform young human beings, to teach them to be different-better, more successful and so on-than their parents. This effort to change, to improve, is the most striking feature of present schooling as compared to traditional, tribalistic education.

The problem of values is a more general one, common to all fields of human activity, but often education is looked upon as the instrument for inculcating values.

Our present system of education lacks value education. Value education is the need of the hour. One should grow as respectful citizen of the society and must learn to respect his own members of family. He should behave in a manner, which provides an impression of him having a good social background

Values are usually influenced by the changing philosophical ideologies, cultural and religious perspectives, social, political and geographical conditions. In modern emerging Indian society, there has been a revolutionary change in the field of values due to many factors in addition to the influence of westernized culture, industrialization, moderanisation, urbanization, globalization and multinationals. Therefore, it is necessary to make a synthesis of the traditional and modern social values. Now it is very essential to concentrate on holistic approach of education so that all types of values may inculcate in the learner group for their all round, harmonious development. It is very amazing that in the modern materialistic society, the individual has totally concentrated on the economic value and by all means, he bothers to earn money and it seems that this is the only prime aim of one's life now.

It is therefore essential to explore and identify concrete devices for the incorporation of values in education. Education should be a strong instrument to attain our national goals. Value education is at the root of this process, as values incorporate, digested in the system will enable people to achieve these goals.

6.1.5 Purpose of the Study

Through value education, we may promote a balanced development of physical, mental, social, cultural, emotional, moral and spiritual aspects of the learners so that we may produce balanced and adjusted citizens who strive to promote social progress and welfare.

In the context of social change, the main objective of education is not only to impart information. But to inculcate the values of humanism, democracy, socialism, secularism, altruism and integration.

The present study aims at investigating the pattern of the Moral Values of the Intermediate students related to certain variables. The purpose of the study is an attempt to answer the following aspects:

1. What is the position of values in the present scenario?
2. Whether there is any relationship between personality factors and moral values of the students?
3. Whether there is any relationship between study habits and moral values of the students?
4. Whether there is any relationship between self-concept and moral values of the students?
5. Whether the socio-demographic variables have any impact on Moral Values of the students?

6.1.6 Scope of the Study

The main intention of the study is to make a survey of Moral Values of Intermediate students in Rural and Urban areas;

Government, Aided and Private Colleges; Residential and Non-residential; Boys and Girls; Group Subjects and Medium of Study.

The study attempted to identify the type of relation between the dependent variable (Moral Values) and independent variables viz., Personality Factors, Study Habits, Self-concepts, Socio-Demographic variables.

6.1.7 Objectives of the Study

The study is designed with the following specific objectives:

1. To study the attitude of Intermediate students towards Moral Values.
2. To study the influence of Personality Factors on the attitude of students towards Moral Values.
3. To study the impact of Study Habits on the attitude of students towards Moral Values.
4. To study the influence of Self-concepts on the Moral Values of Intermediate Students.
5. To know the influence of Socio-Demographic variables on the attitude of students towards Moral Values.

6.1.8 Hypotheses

Based on the above objectives, the following hypotheses were formulated for the purpose of the study.

1. In general there would not be good Moral Values among Intermediate students.
2. There would be no significant influence of the main effects namely sex and college on the Moral Values.
3. There would be no significant interaction effect of sex x college on Moral Values.
4. There would be no significant influence of the main effects of community and caste on Moral Values.

5. There would be no significant interaction effect of community x caste on the Moral Values.
6. There is no significant influence of Personality Factors on the attitude of students towards Moral Values.
7. There is no significant impact of Self-concepts on the attitude of students towards Moral Values.
8. There wouldn't be significant influence of Study Habits on the attitude of students towards Moral Values.
9. There is no significant influence of Socio-Demographic variables on the attitude of students towards Moral Values.
10. Socio-Demographic variables, Personality Factors, Self-concepts and Study Habits would not turnout to be the significant predictors of Moral Values.
11. No independent variable out of 55 turnouts to be significant predictor of Moral Values.

5.1.9 Variables Included in the Study

The review of literature in the field of Moral Values reveals the fact that the Moral Values of the students have been influenced by a number of psycho-sociological variables collectively. Hence the following psycho-sociological variables are included in the study. Out of total variables 55 are independent variables and one is dependent variable. 22 were Socio-Economic Factors and Socio-Demographic variables for which information was gathered through a personal data sheet.

A.Independent Variables

1. Socio-Demographic Variables.

1. College
2. Age
3. Family Annual Income
4. Educational Qualification of Father

5. Educational Qualification of Mother
6. Father Occupation
7. Mother Occupation
8. Birth Order
9. Total Members in the Family
10. Residence
11. Sex
12. Community
13. Caste
14. Native Place
15. Economic Position
16. Medium of the Study
17. Religious Festivals
18. Religious Discourses
19. Visiting Temple
20. When you go wrong who corrects you,
21. Type of Family
22. Group Subjects

2. Psychological Variables.

a) *Personality Factors of HSPQ.*

1. Factor A (Reserved vs. Outgoing)
2. Factor B (Less Intelligent vs. More Intelligent)
3. Factor C (Emotionally less stable vs. More Intelligent)
4. Factor D (Phlegmatic vs. Excitable)
5. Factor E (Obedient vs. Assertive)
6. Factor F (Sober vs. Happy go lucky)
7. Factor G (Moral Standards vs. Super ego strength)
8. Factor H (Shy vs. Venturesome)

9. Factor I (Though minded vs. Tense minded)
10. Factor J (Vigorous vs. Doubting)
11. Factor O (Placid vs. Apprehensive)
12. Factor Q_2 (Group Dependent vs. Controlled)
13. Factor Q_3 (Undisciplined vs. Controlled)
14. Factor Q_4 (Relaxed vs. Tense)

b) Self-concepts

1. Health and Sex Appropriateness
2. Abilities
3. Self-confidence
4. Self-acceptance
5. Worthiness
6. Present, Past and Future
7. Beliefs and Convictions
8. Feeling of Shame and Guilt
9. Sociability
10. Emotional Maturity
11. Self-concepts Total Score

c) Study Habits

1. Home environment and planning of work
2. Reading and note-taking
3. Planning of subject
4. Habits of concentration
5. Preparation for examinations
6. General habits and attitudes
7. School environment
8. Study Habits Total Score

B. Dependent Variable:

Attitude scores of Intermediate Students towards Moral Values are taken as the dependent variable.

5.1.10 Research Tools

The tools used for present study are:

1) Attitude Scale of Moral Values (MV).
2) High School Personality Questionnaire (HSPQ)
3) Study Habits Inventory
4) Self-concepts Scale
5) Socio-Demographic Scale

6.1.11 Sample

The sample of the investigation consisted of 1200 Senior Intermediate College Students. The stratified random sampling was applied. There are three types of managements Aided, Private and Government in intermediate education system both in rural and urban areas. 16 colleges were selected in the above mentioned areas of management and locality by covering all the revenue divisions in the Chittoor District of Andhra Pradesh State. In total 600 girls and 600 boys were included in the above study. The sample frame is $3 \times 3 \times 2$ factorial design with three types of managements situated in three types of locality namely: 1) City/municipal town, 2) Small Town and 3) Village with two divisions in gender.

6.1.12 Collection of Data

The investigator obtained the list of colleges in the district along with strength particulars of the students from the district authorities concerned. Colleges were selected using stratified random sampling technique. The Principals of the colleges were requested to permit the researcher for collection of data in their institutions. The programme and the time schedule were communicated to all the heads of the colleges well in advance and obtained permission from them.

In each college, the required number of senior intermediate students had been selected using random sampling method. The students were well motivated before attempting the tests.

The booklets and answer sheets were distributed among the selected students. The instructions were read out and the purpose of investigation was explained to motivate them to give answers in a proper manner. Sufficient time was provided for the students to give answers to the questionnaires. The investigator took care to ensure that all the questions were answered by the students following the instructions.

Moral Values Inventory and HSPQ were distributed in the morning one after the other with a break of 10 minutes. After the completion of sufficient time the investigator had collected the booklets and answer sheets.

In the afternoon the Socio-Demographic Scale, Self-concept Scale and Study Habits Inventory were distributed one after another to the same group of students with a break of 10 minutes between each test. Students were instructed on how to answer each questionnaire. They were assured that the information given by them would be kept confidential. The investigator requested the students to respond to the questions genuinely to help him to find solutions to the research problems. The investigator helped the students wherever they raise doubts in understanding the questions.

After successful completion of the test, the investigator collected the booklets and answer sheets thanking the students for their good cooperation.

6.1.13 Scoring and Analysis

The Moral Values Inventory and Self-concepts were scored on a 5 point scale by giving weightages 5, 4, 3, 2 and 1 for positive items and 1, 2, 3, 4 and 5 for negative items to the five alternatives-strongly agree, agree, doubtful, disagree and strongly disagree. The study habits inventory was scored in similar manner to the five alternatives-always, often, sometimes, seldom and never. The scoring keys prepared by the concerned authors for HSPQ questionnaire and Socio-demographic scale were employed. The information furnished by the students on socio-demographic variables was also numerically coded in order to suit the data for the computer analysis.

The analysis was carried out on the basis of objectives of the study and hypotheses formulated by employing appropriate statistical techniques. 14 personality factors (HSPQ) were divided into sub-groups on the basis of sten values. Each factor was divided into three groups. Other continuous variables (study habits and self-concepts) were divided into sub-groups on the basis of quartile values.

6.1.14 Statistical Techniques Employed

Frequency distribution tables were prepared for Moral Values for all the groups. Mean, median, mode, range, Quartile Deviation, Standard Deviation, Skewness, Kurtosis, Coefficient of Variation and Standard Error of Mean were calculated wherever necessary. The significance tests like 't' test and 'F' test were employed. Multiple 'R' was calculated by carrying out step-wise regression analysis to predict the Moral Values scores of the pupils. Tables were prepared wherever necessary to present the data. The obtained numerical results were adumbrated by graphical representations.

The significant levels employed with respective symbols are given below:

** Indicates significant at 0.01 level.

* Indicates significant at 0.05 level.

@ Indicates not significant at 0.05 level.

6.2 MAJOR FINDINGS OF THE STUDY

The statistical treatment of the data reveals the following major findings of the study.

A. Distribution Characteristics of Moral Value Scores

1. The mean Moral Value score of the Intermediate Students is 339.68 out of maximum score of 395. The median is 341.622 and mode is 351. The gap among the Mean, Median and Mode is negligible. Hence, the distribution is very nearer to normal distribution.
2. The values of skewness and kurtosis for the Moral Value Scores are -0.631 and 0.958. Hence, the distribution of total Moral Value Scores for the whole group is slightly negative and lepto kurtic.
3. It is found that the mean total Moral Value Scores for female students is significantly higher (344.83) than the male students (334.53). Therefore female students have better Moral Values than male students. The skewness of male and female students are -0.401 and -0.957 respectively and kurtosis of male and female students are -0.022 and 2.40. skewness is slightly negative for both male and female students. Kurtosis for male and female students is less than 3.00. Hence, these two distributions are lepto-kurtic.
4. The mean Moral Value sore for the Christian students is 331.11, less than the Muslim (345.78) and the Hindu (339.89) students. It is found that the Muslim students have significantly better Moral Values than other two communities' viz., the Hindu and the Christian. Skewness is slightly negative for all the three communities and kurtosis is less than 3.00. Hence, these three distributions are lepto-kurtic.
5. It is found that the mean Moral Value Scores for BC (342.39) students is significantly better than SC/ST

(337.22) and OC (341.4) students. It is concluded that BC students have better Moral Values than SC/ST and OC students. Skewness is slightly negative for all the three castes and kurtosis is less than 3.00. Hence, these three distributions are lepto-kurtic.

B. Factorial Designs

1. There is significant influence of sex at 0.01 level on Moral Values of the Intermediate Students (F=49.199). It is in favour of female students.
2. There is significant influence of college at 0.01 level on Moral Values of Intermediate Students (F=17.173). It is in favour of Government Colleges.
3. There is no significant interaction effect of college X sex on Moral Values of Intermediate Students (F=0.405).
4. There is significant influence of community at 0.05 level on Moral Values of Intermediate Students (F=4.037). It is in favour of Muslim community students.
5. There is significant influence of caste at 0.05 level on Moral Values of Intermediate Students (F=4.355). It is in favour of Backward Caste students.
6. There is no significant interaction effect of community X caste on Moral Values of Intermediate Students (0.841).

C. Influence of Socio-Demographic Variables on Moral Values

1. Residence has significant influence on Moral Values of Intermediate Students than hostlers. Day scholars have significantly better Moral Values than the hostellers.
2. Medium of Study has no significant influence on Moral Values of Intermediate Students.
3. Religious festivals have no significant influence on Moral Values of Intermediate Students.

4. Religious Discourses have no significant influence on Moral Values of Intermediate Students.
5. Type of family has no significant influence on Moral Values of Intermediate Students.
6. Age has significant influence at 0.01 level on Moral Values (F= 4.776). The mean value of Moral Value Scores of students whose age is 16 years (344.1612) have better Moral Values than the other two age groups viz., 17 years (338.8300) and 18 and above years (337.0987).
7. Family Annual Income has significant influence at 0.01 level on Moral Values (F= 5.180). The students whose family annual income is Rs. 25,001-50,000 (M=345.5455) have better Moral Values than the other three groups viz., upto Rs. 25,000 (M=339.8915), Rs. 50,001- 1 lakh (M=313.8333) and Rs. above 1 lakh (M=339.6858).
8. Educational Qualifications of Mother has no significant influence on Moral Values of Intermediate Students.
9. Educational Qualifications of Father has no significant influence on Moral Values of Intermediate Students (F=1.480).
10. Father occupation has no significant influence on Moral Value of Intermediate Students (F=0.400).
11. Mother occupation has no significant influence on Moral Value of Intermediate Students (F=2.650).
12. Birth order of the students has no significant influence on Moral Values of Intermediate Students (F=1.975).
13. Total members in the family have no significant influence on Moral Values of Intermediate Students (0.298).
14. Native Place has no significant influence on Moral Values of Intermediate Students (0.643).
15. Family Economic Position has significant influence on Moral Values of Intermediate Students (F=4.555). The

mean value of Moral Values scores of students whose Economic position is medium (M=341.2261) have significantly better Moral Values than the other two groups viz., rich (M=325.0000) and poor (M=336.7675).

16. Visiting Temple has significant influence at 0.05 level on Moral Values of Intermediate Students (F=3.268). The students who are visiting temple occasionally (M=340.6489) have significantly better Moral Values than the other two groups viz., students never visiting temple (M=335.0417) and students visiting temple regularly (M=336.1026).
17. When you go wrong who corrects you has not significant influence on Moral Values of Intermediate Students (F=2.306).
18. Group Subjects has significant influence on Moral Values of Intermediate Students (F=23.059). M.P.C. group students (M=347.1071) have significantly better Moral Values than the other three groups viz., H.E.C. (M=333.1240), C.E.C. (M=344.4811) and Bi.P.C. (M=333.3274).

D. Influence of Psychological Variables

1. The Personality Factors viz., C, I, O, Q_2, Q_3 and Q_4 have significant influence at 0.01 level; Personality Factors-B and E have significant influence at 0.05 level and the Personality Factors-A, D, F, G and H have no significant influence on Moral Values of Intermediate Students.

   It is observed from the mean values that the students with personality characteristics

   (1) High Intelligence;

   (2) Emotionally Stable, Mature, Faces Reality, Calm;

   (3) Obedient, Mild, Easily Led, Docile, Accommodating;

(4) Tough-minded, Rejects Illusions;

(5) Self-assured, Placid, Secure, Complacent, Serene;

(6) Sociably Group Dependent, A Joiner and Sound Follower;

(7) Uncontrolled, Lax, Follows Own Urges, Careless of Social Rules;

(8) Relaxed, Tranquil, Torpid, Unfrustrated, Composed have significantly better Moral Values than the students with personality characteristics (1) Low Intelligence; (2) Affected by feelings, Emotionally Less Stable, Easily upset, Changeable; (3) Assertive, Aggressive, Competitive, Stubborn; (4) Tender-minded, Sensitive, Dependent, Overprotected; (5) Apprehensive, Self-reproaching, Insecure, Worrying, Troubled; (6) Self-sufficient, Resourceful, Prefers Own Decisions; (7) Controlled, Exacting Will Power, Socially Precise, Compulsive, Following Self-image; and (8) Tense, Frustrated, Driven, Overwrought, Fretful. The 'F' values of remaining personality factors viz., A (Reserved Vs Outgoing), D (Phlegmatic Vs Excitable), F (Sober Vs Happy go lucky), G (Moral Standards Vs Super ego strength) and H (Shy Vs Venturesome) are not significant at 0.05 level. It is concluded that the personality factors A, D, F, G and H don't have significant influence on Moral Values of the Intermediate Students.

2. It is observed that the students who scored better on four areas of self-concepts viz., (i) Abilities, (ii) Self Acceptance, (iii) Worthiness, (iv) Present, Past and Future and on total self-concepts have significantly better Moral Values than others.

   It is observed that the students who scored Q_3 and above in the self-concepts areas

   (1) Abilities,

   (2) Self-acceptance,

(3) Worthiness,

(4) Present, Past and Future, and

(5) Self-concepts total score have significantly better Moral Values than the students who scored upto Q_1.

It indicates that better self-concepts leads to better Moral Values.

3)It is observed that the students who scored better on all the seven areas of Study Habits Inventory (SHI) viz., (i) Home environment and Planning of work (SH_1), (ii) Reading and Note taking (SH_2), (iii) Planning of Subject (SH_3), (iv) Habits of concentration (SH_4), (v) Preparation for Examination (SH_5), (vi) General Habits & Attitudes (SH_6) and (vii) School Environment (SH_7) and Total Study Habits score (SHT) have significantly better Moral Values at 0.01 level. It shows that better study habits leads to better Moral Values.

E. Step-wise Multiple Regression Analysis

It is found that the best multiple regression equations for predicting Moral Values of Intermediate Students are:

1. With the help of 22 socio-demographic variables.

   MVS = 358.355+9.638 (S)-9.825 (C)-6.617 (R)-4.074 (A) +2.271 (Ca)

The variance explained with the help of the above 5 variables is 9.3 %.

2. With the help of HSPQ (14 personality factors).

   MVS = 358.476 -3.965 (Q4) -3.887 (Q3) -2.798 (O) +2.258(G)

   The variance explained with the help of the above 4 variables is 5.2 %.

3. With the help of self-concepts (10 areas + Total self-concepts)

$$MVS = 321.351 + 6.093\ (SC_2) + 3.304\ (SC_5) - 2.725\ (SC_9) + 2.634\ (SC_4)$$

The variance explained with the help of the above 4 variables is 6.1 %.

4. With the help of study habits (7 areas + Total study habits)

   $$MVS = 322.239 + 5.813\ (SHT) + 3.090\ (SH_5)$$

   The variance explained with the help of the above 2 variables is 4.3 %.

5. With the help of 55 independent variables (All the independent variables in the study)

   $$MVS = 351.500 + 3.797\ (SC_2) + 8.736\ (S) - 7.649\ (C) - 8.037\ (R) + 3.533\ (SHT) - 3.658\ (A) - 2.669\ (HE) + 2.372\ (SC_4) - 2.010\ (SC_9).$$

   The variance explained with the help of the above 9 variables is 13.6 %.

6.3 CONCLUSIONS

In the light of the findings presented in the preceding pages, the following conclusions are drawn:

1. In general the Intermediate Students have better Moral Values.
2. The frequency distributions of Moral Values of Intermediate Students in sex, community and caste are very nearer to normal distribution.
3. All the Intermediate Students do not have same Moral Values.
4. Community has its own influence on Moral Values of Intermediate Students.
5. Caste has its own influence on Moral Values of Intermediate Students.
6. Medium of Study, Type of Family, College (management), Age of the Student, Family Annual

Income, Family Economic Position, Visiting Temple and Group Subjects have its own significant influence on Moral Values of Intermediate Students.

7. Residence, Sex, Religious Festivals, Religious Discourses, Educational Qualifications of Mother, Educational Qualifications of Father, Father's Occupation, Mother's Occupation, Total Members in the Family, Native Place, When you go wrong who corrects you have no significant influence on Moral Values of Intermediate Students.
8. There is no significant interaction effect of college X sex on Moral Values of Intermediate Students.
9. There is no significant interaction effect of community X caste on Moral Values of Intermediate Students.
10. HSPQ factors B, C, E, I, O, Q_2, Q_3 and Q_4 have their significant influence on Moral Values of Intermediate Students. The remaining facts A, D, F, G, H and J have no significant influence on Moral Values of Intermediate Students.
11. The Five areas of self-concepts viz., 'Abilities', 'Self Acceptance', 'Worthiness', 'Present, Past and Future', 'Sociability' and total score of self-concepts have significant influence on Moral Values of Intermediate Students. The areas 'Health and Sex Appropriate-ness', 'Self confidence', 'Beliefs and Convictions', 'Feeling of Shame and Guilt' and 'Emotional Maturity' have no significant influence on Moral Values of Intermediate Students.
12. All the 7 areas of study habits and total score of study habits have significant influence on Moral Values of Intermediate Students.
13. It is possible to predict the Moral Values of Intermediate Students with the help of different sets of independent variables.
14. It is possible to develop the regression equations for predicting the Moral Values of Intermediate Students

with the help of all the independent variables in the study.

6.4 EDUCATIONAL IMPLICATIONS AND RECOMMENDATIONS

Values are the guiding principles decisive in day to day behaviours as also in critical life situations. In this age of rapid social change influenced by technology, there appears a value crisis in the society. Some values seem to perish, some submerge into others, some new have emerged and some new ones are gaining credibility.

A value is a relationship between a person and an environmental situation which evokes an appreciative response in the individual. Moral values are inseparably related to values in general. Frequently values are divided into types, such as bodily values, economic values, social values, aesthetic values, religious values etc., while there are values which are primarily economic, aesthetic and so on, any human values may also be a Moral Value. To the extent that any activity increases or diminishes the worth of human life, it takes on a moral significance. Values are thus both individual and social.

Durkheim has pointed out that the first element of morality is a spirit of discipline, the second element being, according to him, attachment to social groups. The former is concerned with the development of character of the individual and the latter with the relationship he must bear with others in the society. Both these depend upon the education and training that the individual receives during childhood and adolescence. Children brought up in a laissez-faire can hardly be expected to develop morality to any desired extent.

Educational institutions have to work in a way that the whole child is taken care of and it is possible when the goal before them is to work with the children as how to learn to live.

Teacher plays an important role in the field of education. Today's education is child-centred. The teacher is the maker of the future of the child. The children of today are the citizens and leaders of tomorrow. So, it is necessary to take care about children.

The quality of a nation depends upon the quality of its citizens; the quality of citizens depends upon the quality of their education; the quality of education depends upon the quality of teachers and the quality of teachers depends upon the quality of teacher education. We want value-oriented teacher education (Manchala, 2007).

The home and the school with the influence of parents and teachers have a role to meet and decide how to lead the child from darkness to light, from untruth to truth and from mortality to immortality.

In the family the child is a group member in a clan/family and in the school, the teacher mentors his association in groups. Curricular programmes in the areas of social studies, language and science could help inculcating moral qualities like righteousness, love, self control and truthfulness. Poetry could develop finer sensitivities. Mathematics can help in rationality and logistics.

Types of Activities Schools/Colleges could pursue for value mutation:

- School/College Assembly
- Special Assembly
- Students Panchayat
- Classroom Activities
- Hobby clubs
- Cultural and Literary Activities
- Talks on Values
- Stories

- Celebration of Special Days
- Auxiliary Activities
- Classroom Projects

The above stated values and activities are not an end.

On the basis of the results of this investigation, the following recommendations are made.

1. Government College students have high Moral Values than Aided and Private College students. Aided and Private College should follow all the instructions given by the Government Colleges.
2. Lower age is positively related with Moral Values. Take necessary steps to minimize wastage and stagnation at lower classes.
3. Family Annual Income is positively related with Moral Values. Government should take special interest to increase annual income of the family by providing more job opportunities.
4. Caste and Community are positively related with Moral Values. Government should increase community development programmes with the help of NGOs.
5. Family Economic Position is positively related with Moral Values. Government should take necessary steps to increase the status of economic position of the family.
6. Visiting Temple is positively related with Moral Values. Encourage students to visit temple atleast twice in a week.
7. Group Subjects is positively related with Moral Values. Teacher should take some more care at the time of teaching. Special care may be taken with regard to arts group students. Inculcate more values when ever it is necessary.
8. Some of the Personality Characteristics are related to Moral Values and hence special care may be taken for

developing such Personality Characteristics among students.

9. Self-concepts are related to Moral Values. Necessary self-concepts may be develop among students.
10. Study Habits are positively correlated with Moral Values. Better study habits may be developed among Intermediate Students.
11. Necessary infrastructure facilities and physical facilities may be created in Intermediate Colleges. Congenial atmosphere may be developed in Intermediate College. It inculcates sound health value.
12. Value-oriented teaching is necessary.
13. Special care may be taken for pre-primary, primary and upper primary students (the children have high grasping power below age 14 years).
14. Speeches of great persons (role models) may be provided at least once in a month.
15. Separate Moral Education subject may be introduced.
16. A common subject like Science & Civilization, Indian Heritage and Culture may be introduced to inculcate all types of social and human values.
17. Special classes may be provided for Telugu medium students to inculcate more values.
18. Highly qualified, committed and dedicated teachers may be recruited in the colleges.
19. The Intermediate Board should plan special training courses to the principals of Intermediate Colleges for making their administrative styles more acceptable, more effective, more dynamic and more humane.
20. Working with community has to be insisted upon. Appropriate areas have to be allocated. Surveys, interviews, observation, demonstration, exhibition etc. may be organized and reported back to the authorities. Credits and incentives should also be introduced.

21. Inter-institute/District/State/Country visits may be arranged for exchange of ideas and sharing of experiences.
22. Special care/attention should be given to the educationally challenged personnel to inculcate values.
23. Stories, illustrations and events mainly from Indian nation and its literature from various religions that included in value oriented education leads to national integration.
24. The psychology of learning says that rewards motivate the students towards better learning and under-standing, resulting greater achievement. It increases the confidence in the students. Teachers have to encourage the students to do a certain activity and praise them for their work.

6.5 LIMITATIONS OF THE STUDY AND SUGGESTIONS FOR FURTHER RESEARCH

The following limitations and suggestions are considered for further investigation.

1. The study is limited to the students of Senior Intermediate only. It is advised to extend it to Primary School, High School, DIET, Degree, B.Ed, Engineering, Medicine, P.G. students and Research Scholars.
2. The attitude of students is measured through the Moral Values Attitude Inventory constructed by the investigator. Use other scales of Moral Values.
3. Attitude of Moral Values of the students depend on Psychological, Sociological, Economic and Environmental factors. No factor can be studied in isolation.
4. Due to laborious calculations, only certain variables are studied in this investigation. It may be extend to other variables.
5. This is a presage study in the area of Moral Values. Studies of presage-process, presage-product, process-product and presage-process-product may be undertaken

in the area of Moral Values.

6. The study is confined to 16 intermediate colleges in Chittoor District of Andhra Pradesh only. It may be extended to other districts of Andhra Pradesh and to the other states.
7. This study is confined to 1200 senior intermediate students. It is suggested that a more detailed study can be made covering more number of senior intermediate students.
8. Research studies may be conducted to see the relationship between students Moral Values and teacher behaviour in the class room.
9. Prediction of Moral Values in Intermediate Students may be attempted with some more independent variables like moral adjustment, social adjustment, interests, aptitudes etc., in order to get further insight into the problem.
10. This study has not included any institutional variables such as year of establishment, facilities available, results produced, titles and awards obtained etc. Institutional variables may help us to identify the variations between good and poor institutions. Studies in this direction may help us to improve the status of education.

Let there be an optimistic view on educational issues like these in the years to come.

"The cultivation of Human Values alone is Education".

"There is one religion; the religion of Love. There is one class; the class of Humanity. There is one language; the language of the Heart".

"If there is righteousness in the heart,

There will be beauty in character.

If there is beauty in character,

There will be harmony in the home.

When there is harmony in the home,

There will be order in the nation.

When there is order in the nation,

There will be peace in the world".

(So, be righteous; avoid all prejudices against others on the basis of caste, creed, colour, mode of worship, status or degree of affluence. Do not look down on any one; look upon all as Divine as you really are.)

—Sri Sathya Sai Baba

Bibliography

Allport *et al*. (1964): "Study of Values: A Scale for Measuring Dominant Interests in Personality", 3rd Edition, Boston Houghton, Miffin.

Allport, G.W. (1937): "Personality - A Psychological Interpretation", Hort, New York.

Allport, G.W. (1949): "Personality - A Psychological Interpretation", Constable and Co., London.

Allport, G.W. (1951): "New Knowledge in Human Values", Houghton Mifflin Co., Boston.

Allport, G.W. Vernon. P.E. and Lindzey, G (1951): "A Manual of Study of Values", Houghton Mifflin Co., Boston.

Annamma, A.K. (1985): "Values Aspirations and Adjustment of College Students", in M.B. Buch (Ed.,) Fourth Survey of Research in Education, NCERT, New Delhi.

Archana and Mona Sharma (2002): From "Study Habits of Intermediate Students in Relation to Certain Psycho-sociological Factors", by Rajani, M. (2004), Ph.D. Thesis, S.V.U., p.53.

Arokiaswamy, S. (1993): "Value Perception of the First Degree Students in Colleges Affiliated to the Madurai Kamaraj University in Relation to certain Personality and Environmental Factors", Ph.D Thesis, M.K. University, Madurai.

Bannon, S. (1982): As quoted in Chaya, C.V. (2001), "A Study of Moral Judgement of 10th Standard Students in relation to their Parental Behaviour, Child Rearing Practices, Emotional Maturity and Personality Traits", an unpublished Ph.D. Thesis, submitted to Bangalore University, Bangalore, pp. 117-118.

Banvi, K. (1992): "A study of the Values of College Students in Nagalnad in relation to their Self-concepts-M.B. Buch (Edu) Fifth Survey Education, Vol.II, p.1334, New Delhi.

Bawa, S.K. (2003): "Changing Value System through Women Oriented T.V. Programme". *Journal of All India Association for Educational Research*, Vol. 15(3-4), Sep.-Dec., 6-8.

Begum Shabina, R.B: (1983). "The Effect of Personality Traits on the Moral Judgement of X Standard Students", unpublished M.Ed., Dissertation, Bangalore University, Bangalore.

Best, J.W. (1959): "Research in Education", U.S.A., Prentice-Hall, Inc., Englewood Cliffs, Chapter 3, pp. 31-83.

Bhardwaj, B.P. (1999): "Institutional Climate of DIETs in relation to Morale and Job Satisfaction of Teacher Educators and Academic Achievement of Pupil-Teachers". Ph.D. Edu., Chaudhary Charan Singh University, Meerut.

Bhargava (1986): "A study of Moral Judgement among Children at a concrete and Formal Operational Stages and its relationship with variables of Home and Educational Environment", *Dissertation Abstract International*, May, Vol.51, No.10, p.6231-A.

Bhargava, M. (1997): "Modern Psychological Testing and Measurement", Agra Har Prasad Bhargava.

Bhatnagar, J.N. (1979): "Investigation into the Values, Aspirations and Personality Traits of Adolescents of Rajastan', in M.B. Buch (Edu) Third Survey of Research in Education 1978-1983 NCERT, New Delhi.

Bhushan, L.I. (1970): "Religiosity Scale", *Indian Journal of Psychology*, 45(4), 335-342.

Bhushan, L.I. (1971): Religiosity as a function of age, education and sex. *Indian Psychological Review*, 8(1), 1-4.

Bhushan, L.I. (1972): Manual of Religiosity Scale (in Hindi), National Psychological Corporation, Labh Chand Market, raja Mandi, Agra-2.

Blasi, A. (2004): "Moral functioning: Moral understanding and personality" in Lapsley, D.K. and Narvaez, D. (Edu.), *Morality, Self and Identity.*

Britanica World Language Dictionary (1961): A Dictionary, Funk & Wagnalls Company, New York, Vol.2, p.1126.

Bull, N.J. (1969): "Moral Education", Routledge and Kegan Paul Ltd., London.

Bull, Norman, J. (1969): "Moral Judgement from childhood to Adolescence", Routledge and Kegan Paul, London.

Bush (1981): "A comparison of the effect of Kohleberg's Dilemmas Vs Alerato Dilemma in the Moral stating of Adolescents", *Dissertation Abstract International*, June 1982, Vol.42, No.12, p.5010-A.

Carl Rogers (1969): "Freedom to Learn", Merill, Ohio.

Cattell (1935, 1940, 1949, 1961 and 1971): As quoted by Lakshmi, N. (1996), "Problems of Scheduled Caste, Scheduled Tribe and Non-Scheduled Caste Girls of Secondary Schools in relation to a few Social and Psychological Factors", an unpublished Ph.D. Thesis submitted to Bangalore University, Bangalore, p. 158.

Cattell, B. (1969): "Handbook for Junior-Senior High School Personality Questionnaire", Illinois: Institute of Personality and Ability Testing.

Cattle, R.B. (1950): "The Main Personality Factors in a Questionnaire, Self-estimated Material", *Journal of Social Psychology*, Vol. 6, pp.26-32.

Central Ministry of Education (1981): As quoted in Sapru Alka (1982), "A study of a few socio-psychological factors in relation to Moral Judgement of IX standard students of a few high schools of Bangalore City", an unpublished M.Ed. Dissertation, Bangalore University, Bangalore, p.19.

Chand, S.K. (1992): "A Study of Personal Values of Adolescent Boys and Girls in relations to Socio-economic Status and Academic Achievement".

Chandrakumar, P.S. and Arokiaswamy, S. (1974): "Gender Differences in the Value Orientation among the College Students". *Journal of Community Guidance and Research*, Vol 11(3), 187-193.

Chaturvedi, Archana (2001): "Personality Pattern; Moral Values and Natural Awakening among Students Studying in Schools of Different Cultural Associations". *Indian Journal of Educational Research*, Vol. 9(1), p.39-43.

Chaya A Heblikar (2001): "A study of Moral judgment of 10th standard students in relation to their parental behaviour, Child rearing practices, Emotional Maturity and Personality Traits", an unpublished Ph.D. Thesis, submitted to Bangalore University, Bangalore.

Chaya, C.V. (1993): "Moral Judgement among students of Eighth standard in relation to their Sex, Intelligence, Religiosity and Socio-economic Status", unpublished M.Ed. Dissertation, Bangalore University, Bangalore-56.

Chaya, C.V. (1996): "A Study of Moral Judgement of Ninth Standard Students in relation to their Parental Behaviour and Values", unpublished M.Ed. Dissertation, Bangalore, Bangalore.

Christine J. Yeh, Robert T. Carler and Alex L. Pieterse (2004): "Cultural Values and Racial Identity Apartheid among Asian American Students. An Exploratory Investigation". *Journal of Counselling and Values*, Jan. 2004, Vol. 48, pp.82-95.

Connor Navy, O. and Rovree, O. (1982): "Sex and Leadership differences in Moral perspective and field dependence and Moral Judgement", *Dissertation Abstract International*, August Vol.43, No.2, p.405-A.

Dawson (2002): "New Tools, New Insights: Kohlberg's Moral Judgement stages revisited", *International Journal of Behavioural Development*, March, Vol. 26(2), pp.154-166.

Debruin Ellun, N.M. and Van Large Paul, A.M. (1999): "Impression Promotion and Co-operation Behaviour": European *Journal of Social Psychology*, March Vol. 29 (2-3), pp.305-328.

Deguchi Yasuyukin and Ohkawa Chilkara (2000): "A study on the Empathy of Juvenile Delinquents: Relationship between Empathy + Offence type and Empathy + Moral Judgement", *Japanese Journal of Criminal Psychology*, Vol. 38(2), pp.17 to 36.

Devi, M.I. (2002): "An Evaluation of the Realisation of Moral, Secular and Democratic Values in the Textbook Content in Telugu Language at Primary and Secondary Levels in Andhra Pradesh". Ph.D., Edu., Nagarjuna University, Guntur.

Dhull, I. and Khatri, N. (2002): "Effect of Value Clarification on Moral Reasoning of Children in relation to Parental Attitude". *Journal of Value Education*, Vol. 2(2), July, p.119-128.

Dictionary of Education (1973): As quoted in Apsar Pasha, S.A. (1986), "Insecurity among Scheduled Caste, Scheduled Tribe and Non-Scheduled Caste Students of High Primary Schools in relation to their Social Maturity", unpublished

M.Ed. Dissertation, Bangalore University, Bangalore, p.136.

Dockstander (1979): "Comparative study of Development Sex difference in Moral Reasoning", *Dissertation Abstract International*, September, Vol. 40, No. 3, page.1239-A.

Dolers (1977): "A Study of Two Methods of Training upon the Development of Moral Judgement in Young Children", *Dissertation Abstract International*, Vol.3.7, February, p.4828-A.

Durheim Emile (1961): "Moral Education", The Free Press of Glencoe Inc, New York.

Durkheim, E. (1925): "Education Morale", translated by Everett, Wilson, K. and Herman Schnurere (1973), New York, The Free Press.

Durkheim, E. (1953): "Sociology and Philosophy", Glencoe Illinois Prepress.

Dwivedi, Om Prakash.D. (2002): "A Study of Character Traits of Junior High School Boys and their Educational Implications". *National Journal of Education*, 7(2).

Education Commission (1964-66): As quoted in Sapru Alka (1982), "A Study of a Few Socio-Psychological Factors in relation to Moral Judgement of IX standard students of a few high schools of Bangalore City", an unpublished M.Ed. Dissertation, Bangalore University, Bangalore, p.18.

Edward, J.B. (1965): "Some Moral attitude of boys in a Secondary Modern School - Part I", *Education Review* (1965) 17, pp.114-127.

Edwards, J.B. (1974): "A developmental study of the acquisition of some Moral concepts in children aged 7 to 15", *Educational Researches*, Vol. 16(2), 83-93.

Elbedour Salman *et al*. (1997): "The impact of political violence on Moral Reasoning in Children", *Child Abuse and Neglect*, Nov. Vol. 21(11), pp.1053-1066.

Fifis Baniel Francis (1978): "The relationship of predictive Ability, Empathy, Intelligence and Sex to Moral Judgement in Adolescents", *Dissertation Abstract International*, Vol.39, No. 12, p.7162-A.

Gali Vijayalakshmi (2006): "Prioritisation of Secondary School children's Values by their Parents and Teacher". *Educational Tracks*, Vol.6. No.7, pp.34-37.

Garg (1983): "A Study of Children's Perception of Parental Disciplinary Practice and its relation to Development of Personality Needs, Moral Judgement and Problem-Solving Ability" as quoted in Buch, M.B. (Edu.) *Research in Education*, Vol. IV, 4th Edition, p. 457.

Garrett, H.E. (1973): "Statistics in Psychology and Education", a Textbook, Vakils, Feffer and Simons Pvt. Ltd., Bombay, India, pp.213-215, 337-370.

Gaur, R.S. (1975): "A study of Values and Perceptions of High School Students of the State of Rajasthan and their relation to Learning". In M.B. Buch (Edu.) Second Survey of Research and Development, Baroda.

Gibbs *et al.* (1986): "Construction and Validation of a multiple choice measure of Moral Reasoning", *Child Development*.

Good and Cartwright (1998): "The Development of Moral Judgement among Undergraduate University Students", *College-Student Journal*, June Vol. 32 (2). Pp.270-276.

Good, C.V. Barr, A.S., and Scates, D.E., (1941): "Methodology of Educational Research", New York, Appleton Century Crofts, Inc., Chapter III, pp.104-184.

Gorden, H.P. (1941): "Study Habit Inventory Scores and Scholarship", *J. of Applied Psychology*, Vol.25, pp.168.

Guilford (1950): "Fundamental Statistics in Psychology and Education", A Text Book, International student edition, McGraw-Hill Book Co., Inc., New York.

Guilford, J.P. (1954): "Psychometric Methods" A Text Book, McGraw-Hill Publishing Company, New York, pp.47, 373, 374, 378, 417.

Gupta (1977): As quoted by Narayanaswamy (1994), "Moral Judgement among Students of Higher Primary School in relation to their Sex, Type of School, Standard and Self-concepts", unpublished M.Ed. Dissertation, Bangalore University, Bangalore, p.77.

Gupta (1984): As quoted by Chaya C.V (1993), "Moral Judgement among students of Eighth Standard in relation to their Sex, Intelligence, Religiosity and socioeconomic Status", unpublished M.Ed. Dissertation, Bangalore University, Bangalore, p.46.

Gupta, Ranjana, (1989): "A study of the Values and Moral Judgement of Adolescents of two representative centers of Western and Eastern U.P", Ph.D. (Edu.) Agra Uni.

Gupta, S. (1982): "Relationship between Reading Ability and Father's Profession and Birth Order", in Buch, M.B. (Edu.), 1986, *Thrid Survey of Research in Education (1978-1983)*, NCERT, New Delhi, p.652.

Gupta, S.P. (1974): "Statistical Methods". A Textbook, Sultan Chand and Sons, New Delhi.

Henry (1989): As quoted in Ayesha Noor (2001), "A comparative study of the effect of Personality Traits on the Moral Judgement of Xth Standard Students in Bangalore Urban Secondary Schools", unpublished M.Ed. Dissertation, Bangalore University, Bangalore, p. 43.

Hill, Kenneth Edwin (1996): "Critical Thinking and its relation to Academic, Personal and Moral development in the College Years", *Dissertation Abstract International*: Section B - *The Science and Engineering*, February, Vol.56 (8-B), p.4603.

Hilton (1978): "The relationship between the level of Moral Judgement of High School students and their levels of interpersonal trust, socio-economic status and Intelligence", *Dissertation Abstract International*, Vol. 39, No.6, p.3375-A.

Humphries *et al.*., (2000): "Predictors of Moral reasoning among African American Children: Preliminary Study", *Journal of Black Psychology*, February, Vol. 26(1), pp.51-64.

Joahi, A. (2002): "Classroom Morale in terms of Locus of Control, Creativity and Parental Encouragement of the Higher Secondary Students in Hindi Medium Schools (Boys and Girls)". *National Journal of Education*, 7(2), 89-94.

John Bellingham (2004): "Dictionary of Education". Academic (India) Publishers, New Delhi, India.

Johnson (1979, 1981): "A Study of determine the effect of Moral Judgement among VII Grade students utilizing the Kohlberg's theory of Moral Judgement on selected children's stories", *Dissertation Abstract Internationl*, December 1971, Vol. 42, No.6, p.2471-A.

Johnson (1981): As quoted in Chaya C.V. (1993): "Moral Judgement among students of Eighth standard in relation to their sex, intelligence religiosity and socio-economic status", unpublished M.Ed. Dissertation, Bangalore University, Bangalore-56, p 120.

Johnson Dale Allen (1978): "An Experimental study in developing Moral Judgement", using different instructional patterns with laws of *Dissertation Abstract International*, Vol.39, p.2724-A.

Johnson R.C. (1962): "A Study of Children's Moral Judgement", *Child Development*, Vol. 33, pp.327-354.

Kalamani, M. (1991): "A study of the problems of Adolescents and their Value System", Ph.D. (Edu), Madurai Kamaraj University.

Koexning Amy Lynn (2001): "Moral Development – The effects of childhood Maltreatment on pro-social behaviours and transgressions", *Dissertation Abstract International* – Section B: The science and Engineering, April, Vol. 61 (9-B), p.4990.

Kohlberg (1958): As quoted in Vajaja, "A study of Moral Judgement among 9th and 10th standard students in relation to their self confidence, sex, socioeconomic status and the type of school", an unpublished M.Phil. Dissertation, Bangalore University, Bangalore, p.15.

Kohlberg (1964): As quoted in Chaya (1993), "Moral Judgement among students of Eighth Standard in relation to their Sex, Intelligence, Religiosity and Socio-economic Status", unpublished M.Ed. Dissertation, Bangalore University, Bangalore, p.52.

Kohlberg (1966): "Social Psychology", Holt Rinehart and Winston, New York.

Kohlberg (1984): As quoted in Piaget Kathleen and Wright Lois (1998), "The Moral reasoning abilities of neglected children", Paper practice, Orlando, Florida, January 26, 1998, p.1.

Kohlberg and Turiel (1971): "'From is to ought' Cognitive development and Epistemology", New York academic press.

Kohlberg Lawrence (1981, 1984): As quoted in bear and Gubbs (1977), p.3, as quoted in Paget Kathleen and Wright Lois, "Moral reasoning conference on Research for social work practice", Orlando, Florida, January 26, 1998, p.1.

Kohlberg, L. (1966): "A Cognitive Development Analysis of Children's Sex role Concepts and Attitudes" pp.82-173 in Eleanor E Maccoby (edu.).The development of Sex differences, Stanford, California: Stanford University press, 1966.

Kohlberg, L. (1969): "Stage and Sequence: The cognitive developmental approach to socialization", pp.347 to 480 in Gostin, D.A. (ed.), Handbook of Socialization Theory and research, Chicago, Rand McNally, 1969.

Kohlberg, L. (1971): "Stages of Moral development as a basis for Moral education", in Beek, C.M., Crittenden, B.S. and Sullivan, E.V., Moral Education: Interdisciplinary approaches, Toronto; University of Toronto Press, pp.23-92.

Kolhberg, L. (1963): "Moral development and identification", in H.W. Stevenson (ed.), Child Psychology: Yearbook of the national society for the study of education, Part-I, Chicago University.

Kothari Education Commission (1964-66): It is also known as "Indian Education Commisiion", with Kothari as its Chairman, p.46.

Lagerspetz (1988): "Moral approval of aggression and sex role identity in officers, Trainees, Conscientious objectors to Military Service and in a Female reference Group", Aggressive Behaviour, Vol. 14(5), pp.303-313.

Lewis (1982): "The relationship of Moral development and cognitive development within gifted students examined in the light of variables of Sex, SES and Age", *Dissertation Abstract International*, June 1982, Vol. 42, No.12, Part-I, p.5088-A.

Madhu Raj (1996) (Ed): "Encyclopedic Dictionary of Psychology and Education", Anmol Publications Pvt. Ltd., New Delhi, Vol. 1 & 3, pp.8, 18, 210, 211, 1482, 1765, 1768 and 1785.

Mahamoodali (1998): "Personal Values, Career Aspirations, Academic Achievements and Socio-economic Status as Determinants of Educational Choices at Senior Secondary Level", Ph.D., Aligargh Muslim University.

Manar, R.N. (1974): "A study of Attitudes, Self-concepts and Values of Professional and Non-professional College Students and relation of these variables will then Achievement", Ph.D. (Edu), Meerat University, Meerat, U.P., India.

Manchala, C. (2007): "Achievement of B.Ed. Students", Ph.D. Thesis, S.V. University, Tirupati, Discovery Publishing House, New Delhi, India

Mangal, S.K. (2002): "Statistics in Psychology and Education", a Textbook, Second Edition, Prentice-Hall of India Pvt. Ltd., New Delhi.

Mani, M.N.G. (2000): "Visual Efficiency of Low Vision Children". *Journal of Educational Research and Extension*, Vol. 37, No.3, pp-17-25.

Maslow Abraham (1974): "Some Factors relating to Under-Achievement in English of Secondary Pupils", Ph.D. (Edu), Kerala University.

Maslow, A.W: (1959). "New Knowledge in Human Values", Harper & Row, Evanston Publications, New York.

Mathur, S.L. (2003): "A Study of Effectiveness of Science of Living in Developing Human Values on School Children of Ladnun". Research Project, Jain Vishva Bharati, Ladnun Rajasthan (ERIC, NCERT).

Mehta, P. (2000): "Social Values and Futuristic Perceptions of College Girls in Delhi: A Study of Sociology of Youth Culture". Ph.D., Faculty of Education, Jamia Milla Islamia, New Delhi.

Ministry of Education (1948): "Report of the University Education", GoI, New Delhi.

Ministry of Education (1952): "Commission Report of Secondary Education Commission", GoI, New Delhi.

Ministry of Education (1962): "Report of the University Education Commission", GoI, New Delhi.

Ministry of Education (1964): "Report of the Committee on Religious and Moral Instructions", GoI, New Delhi.

Ministry of Education (1964-66): "Report of the Indian Education Commission", Kothari Commission.

Ministry of Education (1966): "Education and National Development", NCERT, New Delhi.

Ministry of Education (1971): "Report of the Indian Education Commission", NCERT.

Ministry of Education (1977): "Report of the Review Committee on the Curriculum for the 10 years school", GoI, New Delhi.

Ministry of Education (1981): "Working Group for the Review of Teacher's Training Programmes and Inculcation of Ethical and Social Values in Education Recommendation of the High Level Seminar on Value Orientation Education", Simla: 27-05-1981.

Ministry of Education (1986): "National Policy on Education". Govt. of India.

Mohundro (1976): "Stages of Moral Reasoning and value Hierarchies of sixth grade students", *Dissertation Abstract International*, February 1978, Vol. 37, No.8, p.5026-A.

Natarajan, R. and Balan, K. (2003): "A Study of Morale of Elementary School Teachers". The Primary Teacher, 28(2), April, 5-9.

National Council of Educational Research and Training (1975): "The Curriculum for the Ten Year School".

National Policy of Education (NPE) (1986): "A report of Ministry of Human Resource Development", New Delhi, India.

NCERT Seminar (1981). As quoted in Sapru Alka (1982): "A study of a few socio-psychological factors in relation to Moral Judgement of IXth standard students of a few high schools of Bangalore City", an unpublished M.Ed. Dissertation, Bangalore University, Bangalore, p.19. New Delhi.

Pandey, K. (2004): "Study of Awareness and Inculcation of Values Inherent in the Fundamental Duties in Indian Constitution among Primary and Secondary School".

Pandey, P. (1994): "A Psycho-linguist Study of Democratic Values in relation to Mono-bi, and tri-lingualism", *Indian Psychological Abstract and Reviews* (1) 159, Full Article in *Psycho-lingua*, 1991, 21(2), 111-113.

Parikh (1968): "A study on development of Moral Judgement and its relation to family environmental factors in Indian and American families", as quoted in p.23 of Chaya C.V. (1993), "Moral Judgement among students of eighth standard in relation to their Sex, Intelligence, Religiosity and Socio-economic status", unpublished M.Ed. Dissertation, Bangalore University, Bangalore.

Pashupathi, M. *et al.*. (2001): "Seeds of wisdom: Adolescents' knowledge and Judgement about difficult life problems", *Developmental Psychology*, May 37(3), pp. 351-361.

Patel, B.V. (1975): "Study Habits Inventory", psychological Laboratory, Ludhiana.

Patel, C.K. (1979): "A study of Prevalent Value System of the Secondary Teachers of the High Schools of South Gujarat", in M.B. Buch (Edu) Third Survey of Research in Educational 1978-1983, NCERT, New Delhi.

Patel, M.G. (1981): "A study of the Prevalent Value System of the Students of South Gujarat Studying in Standard X & XI", Ph.D. thesis (Edu.), South Gujarat University, Surat.

Patel, B.V. (1976): "A Study of the Reading Ability and Intelligence in the Context of Study Habits", *Journal of Education and Psychology*, Vol. 34, No.1, pp.19-29.

Piaget Jean (11932, 1965, 1968): "The Moral Development of the Child", Routledge and Keganpaul Ltd., New York.

Piaget Kathleen and Wright Lois (1998): "The Moral Reasoning Abilities of Neglected Children", paper presented at the

International Conference Research for social work practice, Orlando, Florida, January 26, 1998.

Piaget, J. (1932): "The Moral judgment of the child", Kegan Paul, Trench, Trubner and Co. Ltd., London.

Radhakrishnan Commission (1948): As quoted in Sapru Alka (1982), "A study of a few socio-psychological factors in relation to Moral Judgement of IX standard student of a few high schools of Bangalore City", an unpublished M.Ed. Dissertation, Bangalore University, Bangalore, p.18.

Radhakrishnan, S. (1929): "Indian Philosophy", The Macmillan Company, New York, Vol.I, 341-475.

Rama Rao (1994): "Moral Education - A Practical Approach", Published by Remakrishna Institute of Moral and Spiritual Education, Yadavagiri, Mysore.

Ramachandra Reddy B. (2007): "Teaching Behaviour of High School Teachers", Ph.D. Thesis, S.V.University, Tirupati, Published by Discovery Publishing House, New Delhi, India

Ray Chaudhary, S.K., Alloport *et al.*, (1988): "Study of Values (1958 Modification) in Indian Situations", The Indian Psychological Bulletin Vol. 4, Part. I.

Reddy, D.V. (1987): "A Study of Moral Judgement in relation to Intelligence, Personality and other variables", unpublished Ph.D. Thesis.

Reddy, S.G. and Reddy, G.P. (2004): "Life Values: A Study on M.B.A. Students". Indian Journal of Applied Psychology, Vol. 41. 13-16.

Reddy, V.D. (2004): "Attitude towards Value-oriented Education in Primary School children in Chittoor District". Journal of Educational Research and Extension, Vol.41 (2), 42-47.

Report of the Review Committee on National Policy of Education (1991): "Ministry of Human Resource Development", New Delhi, India.

Saraswat, R. (1982): "A study of Self-concepts, in relating to Adjustment, Values, Academic Achievement, Socio-economic Status and Sex of High School Students of Delhi", Ph.D. (Social Sciences), IIT, New Delhi. In Butch (Edu.) *IVth Survey of Research in Education*, Vol., p.427 New Delhi-NCERT.

Sathya Sai Baba (1972): "Sathay Sai Institute of Human Values", Anantapuram.

Sati, B.D. (1992): "Comparative Study of Needs, Values, Aspirations and Adjustments in relations to Academic Achievement of S.C. and other Students of Secondary Schools of Kumaun", Ph.D. (Edu.), Kumaun University.

Seshadri, C.S. (1981): "The Concept of Moral Education Column", *Comparative Education,* Vol. 17, No.3.

Sharma, Meenu, (1992): "A study of Teachers Socio-economic Status and Values with Reference to then Attitude", Ph.D. (Edu.), Agra University, Agra.

Sibia, Sukhvinder (1990): "Value Patterns of Children at Piagetian Concrete and Formal Stages of Development", Ph.D. (Edu.), Punjabi University.

Siefering (1981): "Intelligence, Sex and Behavioural correlates of Moral Reasoning of public Junior High School Students", *Dissertation Abstract International*, October, Vol. 42, No.4, p. 1960-A.

Singh (1984): As quoted in Ramakrishnaiah V (1996), "A study of Moral Judgement of IX standard urban and rural students in relation to their personality values and some selected social variables", unpublished M.Ed. Dissertation, Bangalore University, Bangalore, p.78-79.

Singh, D.V. (1999): "Values in School-based Curricula". The Primary Teaacher, Vol. 24(4), 06-13.

Singh, R.P. (1997): "A study of Values of Urban and Rural Adolescent Students", *Indian Educational Abstract,* 2, 38

(Full Article in Praachi-*Journal of Psycho-cultural Dimensions* 9(1), 7-11.

Singh, R.S. (1983): As quoted by Prabhu, K.H. (1996), "A study on the Moral judgement of IX standard students in relation to their parent-child interaction, modernization and their level of Anxiety", unpublished M.Ed. Dissertation, Bangalore University, Bangalore, p. 61.

Smith, J.E. (1958): "Values Conviction and Higher Education New Haven 11, Connecti", The Edward W. Hazer Foundations, 1958.

Somnath Chatterjee (2009): "Criminalisation of politics cause of cynicism; Somnath"; *The Hindu*, daily, Sunday, March 15, 2009, Andhra Pradesh edition, p.4 columns 5 to 8.

Srivastava, A.K. (1967): "An Investigation into the factors related to Educational under Achievement", Ph.D. Thesis, Patna University, Patna.

Srivastava, S.S. (2004): "A Study of School Activities Promoting Values Inherent in Fundamental Duties Mentioned in the Indian Constitution". Research, Bhartiya Shiksha Shodh Sansthan (ERIC, NCERT).

Sukia, S.P., Mehrotra, P.V. and Mehrotra, R.N. (1980): "Elements of Educational Research", A textbook, Allied Publishers, Bombay, India, pp.101-102.

Talesara, H. (2004): "Development of Values through Jeevan Vignan: An Experimental Study". Teacher Research Report, ERIC, NCERT.

The Oxford English Dictionary (1961): Oxford University Press.

U.N.O. (1948): "Universal Declaration of Human rights".

Verma, B.P. and Tyagi. R. (1988): "A study of Sex differences in Values of Senior Secondary School Teachers", The Progress of Education 62(9), 198-200.

Westermark (1912): As quoted in Sapru Alka (1982), "A Study

of a Few Socio-Psychological Factors in relation to Moral Judgement of IX Standard Students of a few High Schools of Bangalore City", an unpublished M.Ed. Dissertation, Bangalore University, Bangalore, p.13.

Wiron, Donglar (1982): "The Teaching of Values in the College Classrooms, Faculty and Students Perception at the Three Contrasting". *Dissertation Abstracts International*, Vol. 43, January 1983.

Wright and Cox (1967): "A Study of the relationship between Moral Judgement and Religious Belief in a sample of English Adolescents", *Journal of Social Psychology*, Vol. 72, pp.135-144.

Yadava, Sharma and Gandhi (2001): "Aggression and Moral Disengagement", *Inter-personality and Clinical Studies*, September, Vol. 17(2), pp.95-99.

Zamen, G.S. (1982): "A study of Social, Religions and Moral Values of Students of Class XI and their relationship with Moral Character Grants and Personality Adjustment", Ph.D. (Edu.), Avadh Univeristy, U.P., India. In Buch (Edu.) *IVth Survey of Research and in Edu*. Vol.1, p. 217, New Delhi, NCERT).

Zupancic and Horvat (1990): "The Role of Moral Judgement in Child's School Functioning", *Psychology Journal*, Vol.32 (1-2), pp.111-118.

INDEX

A

Absolutism 116
Acharya 8
Activities in schools/colleges 65
Adjustment Inventory 68
adolescents 49
Adoption of the instrument HSPQ 155
Aleixo 56
Alloport 9
Alternative Dilemma Questionnaire 40
Altruism scale 58
American secondary school students 55
Annamma 52
Annelobo, Stella 73
Anouilh, Jean 115
Appraisal 105
Aristotle 2, 115
Arokiasamy 53
Asimov, Isaac 115
Ayer, Sir Alfred Jules 115
Ayn Rand 5

B

Bannon 40
Beattie, Bill 5
Bedouin children 43
Begum Shahina 51
Behavioural values 28
Berkeley Free Speech Movement 101
Best 35
Bhagavadgita 8
Bhushan, Anand 66
Birth order 202
Book-smart 7
Boyhood state 15
Bush 39

C

California psychological inventory 55
Carol Gilligan 104
Caste 116
Central Advisory Board of Education 29
Chand, S.K. 42
Chandrakumar, P.S. 38
Characteristics of a real teacher 8
Charity 110
Chatterjee, Somnath 88
Chaturvedi, Archana 56

Chittoor District 130
Civics 7
Clough, Shepard B. 9
College and Sex' on Moral Values 186
Committees and commissions 28
Communication 64
Communities 51
Community 162
Community and Caste 189
Community roles 7
Community-caste on moral values 189
Concept of value oriented education 71
Concern 110
Concurrent Validity 138
Conformists 49
Connor, N.O. 40
Construct validity 138
Content validity 136
Conventional morality 94
Cowardice 110
Creative writing 64
Criminalisation of politics 88
Criterion validity 139
Curriculum 163

D

Dawson 45
Debruin, E. 56
Defining Issues Test 40
Deguchi, Y. 44
Demographic factors 163
Dependent variable 125
Dewey, John 9
Dharma 13
Dignity 12, 110
Distribution characteristics 170, 249
Dockstander 39
Dolres 48
Domain theory 88, 102

E

Education Commission (1964-66) 11
Educational implications 257
Educational theorists 118
Ehavioural Values 28
Einstein 14
Elbedour, Salman 43
Ethics 108
Evans 39
Extra-curricular activities 31

F

Face validity 137
Factorial designs 250
Fairness 110
Falding, Hardold 46
Family economic position 205
Festivals 32
Fifis, Daniel Francis 49
Freedom to learn 9
Freeman 38
Fundamental Duty Adherence Questionnaire 70
Fundamental Duty Awareness Inventory 70
Fundamental values 12

G

Gail M. Inlaw Classification 26

Games and sports 32
Gandhi (Mahatma) 10, 34, 111
Gandhi 98
Gandhi's Classification 26
Gaur, R.S. 47
General classification 27
Giving 24
Gogate 111
Goldman, Emma 5
Gongre 39
Good Interpersonal Relationships 94
Good, C.V. 36, 115
Goodness 30
Gothard, Bill 24
Grammar schools in England 37
Greed 111
Group subjects 208
Guiding principles 15
Gupta 39

H

Hartog Committee (1929) 29
Heinz dilemma 99
Henry Brooks Adams 114
High school personality questionnaire 142
Hilton 49
History 63
Home 162
Honesty 110
Hostein 38
Human civilization 11
Humanities 63
Hypotheses 242

I

Ideals 12
Ideals of virtue 30
Independent Variables 123
Indian Council of Philosophical Research 74
Individualism and Exchange 93
Indrani 73
Influence of 'Religious Discourses' 194
Influence of 'Religious Festivals' 193
Influence of 'Residence' on Moral Values 192
influence of age 196
influence of educational qualifications of father 199
influence of educational qualifications of mother 198
influence of family annual income 197
Influence of psychological variables 252
Influence of type of family 195
Integrity 110
Intellectual development 92
Intelligence 41, 162
Intrinsic Validity 137
Investigation 127
Item validity 136

J

Jealousy 7
Jewish children 43
Johnson 39, 40
Johnson, Lyndon B. 3
Joint families 110

Jorge Luis Borges 34
Judgement abilities 50

K

Kalamani 52
Kamen, Dean 2
Kane 37
Kant 98
Keiser, Mohamood 66
Kenney 50
Kindness 110
King, Martin Luther 98
Koexing 44
Kohlberg 38, 104
Kohlberg's measure of moral reasoning 39
Kohlberg's method 92
Kohlberg's six stages 93
Kohlberg's stages of reasoning 38, 93
Kohlberg's Theory of Moral Development 92
Kothari Commission 29
Kulshreshtha 60
Kumari, Prabhavathi 65

L

Lagerspetz 43
Learning subjects 7
Lewis 40
Literature 64
Locality 116
Louis Raths 9

M

Mahabharata 237
Mahamoodali 43
Maintaining the social order 96
Major findings 249
Malaysian secondary school students 55
Mandela, Nelson 2
Manliness 30
Marrie 41
Mathur, S.L. 57
Measure of Character Structure 68
Mehta 56
Mercy 24
Mohundro 38
Moral 114
Moral absolutism 116
Moral agency 116
moral and social values 51
Moral approval of aggression 43
Moral behaviour 100
Moral codes 117
Moral curriculum 117
Moral development 117
Moral education 13, 117
Moral instruction 65
Moral judgement 37, 48, 49, 52, 54, 86
Moral judgement skills 50
Moral judgement test 68
Moral levels 86
Moral paradigms 45
Moral particularism 118
Moral realism 89
Moral relativism 119
Moral stages 86
Moral thought 100, 101
Moral universalism 119
Moral value scale 58

Moral values 28, 78
Moral Zeitgeist 119
Morality 114
Morality and convention 102
Morality of care 104
Morality: three principal meanings 107
Mother occupation 201
Multiple regression analysis 254

N

Nagaland College students 61
Nai Talim 26
National Policy on Education (1986) 29, 30
National Resource Centre for Value Education 81
Native place of the students 204
Nature of Personality 142
NCERT 30, 72, 73
Numerical values 130

O

Obedience 93
Objective responsibility, 89
Objectives 242
Occasions 32
Organisation of items 141
Organization 25
Other forms of cognition 101
Outdoor activities 32

P

Parikh 38
Parker 9
Parker's Classification 27
Pearson's correlation co-efficient 87
Peer relations 61
Personal Information sheet 84
Personal values 27
Personality 162
Personality 46
Personality factors 209
Peters, J. 14
Piaget's Stages of Moral Judgment 88
Plato's classification 27
Post-conventional morality 97
Pragmatists 74
Pre-conventional morality 93
Predictive validity 138
Prerequisites of a good test 127
Priya 39
Prizes 15
Problem of value education 11
Programme of Action (POA) Document, 1992 81
Programme of Action 29
Prolonged deprivation Scale 68
Prophecy 25
Psychological variables 124
Punishment orientation 93
Purpose of the Study 241

Q

Qualities 12

R

Radhakrishnan Commission (1948) 29
Raj.Madhu 139
Ramayana 237
Rangaswamy 86
Ranu, Sarbjit Kaur 54

Rao, Nagarjuna 72
Rashtriya Panchasheela 73
Rawls 98
Recommendations 257
Reddy, V.D. 77
Reliability 139
Reliability and Validity 164
Religion 115
Research in moral values 32
Resurgence of interest 11
Ridler, Vivan 116
Rogers, Carl 9
Rowahan, Ravan Hushim 47
Rowntree, Derek 10

S

Samoohik Mansik Yogyata Pariksha 59, 68
Saraswat 60
Saraswathi Shishu Mandirs 56
Sat Yuga 111
Sati 42
School 163
Science of living 57
Scope of the study 241
Scoring and analysis 168
Scoring of the items 141
Scoring procedure for HSPQ 156
Secondary Education Commission 29
Seeing your peer 7
Selection of the tool HSPQ 143
Self-concept 60
Self-concepts 59, 227
Self-concepts on moral values 212
Self-confidence 48
Sen Gupta, Alpana 58
Serving 25
Shamshuddin 83
Shishu Mandirs 56
Siefering 50
Situational tests 68
Social contract and individual rights 97
Social sciences 64
Social values 28
Social, moral and spiritual values in education 30
Socio-demographic scale (SDS) 140
Socio-demographic variables 36, 123, 191, 250
Socio-economic levels 40
Spiritual values 28
Spirituality 7
Split-half reliability 140
Spranger's classification 27
Sri Prakasa commission 29
Statistical techniques employed 168
Street-smart 7
Student leaders 49
Study Habits 229
Study habits 62, 215
Study habits inventory 161
Sukhia 35
Sukhvinder, Sibia 52

T

Teaching 25
Tension 7
Test-Retest Reliability 140

Theories of moral development 88
Tools used 166
Total members in the family 203
Truth 30
Tuchman, Barbara W. 34

U

UNESCO 30
Universal principles 98

V

Validity 141
Validity and reliability of HSPQ 156
Validity of the inventory 159
Value 114
Value education 15
Value of superior 41
Values 12, 16
Values through co curricular activities 31
Values through curriculum 30
Vedas 8
Verma 42
Vijayalakshmi 84
Virtues 12
Visiting temple 206
Vivekananda (Swami) 72
Vocational training 7

W

Wark 42
Wiron, Donglar 50
Women-oriented TV Programme 75, 76
Woodruff 46
Words Related to Moral 120
Wright 37

Y

Yadava 45
Yagnavalkya 13

Z

Zale 37
Zamen 51
Zeitgeist 119
Zupanic 42

❑❑❑